Letts study aids

Revise French

A complete revision course for O level and CSE

Gloria Richards BA(Hons.), LLCM, Dip.Ed.

Head of French Department, Brynteg Comprehensive School, Bridgend

Charles Letts Books Ltd
London, Edinburgh & New York

First published 1982
by Charles Letts (Books) Ltd
Diary House, Borough Road, London SE1 1DW
Reprinted 1983

Design: Ben Sands
Illustrations: Yvonne McLean
Maps: Illustra Design Limited

ISBN 0 85097 427 5

Printed and bound by
Charles Letts (Scotland) Ltd

Contents

Preface

This book is designed as a revision guide for candidates studying for O-level and CSE examinations in French. It has been written after analysing the requirements of all the Examination Boards in England, Northern Ireland, Scotland and Wales, whose syllabuses are summarised for you in tabular form.

The book contains a revision of all the major grammatical points and vocabulary elements required for O level and CSE. It includes hints on revision and examination technique as well as questions from recent past papers.

With careful and consistent use, this book should help candidates gain confidence in all the skills which are tested in O-level and CSE French examinations. Different Examination Boards place different emphasis on the various skills – reading, listening, speaking and writing in the foreign language – but all are tested in some form or another, and this book provides practice in all aspects of all the examinations.

Gloria D. Richards

1981

Acknowledgements

I wish to express my thanks to the following people for their help in producing this book:

Joan Delin, Richard Lees and Keith Way, who acted as consultants, for their invaluable help and advice;
my father, Samuel Blythe Farnsworth, for the maps;
Pat Rowlinson and the staff of Letts for their guidance and professional advice;
and my husband and daughter for their unfailing support and encouragement.

The author and publishers would also like to thank the following Examination Boards for their permission to reproduce questions from past papers:

Associated Examining Board (AEB)
Associated Lancashire Schools Examining Board (ALSEB)
East Anglian Examinations Board (EAEB)
East Midland Regional Examinations Board (EMREB)
Joint Matriculation Board (JMB)
London Regional Examinations Board (LREB)
Oxford Delegacy of Local Examinations (Oxford)
Oxford and Cambridge Schools Examination Board (O & C)
Northern Ireland Schools GCE Examinations Council (NIEC)
Scottish Examination Board (SEB)
South East Regional Examinations Board (SEREB)
Southern Universities' Joint Board for School Examinations (SUJB)
South Western Examinations Board (SWEB)
Welsh Joint Education Committee (WJEC)

The author wishes to point out that the answers given in Part III are not supplied by the Examination Boards but are her own suggestions.

Introduction

The aim of this book is to help you revise for either an O-level or a CSE examination in French. Its main objective is to help you revise and practise those skills which will be tested in the examination itself. The key to success in French examinations at these levels lies in the thorough preparation and practice of certain skills – reading, listening, speaking and writing in the foreign language. You must show the examiner that you are proficient in all these skills.

The first thing you must do is to make sure that you know which types of tests are set by your particular Board. You should check the tables on pages vi–ix to find out which types of test you will have to take. If you would like to have further details, you should write to your Examination Board to obtain its current syllabus. The names and addresses of all the Examination Boards are given on page x.

No candidate will be required to take *all* the tests covered in this book. Different Examination Boards set different types of test and emphasise different skills. You must make sure, therefore, that you know which combination of tests you will have to take.

The core material in this book covers the most important points of grammar and items of vocabulary which you will be expected to know. As the book is intended to be as complete as possible, you may find that there is more than your particular Examination Board requires you to know. For example, many Examination Boards do not ask for a knowledge of the present subjunctive. It has been included here, however, since it does feature in some syllabuses and as it could also be useful for those candidates who wish to include it in a free composition.

A section on background knowledge is included. This is tested by many CSE Boards, and will also be useful to O-level candidates, as questions of a general nature about France may be included in the oral examination.

After you have revised the topics from the Core Sections which you know will be included in your examination, test yourself by using the tests in Part II. If, when checking your answers, you find that you have not scored highly, go back and revise the relevant sections again and then do the test again. Keep practising until you are really sure that you have understood and can do the tests almost perfectly.

Part III contains advice about how to approach the different types of test, and specimen examination questions. This advice is given after many years' experience as a teacher and as an examiner. Too many candidates do not do justice to themselves because they lack practice in answering the various types of question. Set aside a predetermined period of time each week, not only to revise your topics, but also to practise answers. Sets of past examination papers can be obtained from the Examination Boards and will be of use to you for further practice.

Finally, remember that success is within your grasp if you have:

(a) revised thoroughly the grammatical structures, idioms and vocabulary required by your Examination Board;

(b) paid special attention to key areas where you know you have had difficulty in the past;

(c) practised and perfected your examination technique.

vi Analysis of written examination syllabuses

Board	Level	Syllabus	Translation into French	Translation into English	Reading comprehension	Listening comprehension	Background knowledge	FREE COMPOSITION Letters	Pictures	Topic	Continuation or Dialogue	Story reproduction
AEB	O	I		●	F			●	Op	Op		
AEB	O	II			E+MCF	MCF		●	Op	Op		
Cambridge	O		Op	●	MCF	F+MCF		Op	●	Op	Op	
JMB	O	A	Op	●	E	E			Op		Op	
JMB	O	B	Op	●	MCF	MCF			Op		Op	
London	O		Op	●	MCF	MCE			Op	Op	Op	
NIEC	O			●	F	E		Op	●	Op		
Oxford	O	A	Op	●	E	Op F					●	
Oxford	O	B		●	MCF	MCF			●		●	
O & C	O		Op	●	F+MCF				Op			Op
SEB	O	Trad			E	E	●	●			●	
SEB	O	Alt			E	E	●	●				
SUJB	O		Op	●					Op	●		Op
WJEC	O		●	●	E	E		Op	Op	Op		
Joint 16+	16+				MCF	MCF		●	●			
ALSEB	CSE				F+E	E+MCE	●	●	Op	Op	Op	
EAEB	CSE	North			E	E		●	●			
EAEB	CSE	South			F+E	E		Op	Op	Op		
EMREB	CSE				MCE	MCE					●	
LREB	CSE				MCF+E	E		●	Op	Op		
NIEB	CSE				E	E	C	Op	Op	Op	Op	
NREB	CSE				F+E	E		●	●			
NWREB	CSE				E	E	●	●	●	Op		
SREB	CSE				MCF	MCF		●	●			
SEREB	CSE				MCF	F+E	C	Op		Op		
SWEB	CSE				MCF+E	E		Op	●	Op		
WJEC	CSE			Pr	E	E		Op	●	Op		
WMEB	CSE				MCF+E	E	●	Op	●		●	
WYLREB	CSE				E	E	●	●	Op	Op		
YREB	CSE				MCF	E		Op	●			

Key

C   coursework
E   questions and answers in English
F   questions and answers in French

MC   multiple-choice questions
Op   optional/alternative
Pr   précis

Board	Level	Syllabus	Dictation	Reading	Role-play/continuation	Conversation	Picture questions	Exam taped	External examiner
AEB	O	I	●		●	●	●		●
AEB	O	II			●	●	●		●
Cambridge	O			●		●			●
JMB	O	A	●	●		●			●
JMB	O	B		●		●		●	
London	O		●	●	●	●		S/T	●/T
NIEC	O			●	●	●			●
Oxford	O	A	●	●		●			T
Oxford	O	B	●	●		●	●		T
O & C	O		●	●		●		Op	Op
SEB	O	Trad		●	●	●	●		
SEB	O	Alt		●		●	●	●	
SUJB	O		●	●		●			●
WJEC	O		●			●	●	S	T
Joint 16+	16+				●	●	●	●	
ALSEB	CSE			●		●		●	
EAEB	CSE	North and South			●	●	●	●	
EMREB	CSE				●	●		●	
LREB	CSE			●	●	●	●	● or	●
NIEB	CSE			●	●	●	●	●	
NREB	CSE			●		●		●	
NWREB	CSE			●	●	●	●	●	
SREB	CSE				●	●		●	
SEREB	CSE			●	●	●	●	●	
SWEB	CSE				●	●	●	●	
WJEC	CSE		●	●		●	●	●	
WMEB	CSE			Op	Op	●	Op	●	
WYLREB	CSE					●		●	
YREB	CSE				●			●	

Key

Op   optional/alternative
S   selection of candidates taped
T   teacher examines

Analysis of examination weightings

Board	Level	Syllabus	Number of papers	Time	% written	% oral
AEB	O	I	3 + Oral	(1) 1½ h (2) 2 h (3) ½ h	30% 37% 8%	25%
AEB	O	II	3 + Oral	(1) ¾ h (2) 2 h (3) 50 min	(1 + 3) 38% 37%	25%
Cambridge	O		3 + Oral	(1) 2¼ h (2) ¾ h (3) 40 min	45% 15% 15%	25%
JMB	O	A	2 + Oral	(1) 1½ h (2) 1¾ h	36⅔% 38⅓%	25%
JMB	O	B	2 + Oral	(1) 1½ h (2) 1¼ h	36⅔% 28⅓%	35%
London	O		3 + Oral	(1) ½ h (2) 1 h (3) 1½ h	10% 30% 45%	15%
NIEC	O		1 + Oral	(1) 3 h	60%	40%
Oxford	O	A	4 + Oral	(1) 50 min (2) 1½ h (3) ½ h (4) 50 min	15½% 38½% 11½% 23%	11½%
Oxford	O	B	5 + Oral	(1) 1½ h (2) 35 min (3) ½ h (4) ½ h (5) ¾ h	25% 15% 5% 20% 20%	15%
O & C	O		3 + Oral	(1) 1¾ h (2) ½ h (3) 2 h	37% 7½% 37%	18½%
SEB	O	Trad	2 + Oral	(1a) ½ h (1b) 1¼ h (2) 1¼ h	15% 25% 30%	30%
SEB	O	Alt	3 + Oral	(1) ½ h (2) 1 h (3) ¾ h	13% 27% 13%	47%
SUJB	O		2 + Oral	(1) 40 min (2) 2 h	27½% 42½%	30%
WJEC	O		4 + Oral	(1) 2 h (2) 1½ h (3) 40 min (4) 30 min	40% 24% 10% 6%	20%

Board	Level	Syllabus	Number of papers	Time	% written	% oral
Joint 16+	16+		2 + Oral	(1) 1½ h (2) 1 h 20 min	25% 50%	25%
ALSEB	CSE		2 + Oral	(1) 1¾ h (2) ¾ h	50% 25%	25%
EAEB	CSE	North	2 + Oral	(1) 1½ h (2) 1½ h	25% 45%	30%
EAEB	CSE	South	2 + Oral	(1) 1½ h (2) 1 h	40% 20%	40%
EMREB	CSE		3 + Oral	(1) ¾ h (2) 1 h (3) ¾ h	25% 25% 25%	25%
LREB	CSE		2 + Oral	(1) 2 h (2) 1 h	50% 15%	35%
NIEB	CSE		2 + Oral + coursework	(1) 1½ h (2) 2 h	25% 30%	30% + coursework 15%
NREB	CSE		2 + Oral	(1) 1¾ h (2) 1¾ h	30% 40%	30%
NWREB	CSE		3 + Oral	(1) 1½ h (2) 1 h (3) 1 h	25% 20% 25%	30%
SREB	CSE		2 + Oral	(1) 1½ h (2) 1 h 5 min	25% 45%	30%
SEREB	CSE		3 + Oral + coursework	(1) 50 min (2) 40 min (3) 1 h	15% 15% 20%	50% (including coursework)
SWEB	CSE		2 + Oral	(1) 1½ h (2) 1½ h	35% 30%	35%
WJEC	CSE		3 + Oral	(1) 2 h (2) ⎰ Time (3) ⎱ not specified	40%	60% (including (2) aural comprehension and (3) dictation)
WMEB	CSE		2 + Oral	(1) 1½ h (2) 2 h	30% 45%	25%
WYLREB	CSE		2 + Oral	(1) 2 h (2) 1½ h	40% 20%	40%
YREB	CSE		3 + Oral	(1) 1¼ h (2) ¾ h (3) ½ h	25% 25% 25%	25%

EXAMINATION BOARDS: ADDRESSES

General Certificate of Education – Ordinary Level (GCE)

AEB
Associated Examining Board
Wellington House, Aldershot, Hampshire GU11 1BQ

Cambridge
University of Cambridge Local Examinations Syndicate
Syndicate Buildings, 17 Harvey Road, Cambridge CB1 2EU

JMB
Joint Matriculation Board
Manchester M15 6EU

London
University of London, School Examinations Department,
66–72 Gower Street, London WC1E 6EE

NIEC
Northern Ireland Schools GCE Examinations Council
Beechill House, 42 Beechill Road, Belfast BT8 4RS

Oxford
Oxford Delegacy of Local Examinations
Ewert Place, Summertown, Oxford OX2 7BX

O & C
Oxford and Cambridge Schools Examination Board
10 Trumpington Street, Cambridge; *and* Elsfield Way, Oxford OX2 8EP

SUJB
Southern Universities' Joint Board for School Examinations
Cotham Road, Bristol BS6 6DD

WJEC
Welsh Joint Education Committee
245 Western Avenue, Cardiff CF5 2YX

Scottish Certificate of Education – Ordinary Grade (SCE)

SEB
Scottish Examination Board
Ironmills Road, Dalkeith, Midlothian EH22 1BR

Certificate of Secondary Education

ALSEB
Associated Lancashire Schools Examining Board
77 Whitworth Street, Manchester M1 6HA

EAEB
East Anglian Examinations Board
The Lindens, Lexden Road, Colchester, Essex CO3 3RL

EMREB
East Midland Regional Examinations Board
Robins Wood House, Robins Wood Road, Apsley, Nottingham NG8 3RL

LREB
London Regional Examinations Board
(*formerly*: MREB Middlesex Regional Examinations Board)
Lyon House, 104 Wandsworth High Street, London SW18 4LF

NIEB
Northern Ireland CSE Examinations Board
Beechill House, 42 Beechill Road, Belfast BT8 4RS

NREB
North Regional Examinations Board
Wheatfield Road, Westerhope, Newcastle upon Tyne NE5 5JZ

NWREB
North West Regional Examinations Board
Orbit House, Albert Street, Eccles, Manchester M30 0WL

SREB
Southern Regional Examinations Board
53 London Road, Southampton SO9 4YI

SEREB
South East Regional Examinations Board
Beloe House, 2–4 Mount Ephraim Road, Royal Tunbridge Wells, Kent TN1 1EU

SWEB
South Western Examinations Board
23–29 Marsh Street, Bristol BS1 4BP

WJEC
Welsh Joint Education Committee
245 Western Avenue, Cardiff CF5 2YX

WMEB
West Midlands Examinations Board
Norfolk House, Smallbrook Queensway, Birmingham B5 4NJ

WYLREB*
West Yorkshire and Lindsey Regional Examining Board
Scarsdale House, 136 Derbyshire Lane, Sheffield S8 8SE

YREB*
Yorkshire Regional Examinations Board
31–33 Springfield Avenue, Harrogate, North Yorkshire HG1 2HW

Joint 16+
ALSEB/JMB/WYLREB/YREB

* Yorkshire and Humberside Regional Examinations Board, at the *YREB* address, now embraces
WYLREB and *YREB*

Part I Core Sections

1 Grammar revision

The key to success in both the written and oral sections of O-level and CSE examinations lies in a sure knowledge of French grammar. However extensive your range of vocabulary may be, you will not be able to understand or to be understood with any degree of accuracy unless you have a good working knowledge of the basic sentence structures and grammatical features of the language. Thorough revision and practice of these features will increase your confidence and provide you with a sound base for the examination.

Begin your revision programme in plenty of time so that you will be able to cover all the grammar revision sections and do all the grammar tests in Part II. These short tests are designed to find out whether you have grasped the grammatical points. If at the end of any test you are still unsure of the elements tested, revise the section again and then do the test again.

1 ARTICLES

Remember these points:

(a) The definite articles (**le, la, l', les** = the) are used more frequently in French than they are in English. Remember to use them in such expressions as:

Children like ice cream. **Les** enfants aiment **les** glaces.
Poor Mary has forgotten her book. **La** pauvre Marie a oublié son livre.
He prefers red wine to white wine. Il préfère **le** vin rouge **au** vin blanc.

(b) When preceded by the preposition **à**, the forms of the definite article are:
au, à la, à l', **aux.**
When preceded by the preposition **de,** the forms are:
du, de la, de l', **des.**

(c) The indefinite articles (**un, une, des** = a, some) are omitted when giving people's occupations:
My father is an engineer. Mon père est ingénieur.
Her brothers are students. Ses frères sont étudiants.

(d) The partitive articles (**du, de la, de l', des** = some) are contracted to **de** or **d'** in the following instances:

(i) After a negative:
J'ai des pommes. Je n'ai pas **de** pommes.
Il a de l'argent. Il n'a pas **d'**argent.
N.B. also: J'ai une voiture. Je n'ai pas **de** voiture.

(ii) When an adjective precedes the noun:
des livres   **de** gros livres
des robes   **de** jolies robes

2 NOUNS

Making nouns plural

As in English, the plurals of nouns in French are normally formed by adding 's' to the singular noun, e.g. un garçon, des garçons.

However, there are several important exceptions to this rule which you will be expected to know. Check carefully the following plural forms which do not follow the normal rule:

l'animal (m)	les animaux	*animal(s)*
le bijou	les bijoux	*jewel(s)*
le bois	les bois	*wood(s)*
le cadeau	les cadeaux	*present(s)*
le caillou	les cailloux	*pebble(s)*
le chapeau	les chapeaux	*hat(s)*
le château	les châteaux	*castle(s)*
le cheval	les chevaux	*horse(s)*

le chou	les choux	*cabbage(s)*
le ciel	les cieux	*sky/heaven*
		skies/heavens
l'eau (f)	les eaux	*water(s)*
le feu	les feux	*fire(s)*
		(pl. also = *traffic-lights*)
le fils	les fils	*son(s)*
le gâteau	les gâteaux	*cake(s)*
le genou	les genoux	*knee(s)*
le hibou	les hiboux	*owl(s)*
le jeu	les jeux	*game(s)*
le journal	les journaux	*newspaper(s)*
le mal	les maux	*evil(s)/harm(s)/hurt(s)*
le nez	les nez	*nose(s)*
l'œil (m)	les yeux	*eye(s)*
l'oiseau (m)	les oiseaux	*bird(s)*
l'os (m)	les os	*bone(s)*
le prix	les prix	*price(s)/prize(s)*
le tableau	les tableaux	*picture(s)*
le temps	les temps	*time(s)/weather(s)*
le timbre-poste	les timbres-poste	*postage stamp(s)*
le travail	les travaux	*works*

N.B. also: madame   **mes**dames
            mademoiselle **mes**demoiselles
            monsieur   **mes**sieurs

Family names do *not* change in French when they are used in the plural:
We are going to the Gavarins. Nous allons chez les Gavarin.

3 ADJECTIVES

(a) When you are writing in French, you must pay special attention to the endings of words. Adjectives in English have the same form in the singular and the plural.

> e.g. *singular:* the good boy
> *plural:*   the good boys

In French, you must check the endings of *all* words, especially adjectives.

> e.g. *singular:* le sage garçon
> *plural:*   les sages garçons

(b) Another important difference between English and French is the position of adjectives. In English, adjectives precede the noun:

> the white house; the intelligent girl

In French, all but a few common adjectives are placed *after* the noun:

> la maison **blanche**; la fille **intelligente**

These are the adjectives which **do** precede the noun in French; try to memorise them:

> beau bon excellent gentil grand gras gros jeune joli
> long mauvais même (= *same*) meilleur nouveau petit vieux vilain

Some adjectives change their meaning according to their position:

un **cher** ami	*a dear friend*
un vin **cher**	*an expensive wine*
un **ancien** élève	*a former pupil*
un bâtiment **ancien**	*an old building*
mes **propres** mains	*my own hands*
mes mains **propres**	*my clean hands*

(c) The spelling of adjectives in French changes according to the gender of the noun they are describing, as well as according to whether the noun is singular or plural:

> le **vieux** livre
> la **vieille** maison

An adjective is normally made feminine by the addition of 'e'.
   e.g. joli/jolie
When a word already ends in 'e' it does not change.
   e.g. jeune (m *and* f)

There are also a number of adjectives which have irregular feminine forms. These must be learnt:

Masculine singular	Feminine singular		Masculine singular	Feminine singular	
ancien	ancienne	*old*	gentil	gentille	*nice*
bas	basse	*low*	gras	grasse	*fat*
beau	belle	*beautiful*	gros	grosse	*big*
blanc	blanche	*white*	jaloux	jalouse	*jealous*
bon	bonne	*good*	long	longue	*long*
bref	brève	*brief*	neuf	neuve	*brand new*
cher	chère	*dear*	nouveau	nouvelle	*new*
doux	douce	*sweet*	premier	première	*first*
épais	épaisse	*thick*	public	publique	*public*
entier	entière	*entire/whole*	roux	rousse	*auburn, russet*
faux	fausse	*false*	sec	sèche	*dry*
favori	favorite	*favourite*	secret	secrète	*secret*
fou	folle	*mad*	vieux	vieille	*old*
frais	fraîche	*fresh*	vif	vive	*lively*

Note also the forms **bel, nouvel, vieil.** These are used before masculine singular words beginning with a vowel or 'h'.
   e.g. un **bel** homme
         un **nouvel** élève
         un **vieil** autobus

4 INDEFINITE ADJECTIVES

(a) Autre(s), other
   Les autres élèves sont sages. *The other pupils are good.*
   J'ai une autre robe rouge. *I have another red dress.*

(b) Chaque, each
   chaque élève, *each pupil*
   chaque maison, *each house*

(c) Même(s) same
   Nous avons vu le même film. *We saw the same film.*
   Ils ont les mêmes disques. *They have the same records.*

(d) Plusieurs, several
   J'ai acheté plusieurs livres. *I have bought several books.*

(e) Quelque(s), some
   pendant quelque temps, *for some time*
   Quelques élèves sont arrivés. *Some pupils have arrived.*

(f) Tel, telle, tels, telles, such
Pay special attention to the position of this word.
      un tel homme, *such a man*
      une telle femme, *such a woman*
      de tels hommes, *such men*
      de telles femmes, *such women*

(g) Tout, toute, tous, toutes, all (+ article)
      tout le fromage, *all the cheese*
      toute la famille, *all the family*
      tous les garçons, *all the boys*
      toutes les jeunes filles, *all the girls*

5 COMPARATIVE AND SUPERLATIVE OF ADJECTIVES

(a) The comparative and superlative forms of the adjective are quite simple when the adjective precedes the noun:

more, **plus**	less, **moins**	as, **aussi**
the most, **le (la, les) plus**	the least, **le (la, les) moins**	

stronger, plus fort	*less strong,* moins fort	*as strong,* aussi fort
the strongest, le plus fort	*the least strong,* le moins fort	
la plus forte	la moins forte	
les plus fort(e)s	les moins fort(e)s	

In all three cases **que** is used to complete the comparison. It can mean *as* or *than*.
>   Pierre est plus fort que Jean. *Peter is stronger* than *John.*
>   Les lions sont aussi forts que les tigres. *Lions are* as *strong* as *tigers.*

Be particularly careful with:
>   better, **meilleur**   un meilleur élève, *a better pupil*
>   best, **le meilleur**   le meilleur élève, *the best pupil*

(b) When an adjective follows the noun, it keeps the same position when it is made comparative or superlative:
>   une histoire plus amusante, *a more interesting story*

In the superlative, the definite article must be repeated after the noun:
>   l'histoire **la** plus amusante, *the most interesting story*

(c) 'In' with a superlative is translated by **de**:
>   L'élève le plus intelligent **de** la classe. *The most intelligent pupil in the class.*

6 DEMONSTRATIVE ADJECTIVES

masculine	*feminine*	*plural*
ce	cette	ces

There is a special masculine singular form which is used before a vowel or 'h': **cet**.

These adjectives correspond to the English *this, that/these, those*.

ce livre	*this book, that book*
cet homme	*this man, that man*
cette maison	*this house, that house*
ces élèves	*these pupils, those pupils*

-ci and **-là** may be added for extra emphasis:

>   ce livre-ci, *this book here*
>   ce livre-là, *that book there*, etc.

7 POSSESSIVE ADJECTIVES

	masculine	*feminine*	*plural*
my	mon	ma	mes
your	ton	ta	tes
his/her	son	sa	ses
our	notre	notre	nos
your	votre	votre	vos
their	leur	leur	leurs

(a) Before a singular feminine noun beginning with a vowel or 'h', use **mon, ton, son**:
>   son amie, *his (her) girlfriend*
>   ton histoire, *your story*
>   mon auto, *my car*

(b) son=his *or* her
sa =his *or* her

The difference in usage depends on the gender of the possession and *not* on the gender of the owner:

sa maman, *his mother* or *her mother*
son stylo, *his pen* or *her pen*

8 ADVERBS

(a) Adverbs of manner are normally formed by adding **-ment** to the feminine form of the adjective:

heureuse (f), *happy* → **heureusement,** *happily*
douce (f), *sweet, gentle* → **doucement,** *sweetly, gently*

As usual, there are exceptions to this rule. Here are some of the more common ones:

constamment *constantly*
énormément *enormously*
évidemment *evidently*
gentiment *nicely*
mal *badly*
précisément *precisely*
profondément *deeply*
vraiment *truly, really*

Note the irregular form **mal.**

Of all the adverbs which candidates misspell, the word **vite** *(quickly)* is the word which is most frequently misspelt. **Vite** is now the only spelling of this word. It does *not* have the same ending as the other adverbs above.

(b) One of the most important things to remember about adverbs in French is their position in relation to the verb ... ce the adverb before the verb. In French, the adverb ... b of a sentence. The normal position for the adverb ...

... *Paris.*

... dverb is nearly always placed between the auxiliary ...

... ced at the beginning of a sentence, but there are ... rds as **aussi** and **ainsi** *(thus).* It is better, therefore, ... erb after the verb.

... ore an adjective, **tout** does not agree with the ... begins with a consonant:

... *ite moved.*

... ERBS

These are formed in a similar way to the comparatives and superlatives of adjectives, except that, because they are adverbs, they are invariable. There are no feminine or plural forms of the article.

e.g. Marie chante **le plus fort.** *Mary sings the loudest.*

Note also: best, **mieux**
the best, **le mieux**
e.g. Elle chante le mieux. *She sings the best.*

10 PERSONAL PRONOUNS

(a) Subject pronouns

	singular	*plural*
1	je	nous
2	tu	vous
3	il/elle/on	ils/elles

Remember that **on** is a third person singular pronoun, so the verb must agree with it:

On **va** en ville,

even though in translation we might use another personal form:

They/we are going to town.

(b) Object pronouns

The normal positions are:

1	2	3	4	5	
me					
te	le				
(se)	la	lui			
nous	les	leur	y	en	verb
vous					
(se)					

Je te le donne. *I give it to you.*
Il m'en a parlé. *He talked to me about it.*
Nous les y enverrons. *We'll send them there.*

The object pronouns always keep to this order, except in *affirmative commands*.
In affirmative commands:

 (i) The object pronouns follow the verb and are joined to the verb by hyphens.
 (ii) Columns 1 and 2 change place.
(iii) **Me** becomes **moi**, and **te** becomes **toi**, except before **en** when they become **m'en** and **t'en.**

Examples:
Affirmative statement: *I have given some to him.*
    Je **lui en** ai donné.
Negative statement: *I have not given any to him.*
    Je ne **lui en** ai pas donné.
Affirmative command: *Give some to him.*
    · Donnez-**lui-en.**
Negative command: *Don't give any to him.*
    Ne **lui en** donnez pas.
Affirmative command: *Give them to me.*
    Donnez-**les-moi.**
Affirmative command: *Give me some.*
    Donnez-**m'en.**

11 POSSESSIVE PRONOUNS

These correspond to the English 'mine', 'yours', 'his', etc.

	singular		*plural*	
	masculine	*feminine*	*masculine*	*feminine*
mine	le mien	la mienne	les miens	les miennes
yours	le tien	la tienne	les tiens	les tiennes
his/hers	le sien	la sienne	les siens	les siennes
ours	le nôtre	la nôtre	les nôtres	les nôtres
yours	le vôtre	la vôtre	les vôtres	les vôtres
theirs	le leur	la leur	les leurs	les leurs

Usage

Où est ton billet? Voici **le mien.** *Where is your ticket? Here is mine.*
Je n'ai pas de voiture. Pouvons-nous y aller dans **la vôtre**?
I haven't a car. Can we go there in yours?

In this last sentence 'yours'=your car. Since 'car' is feminine in French **(la voiture),** the feminine possessive pronoun must be used irrespective of the gender of the possessor.

Possession may also be expressed in the following way:
A qui est ce stylo? Il est **à moi.** *Whose pen is this? It's mine.*

12 DEMONSTRATIVE PRONOUNS

These pronouns are used to say *'this one/that one'*, and in the plural, *'these ones/those ones'*.

singular		plural	
masculine	*feminine*	*masculine*	*feminine*
celui	celle	ceux	celles

If you wish to stress 'this/these' or 'that/those', then the endings **-ci** or **-là** respectively may be added:

Voici deux livres. Celui-ci est à moi. Celui-là est à Natalie.
Here are two books. This one (here) is mine. That one (there) is Natalie's.
Ces chaussures sont à 200F, mais celles-là sont à 150F.
These shoes cost 200F, but those cost 150F.

Always check carefully the gender of the pronouns you are using.

Ceci/cela (this/that)
Ecoutez ceci. *Listen to this.*
Qui a dit cela? *Who said that?*

Cela is often shortened to **ça:**
Qui a dit ça? *Who said that?*
Ça, c'est vrai. *That's true.*

13 DISJUNCTIVE PRONOUNS

These pronouns are also sometimes called 'emphatic' or 'stressed' pronouns.

moi	*me/I*	nous	*us/we*
toi	*you*	vous	*you*
lui	*him/he*	eux	*them (m)/they*
elle	*her/she*	elles	*them (f)/they*

The word **-même** may be added to the above words to translate **-self**:

moi-même *myself*
toi-même *yourself,* etc.

Note also **soi-même,** *oneself.* Use this when you are using **on.**
On peut le faire soi-même. *One can do it oneself.*

Disjunctive pronouns should be used:

(a) After prepositions:
devant moi, *in front of me*
sans eux, *without them*
chez elle, *at her house*

(b) To emphasise a pronoun at the beginning of a sentence:
Moi, je l'ai fait. I *did it.*
Lui, il est venu. He *came.*

(c) When a pronoun stands alone:
Qui l'a fait? – Moi. *Who did it? – I did.*

(d) In comparisons:
Vous êtes plus intelligent que moi. *You are more intelligent than I.*
Il est aussi grand que toi. *He is as tall as you.*

(e) With **c'est** and **ce sont**:
C'est vous. *It's you.*
Ce sont elles. *It's them (f).*

Ce sont is used only with the third person plural.

14 RELATIVE PRONOUNS

(a) qui   who, which (*subject*)
    que   whom, that (*object*)
    dont   whose, of whom, of which

Voici les enfants qui sont sages. *Here are the children who are good.*
Voici les enfants que vous n'aimez pas. *Here are the children whom you don't like.*
Voici le livre dont vous avez besoin. *Here is the book which you need.*

(b) ce qui   that which (*subject*)/what
    ce que   that which (*object*)/what
    ce dont   that of which/what

Dites-moi ce qui est arrivé. *Tell me what has happened.*
Dites-moi ce que vous avez fait. *Tell me what you did.*
Dites-moi ce dont vous avez bcsoin. *Tell me what you need.*

(c)   m. **lequel**   (the . . .) which
     f. **laquelle**   (the . . .) which
    m.pl. **lesquels**   (the . . .) which
    f.pl. **lesquelles**   (the . . .) which

These relative pronouns are used with prepositions:
    Voilà la table sur laquelle vous trouverez vos livres.
    There is the table on which you will find your books.
    Regardez cette maison devant laquelle il y a un agent de police.
    Look at that house in front of which there is a policeman.

The above relative pronouns combine with **à** and **de** to become:

      m. **auquel**   **duquel**
      f. **à laquelle**   **de laquelle**
    m.pl. **auxquels**   **desquels**
    f.pl. **auxquelles**   **desquelles**

Nous irons au jardin public au milieu duquel se trouve un petit lac.
We shall go to the park in the middle of which there is a little lake.
Ce sont des choses auxquelles je ne pense pas.
They are things I don't think about. (penser **à** = to think about)

Lequel etc. may be used on their own as questions:
    J'ai rapporté un de vos livres. – Lequel?
    I've brought back one of your books. – Which one?
    Puis-je emprunter une de tes cravates? – Laquelle?
    May I borrow one of your ties? – Which one?

15 INDEFINITE PRONOUNS

autre, other
    J'ai vendu quelques livres mais je garderai **les autres.**
    I have sold some books but I shall keep the others.

chacun(e), each one
    Regardez ces voitures. **Chacune** est d'occasion.
    Look at those cars. Each one is second-hand.

N'importe is a very useful indefinite pronoun:
    n'importe qui, anybody
    N'importe qui peut le faire. *Anybody can do it.*

    n'importe quoi, anything
    Rapportez n'importe quoi. *Bring back anything.*

    n'importe quel(le)(s), any
    Vous le trouverez dans n'importe quelle épicerie.
    You will find it at any grocer's.

plusieurs, several

    As-tu des disques? Oui, j'en ai plusieurs.
    Have you any records? Yes, I have several.

quelqu'un, someone

    Attendez-vous quelqu'un? *Are you waiting for someone?*

quelques-un(e)(s), some, a few

    Quelques-uns de vos élèves sont paresseux.
    Some of your pupils are lazy.

tout, everything

    Il connaît tout. *He knows everything.*

tout le monde, everybody

    Tout le monde est arrivé. *Everybody has arrived.*

16 CONJUNCTIONS

car, for (because)

Do not confuse this with the preposition **pour.** If you wish to use the word 'for' meaning 'because', remember to use **car.**

    Il a dû rentrer à la maison à pied **car** il avait perdu la clef de sa voiture.
    He had to walk home for he had lost his car key.

Car is an alternative to **parce que** (because).

comme, as

    Faites **comme** vous voulez. *Do as you like.*

depuis que, since (*time*)

    Il a commencé à neiger **depuis que** je suis sorti.
    It has begun to snow since I went out.

donc, so (*reason*)

Do not use this word at the beginning of a sentence, but it may introduce a clause.

    Il est malade, **donc** il est resté à la maison.
    He is ill, so he stayed at home.

lorsque, quand, when

Be very careful when using these conjunctions. The future tense is frequently needed in French after these two conjunctions where in English we use the present tense:

    Je te téléphonerai quand je serai à Paris.
    I shall telephone you when I am in Paris. (i.e. *when I shall be in Paris*)

Similarly, the future perfect is used where in English we use the perfect tense:

    Je viendrai quand **j'aurai fini** mon travail.
    I shall come when I have finished my work. (i.e. *when I shall have finished my work*)

N.B. **Dès que** and **aussitôt que** (as soon as) follow the same rule.

    Dès qu'il sera à la maison, je te téléphonerai.
    As soon as he is at home, I shall telephone you.

parce que, because

    Il n'a pas réussi parce qu'il n'a pas travaillé.
    He didn't succeed because he didn't work.

N.B. there is *no* hyphen between these two words.

puisque, since (*reason*)

    Il travaille dur puisqu'il désire réussir.
    He is working hard since he wants to succeed.

pendant que, during, while

    Pendant qu'il lisait son journal, on a sonné à la porte.
    While he was reading his newspaper, someone rang the door-bell.

tandis que, while, whilst (*contrast*)

    Christophe a bien travaillé tandis que Pierre n'a rien fait.
    Christopher has worked well while Peter has done nothing.

17 PREPOSITIONS

The correct use of prepositions in French can make all the difference between a good and a bad translation or composition. One of the most important things to remember as far as prepositions are concerned is that frequently there is no one single word in French which will translate a particular word in English. Pupils in the early stages of learning French often ask such questions as 'How do you translate "in"?' There are of course several ways of translating 'in', e.g. **dans, en, à,** etc. Usually only one of these will be appropriate in the particular circumstances. Below are some guidelines for the use of some everyday prepositions.

About

à peu près, approximately

> J'ai à peu près cinquante livres. *I have about fifty books.*

à propos de, concerning

> Je voudrais vous parler à propos de votre visite.
> *I should like to speak to you about your visit.*

au sujet de, on the subject of (similar to **à propos de**)

> Il parlait au sujet des vacances. *He was speaking about the holidays.*

de quoi, of what

> De quoi parles-tu? *What are you speaking about?*

environ

> J'arriverai à dix heures environ. *I shall arrive about ten o'clock.*

vers (similar to **environ**)

> Nous partirons vers deux heures. *We shall leave about two o'clock.*

Along

le long de

> Il marchait le long du quai. *He was walking along the platform.*

avancer, to move along

> Avancez, messieurs, s'il vous plaît. *Move along, gentlemen, please.*

dans

> Il marchait dans la rue. *He was walking along the street.*

sur

> La voiture roulait vite sur la route. *The car was going quickly along the road.*

N.B. for *along with* use **avec**:

> Marie est allée au supermarché avec Suzanne. *Mary went to the supermarket along with Susan.*

Among(st)

parmi

> Il a caché le trésor parmi les roches. *He hid the treasure among the rocks.*

entre

> Nous étions entre amis. *We were among friends.*

Before

avant

> Venez avant midi. *Come before noon.*

déjà (already)

> Je l'ai déjà vu. *I've seen it before.*

devant (place)

> Tenez-vous devant la classe. *Stand before the class.*

By

à

> Je viendrai à vélo. *I'll come by bike.*

de

La vieille dame était suivie d'un voleur. *The old lady was followed by a thief.*

en

J'y suis allé en auto. *I went there by car.*

par

Les enfants ont été punis par leur mère. *The children have been punished by their mother.*

près de (= near)

Asseyez-vous près du feu. *Sit by the fire.*

For

depuis

This is a most important preposition which is tested by most Examination Boards.

Depuis is used with the *present* tense to express 'has/have been . . .' in a time clause:

J'apprends le français depuis cinq ans. *I have been learning French for five years.*
Il est ici depuis trois jours. *He has been here for three days.*

Similarly the *imperfect* tense is used to express 'had been . . .':

Il habitait Paris depuis deux ans. *He had been living in Paris for two years.*
Nous l'attendions depuis deux heures. *We had been waiting for him for two hours.*

pendant (= during)

Nous avons travaillé pendant trois heures. *We have worked for three hours.*

pour

For future or pre-arranged time:

Nous serons là pour trois semaines. *We shall be there for three weeks.*

In

à

Les enfants sont à l'école. *The children are in school.*

Other useful expressions:

à l'intérieur, *inside*
à Londres, *in London*
à la mode, *in fashion*
au lit, *in bed*
au soleil, *in the sun*
à voix haute, *in a loud voice*

dans

Ils sont allés dans la salle à manger. *They are in the dining-room.*

de

Elle s'habille de noir. *She dresses in black.*

en

J'habite en France. *I live in France.*
Vous y arriverez en quatre heures. *You will get there in four hours.*
Elle s'habille en pantalon. *She dresses in trousers.*

sous

J'aime marcher sous la pluie. *I like walking in the rain.*

sur

Un sur vingt a un magnétoscope. *One in twenty has a video tape-recorder.*

On

à

à droite, *on the right*
à gauche, *on the left*
à pied, *on foot*
Nous allons à l'école à pied. *We go to school on foot.*
à son retour, *on his/her return*
A son retour, il est allé la voir. *On his return he went to see her.*

dans

Je l'ai recontré dans l'autobus. *I met him on the bus.*

de

d'un côté, *on one side*
de l'autre côté, *on the other side*

en

en vacances, *on holiday*
en vente, *on sale*

par

par une belle journée d'été, *on a fine summer's day*

sur

sur la table, *on the table*

This is the most obvious translation of 'on'; but, as is shown above, there are other words which must be used in certain circumstances.

Remember that with dates, 'on' is *not* translated:
Elle est venue lundi. *She came on Monday.*

Out

dans

Il a pris une lettre dans le tiroir.
He took a letter out of the drawer.

Dans is used here because we think of what the object was *in* just before it was taken out.

hors

hors de danger, *out of danger*
hors d'haleine, *out of breath*
hors de la maison, *out of the house*
hors de vue, *out of sight*

par

Elle regardait par la fenêtre. *She was looking out of the window.*

sur

See also 'in'.
neuf sur dix, *nine out of ten*

Over

au-dessus

Il a tiré au-dessus de ma tête. *He fired over my head.*

par-dessus

J'ai sauté par-dessus le mur. *I jumped over the wall.*

d'en face, over the way (i.e. opposite)
Elle habite la maison d'en face. *She lives in the house over the way.*

plus de (more than)
J'ai plus de mille francs. *I have over a thousand francs.*

sur

Mettez la couverture sur le lit. *Put the blanket over the bed.*

Since

depuis

See also 'for'.
Il n'a rien fait depuis son arrivée.
He has done nothing since he arrived.

Until

jusqu'à

Nous y resterons jusqu'à minuit.
We shall stay there until midnight.

If you wish to use a clause following 'until', remember that you must then use **jusqu'à ce que** + subjunctive.

> Je resterai ici jusqu'à ce qu'il vienne.
> *I shall stay here until he comes.*

à demain, until tomorrow

Translation of 'up, down, in, out' with a verb of motion

In sentences such as:

> He ran into the house,
> She ran down the street,

it is better to change the preposition into a verb:

> Il **est entré** dans la maison en courant.
> Elle **a descendu** la rue en courant.

You will notice that the verb in the original sentence has now become a present participle + **en.** Remember that **descendre** (which is normally conjugated with **être** in the perfect tense) is here conjugated with **avoir** as the verb has a direct object, 'la rue'.

As you can see from the above examples, there is no simple way of translating one French word with a single corresponding word in English. You must have a sure knowledge of individual French phrases and of the different ways of translating even simple words like 'in' and 'on' if you are to achieve 'Frenchness' in both oral and written work. Careful reading of French passages will help you to become more aware of French expressions. Try to read a few lines of good French each day and make a note of, *and learn,* as many useful phrases as possible.

18 Verbs

The most important part of any sentence is the verb. In almost all examinations, the incorrect use of verbs is heavily penalised. You must make sure, therefore, that you revise the sections on verbs carefully. The main tenses which you must be able to use are: *present, future, imperfect, conditional, perfect and pluperfect.* These are the main tenses that you will be expected to speak and write accurately.

There are also other tenses which you will be required to know, but mainly for recognition purposes. These are the past historic, the future and conditional perfect, and for some Examination Boards, the present subjunctive. You must check to see which tenses are specified by your Examination Board for active use and which will be for recognition purposes only.

French verbs are more difficult to learn than English verbs because each verb has several different forms. English verbs usually have no more than two or three different forms in each tense, e.g.:

I go,	you go,	he goes,	she goes,	we go,	you go,	they go
1	1	2	2	1	1	1

French verbs, however, can have as many as six different forms, e.g.:

je vais,	tu vas,	il va,	elle va,	nous allons,	vous allez,	ils vont,	elles vont
1	2	3	3	4	5	6	6

You must set time aside each week to revise verbs carefully. You must learn all the forms of each verb, paying particular attention to spelling.

The other main difficulty with French verbs is that there are many common irregular verbs which have to be learnt separately as they do not fit into the normal verb patterns. This, too, takes time to check thoroughly.

The sections that follow cover the main types of regular verb and the main irregular verbs in the tenses which you will be expected to know at O level and CSE. Always remember that the correct spelling (including the correct use of accents) is *very* important.

Many verbs are regular and conform to the patterns given below for the various tenses. There are three main types of regular verb, usually referred to by the last two letters of the present infinitive.

Type 1: **-er** verbs, e.g. donn**er** (to give)
Type 2: **-ir** verbs, e.g. fin**ir** (to finish)
Type 3: **-re** verbs, e.g. vend**re** (to sell)

Remember that each type has different endings. Check these endings carefully.

19 THE PRESENT TENSE

Type 1: regular -er verbs

The majority of **-er** verbs in French follow this pattern:

donner – to give

je donne	I give
tu donnes	you (*singular*) give
il donne	he gives
elle donne	she gives
nous donn**ons**	we give
vous donn**ez**	you (*plural or polite singular form*) give
ils donn**ent**	they give (*masculine form*)
elles donn**ent**	they give (*feminine form*)

You will see that the endings for type 1 regular verbs are:
-e, -es, -e, -e, -ons, -ez, -ent, -ent.

These are added to the stem of the verb, i.e. the infinitive **donner** minus the **-er** ending. Other regular verbs follow the same pattern:

regarder → je regard**e**
arriver   → j'arrive[1]
parler   → je parl**e**

Irregular -er verbs

The most common irregular **-er** verbs which occur in O-level and CSE examinations are listed below. Check each one carefully. Not every verb has the same degree of irregularity.

For example, the verb **manger** (to eat) has only one irregularity in the present tense, which is the addition of 'e' in the **nous** form, i.e. nous mangeons. The 'e' is added to keep the 'g' sound soft.

Similarly the verb **commencer** requires a cedilla (¸) in the **nous** form, to keep the 'c' sound soft: nous commençons.

The pattern of the following verbs is more irregular:

jeter – to throw	**appeler** – to call
je jette	j'appelle
tu jettes	tu appelles
il jette	il appelle
elle jette	elle appelle
nous jetons	nous appelons
vous jetez	vous appelez
ils jettent	ils appellent
elles jettent	elles appellent

You will see that the actual endings of the present tense of **jeter** and **appeler** are the same as those for the regular **-er** verbs. The irregularity occurs in the doubling of the consonant.

Some other **-er** verbs are irregular because of the addition or changes of accents, e.g. **espérer, répéter, acheter, lever, mener.** The irregularities in all these verbs occur in the singular and the third person plural forms. Try to be as accurate in your use of accents as you would be with spelling.

espérer – to hope	**répéter** – to repeat
j'espère	je répète
tu espères	tu répètes
il espère	il répète
elle espère	elle répète
nous espérons	nous répétons
vous espérez	vous répétez
ils espèrent	ils répètent
elles espèrent	elles répètent

---

[1] When speaking and writing French remember to omit the 'e' of **je** when it is followed by a vowel or 'h'. N.B. especially **j'habite.**

acheter – to buy	lever – to lift	mener – to lead
j'achète	je lève	je mène
tu achètes	tu lèves	tu mènes
il achète	il lève	il mène
elle achète	elle lève	elle mène
nous achetons	nous levons	nous menons
vous achetez	vous levez	vous menez
ils achètent	ils lèvent	ils mènent
elles achètent	elles lèvent	elles mènent

-er verbs whose infinitives end in **-oyer** or **-uyer** change the 'y' to 'i' in the singular and the third person plural forms:

envoyer – to send	ennuyer – to annoy
j'envoie	j'ennuie
tu envoies	tu ennuies
il envoie	il ennuie
elle envoie	elle ennuie
nous envoyons	nous ennuyons
vous envoyez	vous ennuyez
ils envoient	ils ennuient
elles envoient	elles ennuient

Type 2: regular -ir verbs

The endings for the present tense of these verbs are:
-is, -is, -it, -it, -issons, -issez, -issent, -issent
These are added to the stem of the verb, i.e. the present infinitive minus the **-ir.**

finir – to finish

je finis	nous finissons
tu finis	vous finissez
il finit	ils finissent
elle finit	elles finissent

Irregular -ir verbs

There are several important irregular **-ir** verbs which do not follow the above pattern, e.g.:

courir – to run	dormir – to sleep	fuir – to flee
je cours	je dors	je fuis
tu cours	tu dors	tu fuis
il court	il dort	il fuit
elle court	elle dort	elle fuit
nous courons	nous dormons	nous fuyons
vous courez	vous dormez	vous fuyez
ils courent	ils dorment	ils fuient
elles courent	elles dorment	elles fuient

ouvrir[1] – to open	partir[2] – to leave	venir[3] – to come
j'ouvre	je pars	je viens
tu ouvres	tu pars	tu viens
il ouvre	il part	il vient
elle ouvre	elle part	elle vient
nous ouvrons	nous partons	nous venons
vous ouvrez	vous partez	vous venez
ils ouvrent	ils partent	ils viennent
elles ouvrent	elles partent	elles viennent

[1] Although **ouvrir** is an **-ir** verb, it acts like an **-er** verb in the present tense. Other verbs which are like **ouvrir** include: **couvrir** (to cover), **cueillir** (to pick), **découvrir** (to discover), **offrir** (to offer).

[2] The verb **sortir** has the same pattern as **partir**: je sors, il sort, vous sortez, etc.

[3] The verbs **devenir** (to become), **tenir** (to hold), and **retenir** (to hold back) have the same pattern as **venir**: je deviens, il retient, nous tenons, etc.

Type 3: regular -re verbs

Regular **-re** verbs have the following endings added to the stem:
-s, -s, -, -, -ons, -ez, -ent, -ent.

vendre – to sell

je vends	nous vendons
tu vends	vous vendez
il vend	ils vendent
elle vend	elles vendent

Irregular -re verbs

The verb être is the most irregular of **-re** verbs:

être – to be

je suis	nous sommes
tu es	vous êtes
il est	ils sont
elle est	elles sont

Listed below are some of the more common irregular **-re** verbs.

battre – to beat	**boire** – to drink	**conduire** – to drive
je bats	je bois	je conduis
tu bats	tu bois	tu conduis
il bat	il boit	il conduit
elle bat	elle boit	elle conduit
nous battons	nous buvons	nous conduisons
vous battez	vous buvez	vous conduisez
ils battent	ils boivent	ils conduisent
elles battent	elles boivent	elles conduisent

connaître – to know	**craindre** – to fear	**croire** – to believe
je connais	je crains	je crois
tu connais	tu crains	tu crois
il connaît	il craint	il croit
elle connaît	elle craint	elle croit
nous connaissons	nous craignons	nous croyons
vous connaissez	vous craignez	vous croyez
ils connaissent	ils craignent	ils croient
elles connaissent	elles craignent	elles croient

dire – to say	**écrire** – to write	**faire** – to do, make
je dis	j'écris	je fais
tu dis	tu écris	tu fais
il dit	il écrit	il fait
elle dit	elle écrit	elle fait
nous disons	nous écrivons	nous faisons
vous dites	vous écrivez	vous faites
ils disent	ils écrivent	ils font
elles disent	elles écrivent	elles font

lire – to read	**mettre** – to put	**prendre** – to take
je lis	je mets	je prends
tu lis	tu mets	tu prends
il lit	il met	il prend
elle lit	elle met	elle prend
nous lisons	nous mettons	nous prenons
vous lisez	vous mettez	vous prenez
ils lisent	ils mettent	ils prennent
elles lisent	elles mettent	elles prennent

rire – to laugh	**suivre** – to follow	**vivre** – to live
je ris	je suis[1]	je vis[2]
tu ris	tu suis	tu vis[2]
il rit	il suit	il vit[2]
elle rit	elle suit	elle vit[2]
nous rions	nous suivons	nous vivons
vous riez	vous suivez	vous vivez
ils rient	ils suivent	ils vivent
elles rient	elles suivent	elles vivent

Verbs ending in -oir

In addition to the three main types of verb, there is a fourth group, the infinitives of which end in **-oir.** All of these verbs are irregular. The more common ones are listed below.

avoir – to have	**s'asseoir** – to sit down	**devoir** – to owe
j'ai	je m'assieds	je dois
tu as	tu t'assieds	tu dois
il a	il s'assied	il doit
elle a	elle s'assied	elle doit
nous avons	nous nous asseyons	nous devons
vous avez	vous vous asseyez	vous devez
ils ont	ils s'asseyent	il doivent
elles ont	elles s'asseyent	elles doivent

falloir – to be necessary	**pleuvoir** – to rain
3rd person singular only:	3rd person singular only:
il faut – it is necessary	**il pleut** – it is raining

pouvoir – to be able	**recevoir** – to receive	**savoir** – to know
je peux	je reçois	je sais
tu peux	tu reçois	tu sais
il peut	il reçoit	il sait
elle peut	elle reçoit	elle sait
nous pouvons	nous recevons	nous savons
vous pouvez	vous recevez	vous savez
ils peuvent	ils reçoivent	ils savent
elles peuvent	elles reçoivent	elles savent

voir – to see	**vouloir** – to want
je vois	je veux
tu vois	tu veux
il voit	il veut
elle voit	elle veut
nous voyons	nous voulons
vous voyez	vous voulez
ils voient	ils veulent
elles voient	elles veulent

Reflexive verbs

In addition to the above verbs, you will need to revise the present tense of reflexive verbs. The present tense endings of these follow the patterns already given. The difference is that an extra pronoun, called a reflexive pronoun, precedes the verb.

se coucher – to go to bed

je **me** couche	nous **nous** couchons
tu **te** couches	vous **vous** couchez
il **se** couche	ils **se** couchent
elle **se** couche	elles **se** couchent

---

[1] Although this part of the verb has the same spelling as the first person singular, present tense of the verb **être** (to be), the sense of the rest of the sentence will indicate which verb is being used.

[2] These forms have the same spelling as the past historic tense of the verb **voir** (to see). Once again, the sense of the sentence will indicate which verb and tense are being used.

English translations of the present tense

Do remember, especially when translating from English into French, that the present tense in English has several different forms but in French there is only one present tense. For example, 'I go', 'I am going' and 'I do go' are all translated as **je vais.**

A very common mistake in O-level and CSE examinations is to try to translate the English 'am' and 'do' when attached to another verb. This mistake is always penalised heavily.

20 THE FUTURE TENSE

When you are talking about something which is going to happen in the near future, you can often avoid using the future tense by using the present tense of **aller** plus an infinitive:

Je **vais acheter** des chaussures samedi prochain. *I will buy some shoes next Saturday.*

Using the verb **aller** plus an infinitive instead of the future tense will often add a touch of 'Frenchness' to your compositions. However, you must still be able to recognise and use the correct forms of the future tense.

All verbs have the same endings in the future tense in French. They are:

-ai, -as, -a, -a, -ons, -ez, -ont, -ont.

Type 1: -er verbs

The future endings are added to the whole of the infinitive:

donner

je donnerai – *I shall give*	nous donnerons
tu donneras	vous donnerez
il donnera	ils donneront
elle donnera	elles donneront

Type 2: -ir verbs

The future endings are added to the whole of the infinitive:

finir

je finirai – *I shall finish*	nous finirons
tu finiras	vous finirez
il finira	ils finiront
elle finira	elles finiront

Type 3: -re verbs

The final 'e' of the infinitive is omitted, before adding the appropriate endings:

vendre

je vendrai – *I shall sell*	nous vendrons
tu vendras	vous vendrez
il vendra	ils vendront
elle vendra	elles vendront

The future tense of irregular verbs

Listed below are the future tenses of the common irregular verbs which you will be expected to know. The endings are the same as for all other verbs in the future tense, but you must check carefully the spellings of these irregular verbs.

acheter	j'achèterai	*I shall buy*
aller	j'irai	*I shall go*
apercevoir	j'apercevrai	*I shall perceive, notice*
appeler	j'appellerai	*I shall call*
s'asseoir	je m'assiérai	*I shall sit down*
avoir	j'aurai	*I shall have*
courir	je courrai	*I shall run*
cueillir	je cueillerai	*I shall pick*
devoir	je devrai	*I shall owe, I shall have to*
envoyer	j'enverrai	*I shall send*
être	je serai	*I shall be*
faire	je ferai	*I shall do*

falloir	il faudra	*it will be necessary*
jeter	je jetterai	*I shall throw*
mourir	je mourrai	*I shall die*
pleuvoir	il pleuvra	*it will rain*
pouvoir	je pourrai	*I shall be able*
recevoir	je recevrai	*I shall receive*
répéter	je répéterai	*I shall repeat*
savoir	je saurai	*I shall know*
tenir	je tiendrai	*I shall hold*
venir	je viendrai	*I shall come*
voir	je verrai	*I shall see*
vouloir	je voudrai	*I shall want*

21 THE IMPERFECT TENSE

This tense is *one* of the past tenses in French. You must remember that it is not the only past tense. As its name suggests, it is an 'unfinished' tense and should not be used for completed actions.

The imperfect endings are:

-ais, -ais, -ait, -ait, -ions, -iez, -aient, -aient.

Except for the verb **être,** the imperfect tense is always formed from the stem of the first person plural of the present tense.

e.g.
nous **donn**ons	→	je donnais	*I was giving*
nous **finiss**ons	→	je finissais	*I was finishing*
nous **vend**ons	→	je vendais	*I was selling*
nous **all**ons	→	j'allais	*I was going*

Examples of verbs in the imperfect tense:

finir	**aller**
je finissais – *I was finishing*	j'allais – *I was going*
tu finissais	tu allais
il finissait	il allait
elle finissait	elle allait
nous finissions	nous allions
vous finissiez	vous alliez
ils finissaient	ils allaient
elles finissaient	elles allaient

The verb **être** is the only verb whose imperfect tense is *not* formed in the above way. The imperfect tense of **être** is as follows:

être
j'étais – *I was*	nous étions
tu étais	vous étiez
il était	ils étaient
elle était	elles étaient

You must be very careful in your use of the imperfect tense, especially when translating. The following English expressions can all be translated by the imperfect tense:

(a) I went
(b) I was going
(c) I used to go   **j'allais**
(d) I would go

(a) *I went* to town every Saturday. **J'allais** en ville tous les samedis.
Here 'went' signifies a repeated action in the past which should be translated by the imperfect tense.

(b) *I was going* to telephone you later. **J'allais** te téléphoner plus tard.

(c) *I used to go* to their house every day. **J'allais** chez eux chaque jour.
Here the action is a repeated action in the past as in (a). The imperfect tense is therefore required.

(d) *I would go* (= used to go) to town on Fridays. **J'allais** en ville le vendredi.

Even the word 'would' may need to be translated by the imperfect tense if it means 'used to'. Remember that 'would' is translated by the conditional tense (see below) when you wish to suggest a condition.

22 THE CONDITIONAL TENSE

For most O-level and CSE candidates, this tense will be for recognition purposes only. Candidates may wish, however, to include this tense in their oral exam or in the free composition section. The formation of this tense is really an amalgamation of the stem of the future tense and the endings of the imperfect tense.

Future		Conditional	
je serai	*I shall be*	je ser**ais**	*I should be*
j'aurai	*I shall have*	j'aur**ais**	*I should have*
je finirai	*I shall finish*	je finir**ais**	*I should finish*
je voudrai	*I shall want*	je voudr**ais**	*I should like (want)*

Je voudrais is one of the most useful examples of the conditional tense in French. It is used constantly, especially when shopping or asking for something (e.g. booking a hotel room or campsite, asking the way, etc.). For further examples see the role-play section.

Here is an example of a verb in the conditional tense:

vouloir

je voudrais – *I should like (want, wish)*	nous voudrions
tu voudrais	vous voudriez
il voudrait	ils voudraient
elle voudrait	elles voudraient

There are no exceptions in the formation of the conditional tense. All verbs follow the above rule.

The conditional implies that something *would* happen if something else did. It is often used after or before a clause beginning with **si** (if), which is in the imperfect tense:

S'il faisait beau, j'irais à la piscine.
If the weather was fine, I should go to the swimming pool.

Elle viendrait avec nous, si elle avait assez d'argent.
She would come with us if she had enough money.

23 THE PERFECT TENSE

Both O-level and CSE candidates will need to use this tense in almost all sections of the examination. All Examination Boards include a knowledge of the perfect tense in their syllabuses. You should therefore pay special attention to this tense when revising. In both O-level and CSE examinations more marks are lost through the incorrect use of this tense than for any other single reason.

In French the perfect tense has two main forms:
1 Those verbs which are conjugated with **être.**
2 Those verbs which are conjugated with **avoir** (this is by far the largest group).

1 Verbs conjugated with 'être'

(a) The verbs in the following list are all conjugated with **être**. It is not difficult to learn this list as there are only sixteen verbs.

aller	*to go*	partir	*to leave*
arriver	*to arrive*	rentrer	*to go back*
descendre	*to go down*	rester	*to stay*
devenir	*to become*	retourner	*to return*
entrer	*to enter*	revenir	*to come back*
monter	*to go up*	sortir	*to go out*
mourir	*to die*	tomber	*to fall*
naître	*to be born*	venir	*to come*

Because the above verbs are conjugated with **être,** the past participles will agree with the subject of the verb.

arriver

je suis arrivé(e) – *I have arrived, I arrived*	nous sommes arrivé(e)s
tu es arrivé(e)	vous êtes arrivé(e)(s)
il est arrivé	ils sont arrivés
elle est arrivée	elles sont arrivées

The past participles of all the **-er** verbs in the list above will also end in **-é**:

aller	je suis allé(e)	*I went*
entrer	je suis entré(e)	*I entered*
monter	je suis monté(e)	*I went up*
rentrer	je suis rentré(e)	*I went back*
rester	je suis resté(e)	*I stayed*
retourner	je suis retourné(e)	*I returned*
tomber	je suis tombé(e)	*I fell*

The past participle endings for the other verbs in the list are as follows:

descendre	je suis descendu(e)	*I went down*
devenir	je suis devenu(e)	*I became*
revenir	je suis revenu(e)	*I came back*
venir	je suis venu(e)	*I came*
partir	je suis parti(e)	*I left*
sortir	je suis sorti(e)	*I went out*
mourir	il est mort, elle est morte	*he died, she died*
naître	je suis né(e)	*I was born*

(b) *Reflexive verbs*

All reflexive verbs are conjugated with **être.** For example:

se laver

je me suis lavé(e) – *I washed myself*	nous nous sommes lavé(e)s
tu t'es lavé(e)	vous vous êtes lavé(e)(s)
il s'est lavé	ils se sont lavés
elle s'est lavée	elles se sont lavées

Note the use of **t'** and **s'** before the vowel in the **tu** and **il/elle** forms.

Other reflexive verbs follow this pattern. The only variation will be in the past participle when the verb is not an **-er** verb. For example:

s'asseoir	je me suis assis(e)	*I sat down*
se souvenir	je me suis souvenu(e)	*I remembered*
se taire	je me suis tu(e)	*I became silent*

Special note

In certain cases the ending of the past participle does *not* agree with the reflexive pronoun. This happens when the verb is followed by a direct object. For example:

Elle s'est lavée. *She washed herself.*

Here the past participle agrees with the reflexive pronoun. But:

Elle s'est lavé les mains. *She washed her hands.*

Here the verb is followed by a direct object and the past participle does *not* agree.

2 Verbs conjugated with 'avoir'

Except for the categories given in 1(a) and 1(b) above, all other verbs in French are conjugated with **avoir** in the perfect tense. Remember that the past participles of these verbs do *not* agree with the subject of the verb.

donner	**finir**
j'ai donné – *I have given, I gave*	j'ai fini – *I have finished, I finished*
tu as donné	tu as fini
il a donné	il a fini
elle a donné	elle a fini
nous avons donné	nous avons fini
vous avez donné	vous avez fini
ils ont donné	ils ont fini
elles ont donné	elles ont fini

savoir	j'ai su	*I knew, I have known*
suivre	j'ai suivi	*I followed, I have followed*
tenir	j'ai tenu	*I held, I have held*
vivre	j'ai vécu	*I lived, I have lived*
voir	j'ai vu	*I saw, I have seen*
vouloir	j'ai voulu	*I wanted, I have wanted*

Special note

In certain circumstances, the verbs in 1(a) which are normally conjugated with **être** may be conjugated with **avoir**. This change occurs when the verb has a direct object. For example:

Il a descendu l'escalier. *He went down the stairs.*

Elle a sorti un billet de 100 francs. *She took out a 100 franc note.*

Preceding direct object agreements

Although verbs conjugated with **avoir** in the perfect tense never agree with the subject of the verb, there are occasions when the past participle does agree with the *direct object* when this direct object *precedes* the verb. For example:

1(a) J'ai vu **la maison.**

Here the direct object follows the verb. Therefore, no agreement is made.

1(b) Voici **la maison** que j'ai achetée.

Here the direct object precedes the verb. Therefore, an agreement is made by adding 'e' (since **maison** is feminine) to the past participle.

2(a) J'ai acheté **ces livres.**

No agreement is made as the direct object follows the verb.

2(b) J'ai vu ces livres. Je **les** ai achetés.

The agreement is made here since the direct object **les** precedes the verb.

24 THE PLUPERFECT, FUTURE PERFECT AND CONDITIONAL PERFECT TENSES

When listening to spoken French, or reading French for translation or comprehension purposes, you will need to recognise the following tenses:

(a) the pluperfect tense
(b) the future perfect tense
(c) the conditional perfect tense.

These tenses are formed from the imperfect, future and conditional tenses of **avoir** and **être** plus the past participle of the required verb. If a verb is conjugated with **avoir** in the perfect tense, then it will be conjugated with **avoir** in the tenses given above. Similarly, those verbs which are conjugated with **être** in the perfect tense will still be conjugated with **être** in the above tenses. For example:

Perfect:	j'**ai** fini	*I (have) finished*
Pluperfect:	j'**avais** fini	*I had finished*
Future perfect:	j'**aurai** fini	*I shall have finished*
Conditional perfect:	j'**aurais** fini	*I should have finished*
Perfect:	je **suis** allé(e)	*I went, I have gone*
Pluperfect:	j'**étais** allé(e)	*I had gone*
Future perfect:	je **serai** allé(e)	*I shall have gone*
Conditional perfect:	je **serais** allé(e)	*I should have gone*
Perfect:	je me **suis** lavé(e)	*I (have) washed myself*
Pluperfect:	je m'**étais** lavé(e)	*I had washed myself*
Future perfect:	je me **serai** lavé(e)	*I shall have washed myself*
Conditional perfect:	je me **serais** lavé(e)	*I should have washed myself*

Given below are complete examples of:

The pluperfect tense	The future perfect tense	The conditional perfect tense
aller	**finir**	**se laver**
j'étais allé(e)	j'aurai fini	je me serais lavé(e)
– I had gone	*– I shall have finished*	*– I should have washed myself*
tu étais allé(e)	tu auras fini	tu te serais lavé(e)
il était allé	il aura fini	il se serait lavé
elle était allée	elle aura fini	elle se serait lavée
nous étions allé(e)s	nous aurons fini	nous nous serions lavé(e)s
vous étiez allé(e)(s)	vous aurez fini	vous vous seriez lavé(e)(s)
ils étaient allés	ils auront fini	ils se seraient lavés
elles étaient allées	elles auront fini	elles se seraient lavées

25 THE PAST HISTORIC TENSE

The past historic tense is sometimes used in written French instead of the perfect tense. For most Examination Boards the past historic tense is required for recognition purposes only, in translation from French into English and in written comprehension. As it is a literary tense and not one which is used in conversation, you are unlikely to be asked to write it in dictation or in aural comprehension answers. However, you should be able to recognise it. Some forms of the past historic tense are very different from the form of the infinitive and may cause you difficulty if you have not revised this tense carefully. Check the syllabus of your Examination Board to see if this tense is required for active use or for recognition purposes only.

Type 1: -er verbs

The past historic endings added to the stem of the verb are:

-ai, -as, -a, -a, -âmes, -âtes, -èrent, -èrent.

donner

je donnai – *I gave*	nous donnâmes
tu donnas	vous donnâtes
il donna	ils donnèrent
elle donna	elles donnèrent

Type 2: -ir verbs

The past historic endings added to the stem of the verb are:

-is, -is, -it, -it, -îmes, -îtes, -irent, -irent.

finir

je finis – *I finished*	nous finîmes
tu finis	vous finîtes
il finit	ils finirent
elle finit	elles finirent

You will notice that the singular form of the past historic tense of **-ir** verbs resembles the present tense of the verb. However, by looking carefully at the passage of French with which you are dealing, you will know which tense is being used. The meaning of the passage or the tense of the other verbs used will help you to decide.

Type 3: -re verbs

Type 3 verbs have the same endings in the past historic tense as Type 2 verbs.

vendre

je vendis – *I sold*	nous vendîmes
tu vendis	vous vendîtes
il vendit	ils vendirent
elle vendit	elles vendirent

The past historic of irregular verbs

(a) The following verbs have the same endings as Type 2 and Type 3 verbs above, but the stems of the verbs in the past historic are irregular.

s'asseoir	je m'assis	*I sat down*
conduire	je conduisis	*I drove*
craindre	je craignis	*I feared*
dire	je dis	*I said*
écrire	j'écrivis	*I wrote*
faire	je fis	*I made*
joindre	je joignis	*I joined*
mettre	je mis	*I put*
plaindre	je plaignis	*I pitied*
prendre	je pris	*I took*
produire	je produisis	*I produced*
rire	je ris	*I laughed*
voir	je vis	*I saw*

(b) In the past historic tense certain irregular verbs have the following endings:
-us, -us, -ut, -ut, -ûmes, -ûtes, -urent, -urent.

apercevoir	j'aperçus	*I noticed*
avoir	j'eus	*I had*
boire	je bus	*I drank*
connaître	je connus	*I knew*
courir	je courus	*I ran*
croire	je crus	*I believed*
devoir	je dus	*I had to*
être	je fus	*I was*
falloir	il fallut	*it was necessary*
lire	je lus	*I read*
mourir	il mourut	*he died*
paraître	je parus	*I appeared*
plaire	je plus	*I pleased*
pleuvoir	il plut	*it rained*
pouvoir	je pus	*I was[1] able*

([1]Care must be taken to differentiate between this and the continuous past tense: the imperfect.)

recevoir	je reçus	*I received*
savoir	je sus	*I knew*
se taire	je me tus	*I became silent*
vivre	je vécus	*I lived*
vouloir	je voulus	*I wanted*

Here is an example of a verb in the past historic tense with the above endings:

avoir

j'eus – *I had*	nous eûmes
tu eus	vous eûtes
il eut	ils eurent
elle eut	elles eurent

The verbs **tenir** and **venir** and their compounds (e.g. **revenir, retenir**) have special past historic forms which must be learned separately.

tenir	**venir**
je tins – *I held*	je vins – *I came*
tu tins	tu vins
il tint	il vint
elle tint	elle vint
nous tînmes	nous vînmes
vous tîntes	vous vîntes
ils tinrent	ils vinrent
elles tinrent	elles vinrent

The past historic tense is translated into English in the same way as the perfect tense. The difference between them is that the perfect tense is used when speaking or writing a letter about what has happened in the past, and the past historic tense is used for a literary, narrative account of events in the past.

26 THE SUBJUNCTIVE

The subjunctive is rarely required at CSE level. At O level an easy subjunctive may occur in a passage of French for translation or comprehension purposes, but is rarely required in English to French translation. O-level candidates may wish to use the subjunctive in their free composition.

The present subjunctive is formed from the third person plural, present indicative:

donner	ils donnent	→	**je donne**
finir	ils finissent	→	**je finisse**
vendre	ils vendent	→	**je vende**

The endings for the present subjunctive are:

-e, -es, -e, -e, -ions, -iez, -ent, -ent.

finir

je finisse	nous finissions
tu finisses	vous finissiez
il finisse	ils finissent
elle finisse	elles finissent

There are also several irregular verbs whose subjunctive you may need to recognise:

aller	→	j'aille, nous allions, ils aillent
avoir	→	j'aie, il ait, nous ayons, ils aient
être	→	je sois, nous soyons, ils soient
faire	→	je fasse, etc.
pouvoir	→	je puisse, etc.
savoir	→	je sache, etc.
vouloir	→	je veuille, nous voulions, ils veuillent

Given below are some of the constructions which require the use of the subjunctive:

(a) il faut que . . . *it is necessary that . . .*
Il faut que vous travailliez. *You must work.*

(b) bien que . . . *although . . .*
quoique . . . *although . . .*
afin que . . . *in order that . . .*
avant que . . . *before . . .*
jusqu'à ce que . . . *until . . .*

Je veux vous parler avant que vous sortiez.
I want to speak to you before you go out.

Bien que le temps fasse mauvais, nous allons sortir.
Although the weather is bad we are going to go out.

(c) vouloir que . . . *to wish that . . . (to want)*
préférer que . . . *to prefer that . . .*
regretter que . . . *to regret that . . . (to be sorry that . . .)*

Je veux que vous restiez. *I want you to stay.*
Je regrette que vous soyez malade. *I am sorry that you are ill.*

(d) il est possible (impossible) que . . . *it is possible (impossible) that . . .*
douter que . . . *to doubt that . . .*

Il est impossible qu'il réussisse. *It is impossible for him to succeed.*

There are other tenses of the subjunctive mood and other occasions when the subjunctive is required, but they are not required at this level.

27 THE PASSIVE

The passive in French is formed as in English, using a suitable tense of 'to be' (**être**) plus the past participle of the verb required:

Il **a été mordu** par un chien. *He has been bitten by a dog.*

However, most French people prefer to avoid using the passive by making the verb active in some way. There are a number of ways of doing this:

(a) The agent of a passive sentence can become the subject of an active sentence:

Un chien l'a mordu. *A dog bit him.*

(b) Where the agent is not mentioned, **on** can be used as the subject:

On a vendu cette maison. *This house has been sold.*

(c) Sometimes a reflexive verb can be used:

Les cigarettes se vendent ici. *Cigarettes are sold here.*

Caution

In free composition it is very tempting for candidates to use the passive in French to try to translate their thoughts which are often in the passive in English (e.g. she is called, I am bored, they were saved, etc.). It is always very easy for an examiner to recognise those candidates who have thought out their sentences in English and then tried to translate them into French in the free composition section. Their compositions will be littered with passive-type English sentences clumsily translated word for word into French. The result is a very poor non-French composition. Always try to use a known French construction in your answers and avoid the passive in French where possible.

Similarly, in prose composition beware of English sentences which contain a passive. Sentences such as 'He is called Peter' should be translated with a reflexive verb:

Il **s'appelle** Pierre.

This type of English passive is a very frequent testing point in O-level prose composition and too many candidates fail to recognise it. Check again to make sure that *you* will recognise it in the examination.

28 THE IMPERATIVE

(a) Commands in French are formed from the **tu, nous,** and **vous** forms of the present tense of verbs, omitting the pronouns. For example:

finis!   *finish!* (singular)
finissons!   *let us finish!*
finissez!   *finish!* (plural)

(b) **-er** verbs omit the 's' in the second person singular imperative:

tu portes → **porte**   *carry*
tu vas   → **va**   *go*

N.B. the second person singular imperative of **aller** retains the 's' when followed by 'y':

Vas-y. *Go on/go there.*

(c) The following verbs have irregular imperatives:

avoir   → aie, ayons, ayez
être   → sois, soyons, soyez
savoir → sache, sachons, sachez
vouloir → veuille, veuillons, veuillez

(d) The reflexive pronoun is retained in the imperative of reflexive verbs and follows the rules for object pronouns, i.e. in the affirmative, the pronoun follows the verb and is joined to the verb by a hyphen; the pronoun **te** becomes **toi.**

Dépêche-toi! *Hurry up!*

But in a negative command, the pronoun keeps its original position and spelling:

Ne te dépêche pas! *Don't hurry!*

Here are examples of all three imperatives in the affirmative and in the negative:

se lever – to get up
Lève-toi. Ne te lève pas.
Levons-nous. Ne nous levons pas.
Levez-vous. Ne vous levez pas.

29 THE PRESENT PARTICIPLE

The present participle (e.g. going, looking, selling) is normally formed by adding **-ant** to the stem of the first person plural of the present tense:

aller	nous allons	→	**allant**	*going*
regarder	nous regardons	→	**regardant**	*looking*
finir	nous finissons	→	**finissant**	*finishing*
vendre	nous vendons	→	**vendant**	*selling*
dire	nous disons	→	**disant**	*saying*

The following irregular verbs do *not* form the present participle from the stem of the first person plural of the present tense:

avoir	**ayant**	*having*
être	**étant**	*being*
savoir	**sachant**	*knowing*

Do not, however, try to use the present participle in such expressions as 'I am going', 'they are eating', etc. Expressions such as these should be translated by the present tense – **je vais, ils mangent,** etc.

A present participle is not finite (i.e. not complete in itself). It should be used in such expressions as:

He went home singing. Il est rentré **en chantant.**

Seeing that she was ill, he telephoned the doctor.
Voyant qu'elle était malade, il a téléphoné au médecin.

The use of **en** + present participle, as in the first example above, is one that you are very likely to need. It is a frequent testing point in prose composition and you should also be able to incorporate it into free composition.

En + present participle can also mean 'by/on/when doing . . .':

En rentrant à la maison il a trouvé ses clefs. *On returning home he found his keys.*

En travaillant dur, ils ont réussi. *By working hard, they succeeded.*

Check carefully the following examples where a present participle is used in English but *not* in French:

(a) *He left* without saying *goodbye.*
Il est parti **sans dire** au revoir.

(b) *I shall have breakfast* before leaving.
Je prendrai le petit déjeuner **avant de partir.**

(c) Instead of working, *he went to play football.*
Au lieu de travailler, il est allé jouer au football.

Note the use of the infinitive in the above three sentences. Do not be misled by the English present participle.

(d) After getting up *late, we missed the bus.*
Après nous être levés en retard, nous avons manqué l'autobus.

Note the use of the perfect infinitive after **après.** This construction needs special care because of the reflexive verb. The subject of the main part of the sentence (**nous**) dictates which reflexive pronoun must be used before **être.**

(e) *I saw some boys* fishing *in the river.*
J'ai vu des garçons **qui pêchaient** dans la rivière.

You must check very carefully before using a present participle in French to see if, in fact, you need to use a present participle construction, or if, as in the cases above, you need to use a different construction.

30 VERBS FOLLOWED BY PREPOSITIONS

Some verbs in French can be directly followed by an infinitive:

Je sais nager. *I can swim.*
Tu veux venir? *Do you want to come?*

Many, however, require the addition of a preposition before the following infinitive. Try to learn as many of the following as possible:

aider à   *to help to . . .*
aimer à   *to like to . . .*
apprendre à   *to learn to . . .*
s'attendre à   *to expect to . . .*
commencer à   *to begin to . . .*
consentir à   *to agree to . . .*
continuer à   *to continue to . . .*
se décider à   *to make up one's mind to . . .*
forcer à   *to compel to . . .*
hésiter à   *to hesitate to . . .*
inviter à   *to invite to . . .*
se mettre à   *to begin to . . . .*
obliger à   *to oblige to . . .*
ressembler à   *to look like . . .*
réussir à   *to succeed in . . .*

s'arrêter de   *to stop (doing)*
avoir l'intention de   *to intend to . . .*
avoir peur de   *to be afraid of (doing)*
avoir besoin de   *to need to . . .*

cesser de   *to stop (doing)*
décider de   *to decide to . . .*
défendre de   *to forbid to . . .*
demander de   *to ask to . . .*
dire de   *to tell to . . .*
empêcher de   *to prevent from . . .*
essayer de   *to try to . . .*
faire semblant de   *to pretend to . . .*
finir de   *to finish (doing)*
menacer de   *to threaten to . . .*
offrir de   *to offer to . . .*
ordonner de   *to order to . . .*
oublier de   *to forget to . . .*
permettre de   *to allow to . . .*
prier de   *to beg to . . .*
promettre de   *to promise to . . .*
refuser de   *to refuse to . . .*
regretter de   *to be sorry for . . .*

Certain other words apart from verbs also require a preposition before a following infinitive:

beaucoup à (faire)   *a lot to (do)*
le dernier à   *the last to . . .*
prêt à   *ready to . . .*
le premier à   *the first to . . .*
rien à   *nothing to . . .*

certain de   *certain to . . .*
content de   *pleased to . . .*
le droit de   *the right to . . .*

étonné de   *surprised to . . .*
heureux de   *happy to . . .*
obligé de   *obliged to . . .*
l'occasion de *the opportunity to . . .*
la permission de   *the permission to . . .*
surpris de   *surprised to . . .*
le temps de   *the time to . . .*

Note also the preposition **pour** before an infinitive:

Je suis allé en ville **pour** rencontrer des amis. *I went to town to meet some friends.*
Il est trop malade **pour** venir. *He is too ill to come.*
Vous êtes assez intelligent **pour** comprendre. *You are intelligent enough to understand.*

Some verbs need the preposition **à** before an indirect object:

acheter à quelqu'un   *to buy from someone*
cacher à quelqu'un   *to hide from someone*
conseiller à quelqu'un   *to advise someone*
défendre à quelqu'un   *to forbid someone*
donner à quelqu'un   *to give someone*
dire à quelqu'un   *to tell someone*
emprunter à quelqu'un   *to borrow from someone*
envoyer à quelqu'un   *to send (to) someone*
se fier à quelqu'un   *to trust someone*
montrer à quelqu'un   *to show (to) someone*
obéir à quelqu'un   *to obey someone*
offrir à quelqu'un   *to offer (to) someone*
ordonner à quelqu'un   *to order someone*
penser à quelqu'un   *to think about someone*
plaire à quelqu'un   *to please someone*
prendre à quelqu'un   *to take from someone*
prêter à quelqu'un   *to lend someone*
promettre à quelqu'un   *to promise someone*
raconter à quelqu'un   *to tell someone*
répondre à quelqu'un   *to reply to someone*
réfléchir à quelque chose   *to think (ponder) about something*
ressembler à quelqu'un   *to resemble someone*
voler à quelqu'un   *to steal from someone*

Some verbs need the preposition **de** before an object:

> s'approcher de   *to approach* . . .
> dépendre de   *to depend on* . . .
> jouir de   *to enjoy* . . .
> se moquer de   *to make fun of* . . .
> remercier de   *to thank for* . . .
> se servir de   *to use* . . .
> se souvenir de   *to remember* . . .

31 IMPERSONAL VERBS

You should be able to use the following accurately:

(a) Il y a + all tenses

> **Il y a** beaucoup de monde en ville.
> *There are a lot of people in town.*

> **Il y avait** une grande foule devant la mairie.
> *There was a large crowd in front of the town hall.*

> **Il y a eu** un accident.
> *There has been an accident.*

> **Il y aura** un jour de congé la semaine prochaine.
> *There will be a day's holiday next week.*

(b) Il faut it is necessary
Il fallait it was necessary (*continuous*)
Il a fallu it was necessary (*event*)
Il faudra it will be necessary

> Il me faut rentrer. *I must go home.*
> Il lui fallait travailler dur. *He had to work hard.*
> Il m'a fallu acheter une nouvelle robe. *I had to buy a new dress.*

Remember that you may use **devoir** (*to have to*) in sentences similar to those above, but with a personal subject:

> J'ai dû acheter une nouvelle robe.

For **Il faut que . . .** see section 26 on the subjunctive.

(c) Il reste . . . there remains . . .
> Il me reste vingt francs. *I have twenty francs left.*

Il restait . . . there remained . . .
> Il lui restait deux pommes. *He had two apples left.*

You should be able to recognise the following impersonal verbs:

(a) Il s'agit de . . . It is a question of . . .
> De quoi s'agit-il? Il s'agit d'un vol. *What's it about? It's about a theft.*

(b) Il vaut mieux . . . It's better . . .
> Il vaut mieux rentrer tout de suite. *It's better to return home straight away.*

32 TENSES WITH 'SI'

Check the following rule carefully.
> (a) **Si** + present tense . . . ., (future).
> (b) **Si** + imperfect tense . . . ., (conditional).
> (c) **Si** + pluperfect tense . . . ., (conditional perfect).

(a) S'il vient, je te téléphonerai.
> *If he comes, I shall telephone you.*

(b) S'il venait, je te téléphonerais.
> *If he were to come, I should telephone you.*

(c) S'il était venu, je t'aurais téléphoné.
> *If he had come, I should have telephoned you.*

33 VENIR DE

This expression means 'to have just' (done something).

Remember to use the *present* tense in such expressions as:
  I have just arrived. **Je viens** d'arriver.
Use the *imperfect* tense in such expressions as:
  They had just gone out. **Ils venaient de** sortir.

34 NEGATIVES

ne . . . pas (*not*)	*Check carefully*
ne . . . point (*not at all*)	ne . . . aucun (*not one, not any*)
ne . . . jamais (*never*)	ne . . . guère (*scarcely*)
ne . . . personne (*nobody*)	ne . . . ni . . . ni . . .(*neither . . . nor*)
ne . . . plus (*no more, no longer*)	ne . . . nulle part (*nowhere*)
ne . . . que (*only*)	
ne . . . rien (*nothing*)	

The position of the negative in the sentence

(a) Present tense:
  Je **ne** joue **pas** au tennis. *I don't play tennis.*

(b) Perfect tense:
  Je **n**'ai **pas** joué au tennis. *I didn't play tennis.*

  N.B. exception with 'ne . . . personne':
  Je **n**'ai vu **personne.** *I saw nobody.*

(c) Reflexive verbs:
  Je **ne** me lève **pas** de bonne heure. *I don't get up early.*
  Je **ne** me suis **pas** levé de bonne heure. *I didn't get up early.*

(d) With object pronouns:
  Je **ne** le vois **pas.** *I don't (can't) see him (it).*
  Je **ne** l'ai **pas** vu. *I didn't see him (it).*

Remember that certain negatives may be inverted to become the subject of a sentence:

  Rien n'est arrivé. *Nothing has happened.*
  Personne n'a gagné. *Nobody won.*
  Aucun avion **n**'a décollé. *No plane took off.*

Words like **rien, personne** and **jamais** may be used on their own:
  Qu'a-t-il vu? **Rien.** *What did he see? Nothing.*
  Y êtes-vous allés? **Jamais.** *Did you ever go there? Never.*
  Qui avez-vous vu? **Personne.** *Whom did you see? Nobody.*

Combination of negatives

(a) Plus before **rien:**
  Ils ne font plus rien. *They no longer do anything.*

(b) Jamais before **rien:**
  Il ne nous donnent jamais rien. *They never give us anything.*

(c) Plus before **personne:**
  Je n'y recontre plus personne. *I don't meet anyone there now.*

(d) Jamais before **personne:**
  Je n'y rencontre jamais personne. *I never meet anyone there.*

Negatives before an infinitive

Except for **ne . . . personne,** both parts of the negative precede the present infinitive:

  J'ai décidé de **ne jamais** retourner. *I decided never to return.*
  J'ai décidé de **ne** voir **personne.** *I decided to see nobody.*

Remember that **si** = *yes* after a negative question or statement:

> Ne l'avez-vous pas vu? Si, je l'ai vu.
> *Haven't you seen it (him)? Yes, I've seen it (him).*

N'est-ce pas?

This is a most useful phrase which translates a variety of negative expressions at the end of questions, e.g. . . . haven't we? . . . didn't they? . . . wasn't he? . . . can't she? etc.

> Nous avons réussi, n'est-ce pas? *We succeeded, didn't we?*
> Ils ont gagné, n'est-ce pas? *They won, didn't they?*
> Il était malade, n'est-ce pas? *He was ill, wasn't he?*
> Elle peut venir, n'est-ce pas? *She can come, can't she?*

35 QUESTIONS

There are various ways of asking a question in French.

(a) One of the easiest ways is to use **Est-ce que . . .** at the beginning of the sentence:
> Est-ce qu'il vient? *Is he coming?*

(b) Except for the first person singular of many verbs, inversion may be used:
> Vient-il? *Is he coming?*

(c) Vocal intonation is frequently used in conversation:
> Il vient? *Is he coming?*

Care must be taken when a noun is the subject of a question. Remember that in writing, a pronoun should also be used:
> Votre frère est-il à la maison? *Is your brother at home?*

In conversation, however, vocal intonation might be used:
> Votre frère est à la maison?

Words used to introduce questions

(a) Qui?
Qui est-ce qui? } Who?

Both of the above are used as the *subject* of the question:

> Qui a dit cela?
> Qui est-ce qui a dit cela? } *Who said that?*

(b) Qui?
Qui est-ce que? } Whom?

These two forms are used as the *object* of the sentence:

> Qui as-tu vu?
> Qui est-ce que tu as vu? } *Whom did you see?*

Note that when **est-ce** is used in any question-form the verb and subject are not inverted.

(c) Qu'est-ce qui? What? (as the subject)
> Qu'est ce qui est arrivé? *What has happened?*

(d) Que?
Qu'est-ce que? } What? (as the object)
> Qu'as-tu vu?
> Qu'est-ce que tu as vu? } *What have you seen?*

(e)　m. **Quel** + noun
　　f. **Quelle** + noun
m.pl. **Quels** + noun
　f.pl. **Quelles** + noun } What? which?

> Quels livres? *What (which) books?*
> Quelle maison? *What (which) house?*

(f) Où? where?
> Où habitez-vous? *Where do you live?*

Combien? How much?
> Combien as-tu gagné? *How much did you earn (win)?*

Comment? How?
> Comment vas-tu? *How are you?*

Pourquoi? Why?
> Pourquoi es-tu venu? *Why did you come?*

Quand? When?
> Quand rentres-tu? *When are you going back (home)?*

36 INVERSION

Remember that inversion is required in the following circumstances:

(a) After direct speech:
> 'Asseyez-vous' a-t-il dit. *'Sit down', he said.*

(b) After **peut-être** at the begining of a sentence:
> Peut-être viendra-t-il. *Perhaps he will come.*

However, inversion can be avoided by using **peut-être que**:
> Peut être qu'il viendra.

(c) In certain subordinate clauses:
> Voici la maison où habite ma grand'mère. *Here is the house where my grandmother lives.*

(d) Note also the translation of the following English inversion:
> Qu'elle est jolie! *How pretty she is!*

2 Vocabulary topics

The following lists contain key words for a number of topics which will be of use to you when preparing for the free composition and the oral examination for both O level and CSE. Try to learn as many words as possible during the weeks before the examination. The vocabulary lists are all based on everyday subjects which may be included in the examination.

1 ACCIDENT/INJURY LES ACCIDENTS

ambulance l'ambulance (f)
to break briser; casser
to break one's arm (leg, etc.) se casser le bras, la jambe, etc.
to bump into heurter
to collide (with a person) heurter
to collide (with a vehicle) entrer en collision avec
to crush écraser
to be crushed s'écraser
to damage abîmer
to destroy détrüire
to drown (se) noyer
a fatal accident un accident mortel
Help! Au secours!
to help aider
to hit frapper
to injure blesser
to be injured se blesser, être blessé
to jostle, push bousculer
to knock down renverser
to lose one's way s'égarer, perdre son chemin
a motor accident un accident de voiture
a road accident un accident de la route
a serious accident un accident grave
to be shipwrecked faire naufrage
to spoil gâter
stretcher le brancard
to tear déchirer
to twist one's ankle se fouler la cheville; se donner une entorse

2 AIRPORT L'AÉROPORT

air hostess l'hôtesse (f) de l'air
air sickness le mal de l'air
air terminal l'aérogare (f)
control-tower la tour de contrôle

(the) customs la douane
customs officer le douanier
to fly voler
helicopter l'hélicoptère (m)
hijacker le pirate de l'air
hijacking le détournement d'avion
jet l'avion (m) à réaction
to land atterrir
loudspeaker le haut-parleur
(airport) lounge la salle d'attente
luggage trolley le chariot
passenger le passager
pilot le pilote
plane l'avion (m)
porter le porteur
runway la piste d'atterrissage
(customs) scanner le détecteur
to take off décoller
ticket le billet

3 ANIMALS LES ANIMAUX

badger le blaireau
bear l'ours (m)
bull le taureau
calf le veau
camel le chameau
cat le chat, la chatte
cow la vache
deer le cerf, le daim
doe la biche
dog le chien, la chienne
poodle le (la) caniche
sheepdog le chien de berger
spaniel l'épagneul (m)
donkey l'âne (m)
elephant l'éléphant (m)
flock, herd le troupeau
fox le renard
frog la grenouille
gerbil la gerbille
giraffe la girafe
goat le bouc, la chèvre
guinea pig le cobaye, le cochon d'Inde
hamster le hamster
hare le lièvre
hedgehog le hérisson
horse le cheval
mare la jument
lamb l'agneau (m)
lion le lion
monkey le singe
mouse la souris
ox le bœuf
paw la patte
pig le cochon
rabbit le lapin
rat le rat
rhinoceros le rhinocéros
sheep le mouton; **ewe** la brebis
snake le serpent, la couleuvre
squirrel l'écureuil (m)
toad le crapaud
tiger le tigre
tortoise la tortue
wolf le loup
worm le ver

4 BIRDS LES OISEAUX

blackbird le merle
budgie la perruche inséparable
chicken le poulet
cockerel le coq
crow le corbeau
cuckoo le coucou
dove la colombe
duck le canard
eagle l'aigle (m)
feather la plume
goose l'oie (f)
hen la poule
nest le nid
nightingale le rossignol
owl le hibou
parrot le perroquet
robin le rouge-gorge
seagull la mouette
skylark l'alouette (f)
sparrow le moineau
swallow l'hirondelle (f)
swan le cygne
thrush la grive
turkey le dindon, la dinde

5 CAFÉ/HOTEL/RESTAURANT LE CAFÉ/L'HÔTEL/ LE RESTAURANT

aperitif l'apéritif (m)
bar (counter) le comptoir
bill (hotel) la note
bill (restaurant) l'addition (f)
boarding-house la pension
boarder le pensionnaire
full-board la pension complète
half-board la demi-pension
breakfast le petit déjeuner
chambermaid la femme de chambre
cook le cuisinier, la cuisinière
head cook le chef de cuisine
cover charge le couvert
cup la tasse
dessert le dessert
dinner le dîner
dish le plat
drink la boisson
to drink boire
to eat manger
fork la fourchette
glass le verre
guest l'invité(e)
hotelier l'hôtelier (m)
inn l'auberge (f)
inn-keeper l'aubergiste (m)
lunch le déjeuner
to lunch déjeuner
to have a meal prendre un repas
manager le patron
menu le menu, la carte
to order commander
pavement (café) la terrasse
plate l'assiette (f)
pub le bar, le bistro(t), le cabaret, l'estaminet (m)
room la chambre
double room une chambre à deux personnes

single room une chambre à un lit
sandwich le sandwich
service charge included service compris
spoon la cuiller
supper le souper
table cloth la nappe
to lay the table mettre le couvert
tea (drink) le thé
tea (meal) le goûter
waiter le garçon
head waiter le maître d'hôtel
waitress la serveuse

6 CAMPING LE CAMPING

to boil faire bouillir
to camp camper
to go camping faire du camping
camp bed le lit de camp
camp chair la chaise pliante
camp equipment le matériel de camping
camp fire le feu de camp
campsite le camping
camping stove le réchaud (à gaz)
caravan la caravane
to cook faire cuire
ground sheet le tapis de sol
hammer le marteau
to hitch-hike faire de l'auto-stop
hitch-hiker l'auto-stoppeur (m), l'auto-stoppeuse (f)
lantern la lanterne
(tent) peg le piquet
to pitch the tent dresser, monter, la tente
rucksack le sac à dos
sleeping-bag le sac de couchage
to take down the tent démonter la tente
torch la lampe électrique de poche, la torche électrique
water-container le bidon à eau

7 CAR/GARAGE LA VOITURE/LE GARAGE

bonnet le capot
boot le coffre
break le frein
to break freiner
breakdown la panne
to break down être en panne
breathalyser l'alcotest (m)
bumper le pare-chocs
car l'auto (f), la voiture
clutch l'embrayage (m)
door la portière
driver le chauffeur
driving licence le permis de conduire
driving-mirror le rétroviseur
engine le moteur
headlamp le phare
garage-owner le garagiste
gear-lever le (levier de) changement de vitesse
to change gear changer de vitesse
horn l'avertisseur; le klaxon
to sound the horn klaxonner
indicator light le feu clignotant
lorry le camion
mechanic le mécanicien
moped le cyclomoteur; le vélomoteur
motorbike la motocyclette

mudguard le garde-boue, le pare-boue
oil l'huile (f)
petrol l'essence (f)
petrol-pump le poste d'essence
to fill up with petrol faire le plein d'essence
petrol tank le réservoir à essence
puncture la crevaison; le pneu crevé
radiator le radiateur
to repair (after a breakdown) dépanner
roof rack la galerie
safety belt la ceinture de sécurité
seat le siège
bench-seat la banquette
scooter le scooter
second-hand car la voiture d'occasion
service station la station-service
side light le feu de position
spare wheel la roue de secours
speed la vitesse
steering wheel le volant
step le marchepied
tyre le pneu
to pump up (a tyre) gonfler (un pneu)
van la camionnette
window la glace
windscreen le pare-brise
windscreen wiper l'essuie-glace (m)

8 CINEMA/THEATRE LE CINÉMA/LE THÉÂTRE

actor un acteur
actress une actrice
to applaud applaudir
applause les applaudissements (mpl)
balcony (circle) le balcon
to book (a seat) louer, retenir (une place)
box la loge
character le personnage
concert le concert
documentary le documentaire
entrance l'entrée (f)
exit la sortie
film le film
the 'gods' la galerie
interval l'entracte (m)
opera l'opéra (m)
orchestra stalls les fauteuils (mpl) d'orchestre
performance la représentation
play la pièce
to be present at assister à
programme le programme
scenery le décor
screen l'écran (m)
seat le fauteuil, la place
show le spectacle
stage la scène
star la vedette, la star
ticket le billet
tip le pourboire
usherette l'ouvreuse (f)
wings les coulisses (fpl)

9 CLOTHES LES VÊTEMENTS, LES HABITS

apron le tablier
belt la ceinture
beret le béret

blazer le blazer
blouse le chemisier
boot la botte, la bottine
braces les bretelles (fpl)
button le bouton
cap la casquette, le képi (*police, army*)
cardigan le tricot
coat le manteau
cotton le coton
dress la robe
dressing-gown la robe de chambre
dressmaker le couturier, la couturière
dungarees les bleus (mpl), la salopette
fur la fourrure
glove le gant
handkerchief le mouchoir
hat le chapeau
jacket le veston, la veste
jeans le blue-jean (m)
lace la dentelle
leather le cuir
linen le lin
made-to-measure sur mesure
material l'étoffe (f)
nightdress la robe de nuit
nylon le nylon
overcoat le pardessus
overall la blouse
plastic la (matière) plastique
pocket la poche
pullover le pullover
pyjamas le pyjama
rags les haillons (mpl)
raincoat l'imperméable (m)
ready-made prêt-à-porter
sandal la sandale
scarf l'écharpe (f) (*long*); le foulard (*square*)
shirt la chemise
shoe le soulier, la chaussure
shorts le short
silk la soie
size la taille
shoe size la pointure
skirt la jupe
sleeve la manche
slipper la pantoufle
sock la chaussette
stocking le bas
suit le complet, le costume, le tailleur
sweater le chandail
terylene le térylène, le tergal
tie la cravate
tights le collant
trousers le pantalon
(short) trousers la culotte
trouser-suit un ensemble-pantalon
velvet le velours
waistcoat le gilet
windcheater le blouson
wool la laine

10 COLOURS LES COULEURS

black noir
blue bleu
brown brun

dark foncé
dark brown marron (*invariable*)
green vert
grey gris
light clair
orange orange
pink rose
purple pourpre
red rouge
red (*of hair*) roux
white blanc, blanche
yellow jaune

N.B. When using a compound adjective of colour, e.g. light blue, dark green, do *not* make the adjectives agree with the noun:

la robe ver**te**
but: la robe vert foncé.

11 COUNTRIES/NATIONALITIES LES PAYS ET LES NATIONALITÉS

Countries	Les pays	Inhabitants Les habitants
America	l'Amérique (f)	un(e) Américain(e)
USA	les États-Unis (mpl)	un(e) Américain(e)
Asia	l'Asie (f)	un(e) Asiatique
Austria	l'Autriche (f)	un(e) Autrichien(ne)
Belgium	la Belgique	un(e) Belge
Canada	le Canada	un(e) Canadien(ne)
China	la Chine	un(e) Chinois(e)
Denmark	le Danemark	un(e) Danois(e)
England	l'Angleterre	un(e) Anglais(e)
Europe	l'Europe (f)	un(e) Européen(ne)
Germany	l'Allemagne (f)	un(e) Allemand(e)
G Britain	la Grande Bretagne	un(e) Britannique
Greece	la Grèce	un Grec, une Grecque
Holland	la Hollande	un(e) Hollandais(e)
Italy	l'Italie (f)	un(e) Italien(ne)
India	l'Inde (f)	un(e) Indien(ne)
Ireland	l'Irlande (f)	un(e) Irlandais(e)
Japan	le Japon	un(e) Japonais(e)
Luxembourg	le Luxembourg	un(e) Luxembourgeois(e)
Mexico	le Mexique	un(e) Mexicain(e)
Netherlands	les Pays Bas (mpl)	un(e) Néerlandais(e)
New Zealand	la Nouvelle Zélande	un(e) Néozélandais(e)
Norway	la Norvège	un(e) Norvégien(ne)
Poland	la Pologne	un(e) Polonais(e)
Portugal	le Portugal	un(e) Portugais(e)
Russia	la Russie	un(e) Russe
USSR	l'URSS (f)	un(e) Russe
Scotland	l'Écosse (f)	un(e) Écossais(e)
S Africa	l'Afrique (f) du Sud	un(e) Sud-Africain(e)
Spain	l'Espagne (f)	un(e) Espagnol(e)
Sweden	la Suède	un(e) Suédois(e)
Switzerland	la Suisse	un Suisse, une Suissesse
UK	le Royaume-Uni	un(e) habitant(e) du Royaume-Uni
Wales	le Pays de Galles	un(e) Gallois(e)
Yugoslavia	la Yougoslavie	un(e) Yougoslave

12 COUNTRYSIDE LA CAMPAGNE

to take the air prendre l'air
bank (*of a river*) le bord, la rive
bridge le pont
cave la caverne
cottage la chaumière
countryman le paysan
countrywoman la paysanne
current le courant
field le champ, la prairie, le pré
to flow couler
forest la forêt
hamlet le hameau
hayrick la meule de foin
hill la colline
lake le lac
landscape, scenery le paysage
mill le moulin
mountain la montagne
mud la boue
path le sentier
pebble le caillou (pl: les cailloux)
picnic le pique-nique
to picnic pique-niquer
policeman le gendarme
pond l'étang (m), la mare
river le fleuve, la rivière
road la route
slope la pente
stone la pierre
stream le ruisseau
tree l'arbre (m)
(*see section 20 for the names of the different trees*)
waterfall la cascade, la fontaine
wild flowers les fleurs sauvages (fpl)
wood le bois
wooded boisé
valley la vallée
village le village

13 COMMERCE/INDUSTRY LE COMMERCE/L'INDUSTRIE

bank la banque
boss le patron
business les affaires (fpl)
businessman le commerçant
calculator la machine à calculer, le calculateur
cashier le caissier, la caissière
clerk le commis, l'employé(e) de bureau
commercial traveller le commis-voyageur
computer le calculateur mécanique, l'ordinateur (m)
expenses les frais (mpl)
factory la fabrique, l'usine (f)
job l'emploi (m), la situation
name, make (*of an article*) la marque
manufacturer le fabricant
mine la mine
(coal) mine la mine de charbon
office le bureau
pay (*wages*) le salaire
pay (*salary*) le traitement
profit le bénéfice
secretary le (la) secrétaire
staff le personnel

steelworks l'aciérie (f)
strike la grève
trade (*job*) le métier
trade union le syndicat
typist le dactylo; la dactylo
typewriter la machine à écrire
worker l'ouvrier (m), l'ouvrière (f)
workshop l'atelier
work-site le chantier

14 DATES/FESTIVALS LES DATES/LES FÊTES

anniversary; birthday l'anniversaire (m); la fête
birthday party la réunion d'anniversaire
bank holiday la fête légale
baptism le baptême
Christmas Noël (m)
at Christmas à Noël
congratulations félicitations (fpl)
to congratulate féliciter
Easter Pâques (m)
first of April le jour des poissons d'avril
first of May la fête du muguet; la fête du travail
Hallowe'en la veille de la Toussaint
14th July la Fête Nationale
Shrove Tuesday le mardi gras
New Year's Day le Jour de l'An
New Year's Eve la veille du Jour de l'An
wedding le mariage; les noces (fpl)

Days of the week Les jours de la semaine

Sunday dimanche
Monday lundi
Tuesday mardi
Wednesday mercredi
Thursday jeudi
Friday vendredi
Saturday samedi

All the days of the week in French are masculine, and are written with small letters.

on Monday lundi
on Mondays le lundi
Never use '**sur**' with days of the week.

Months of the year Les mois de l'année
January janvier
February février
March mars
April avril
May mai
June juin
July juillet
August août
September septembre
October octobre
November novembre
December décembre

All the months of the year in French are masculine, and are written with small letters.

in January en janvier, au mois de janvier

15 DIRECTION/DISTANCE LA DIRECTION/ LA DISTANCE

bottom (*end*) le fond
corner le coin

in the distance au loin
in the direction of du côté de
east l'est (m)
elsewhere ailleurs
end le bout
everywhere partout
far loin
here ici
in front devant
inside dedans, à l'intérieur
kilometre le kilomètre
left gauche
on/to the left à gauche
long (de) long
lower (*e.g. floor*) inférieur
metre le mètre
mile le mille
near (tout) près
near to près de
neighbouring voisin
next to à côté de, auprès de
north le nord
nowhere nulle part
outside dehors, à l'extérieur
place le lieu, l'endroit (m)
right droite
on/to the right à droite
side le côté
on all sides de tous côtés
on one side d'un côté
on the other side de l'autre côté
situated (at) situé à
somewhere quelque part
south le sud
space l'espace (m)
straight on tout droit
there là
here and there çà et là
over there là-bas
up there là-haut
upper (*e.g. floor*) supérieur (à l'étage supérieur)
west l'ouest (m)
wide (de) large

N.B.

La maison se trouve **à** 3 kms de l'école.

Le jardin **a** 30 mètres **de long.**
Le jardin **a** 25 mètres **de large.**
Le bâtiment **a** 20 mètres **de haut.**

Le jardin **est long de** 30 mètres.
Le jardin **est large de** 25 mètres.
Le bâtiment **est haut de** 20 mètres.

16 EMOTIONS/FEELINGS LES EMOTIONS/ LES SENTIMENTS

to admire admirer
anger la colère
to get angry se mettre en colère; se fâcher
to annoy ennuyer
anxiety l'inquiétude (f)
to be anxious s'inquiéter
to boast se vanter
to bore ennuyer
boredom l'ennui (m)

care le soin; (*worry*) le souci
to care for, to look after soigner
confidence la confiance
to complain se plaindre
to console consoler
to cry pleurer
to delight enchanter, charmer, ravir
despair le désespoir
to despise mépriser
to disappoint décevoir
to discourage décourager
to disturb déranger
doubt le doute
to doubt douter
to encourage encourager
to endure supporter
to enjoy jouir de
to enjoy (doing something) se plaire à (faire quelque chose)
to enjoy oneself s'amuser
enthusiasm l'enthousiasme (m)
envy l'envie (f)
N.B. avoir envie de *to feel like (doing . . .)*
to expect s'attendre à
to fear craindre
fear la crainte, la peur
to forgive pardonner à
friendship l'amitié (f)
to frighten effrayer; faire peur à
frightened effrayé
grateful reconnaissant
gratitude la reconnaissance
groan le gémissement
to groan gémir
happy heureux (m), heureuse (f)
to hate détester
hatred la haine
to hope espérer
hope l'espoir (m)
horror l'horreur (f)
to be interested in s'intéresser à
joy la joie
to laugh at se moquer de
laughter les rires (mpl)
to laugh rire
to like, love aimer
love l'amour (m)
to mistrust se méfier de
to be in a good mood être de bonne humeur
to be in a bad mood être de mauvaise humeur
nice (*of a person*) sympathique, aimable, gentil(le)
to pity plaindre
pity la pitié
What a pity! Quel dommage!
to please plaire à
pleasure le plaisir
to prefer aimer mieux, préférer
pride l'orgueil (m)
proud fier (m), fière (f)
to relieve soulager
sad triste
sadness la tristesse
to satisfy satisfaire à
to scold gronder
shame la honte
to be ashamed avoir honte (de)
to shout crier

shudder le frémissement
to shudder frémir, frissonner
to sigh soupirer
to sob sangloter
to be sorry regretter
to suffer souffrir
surprise la surprise, l'étonnement
to surprise étonner, surprendre
to be surprised s'étonner
to suspect soupçonner
sympathy la compassion, la sympathie
tears les larmes (fpl)
to burst into tears fondre en larmes
to tease taquiner
terror la terreur
to terrify effrayer, épouvanter, terrifier
to thank remercier
to threaten menacer
to trouble gêner
to trust se fier à
to warn avertir, prévenir
to welcome accueillir

17 EXCLAMATIONS/GREETINGS
LES EXCLAMATIONS/LES SALUTATIONS
Agreed, all right! D'accord!
Cheer up! Courage!
Come now! Allons donc! Voyons donc!
Delighted (to meet you)! Enchanté!
Excuse me! Pardon! Excusez-moi!
Fire! Au feu!
Great! Chouette! Formidable! Mince alors! Sensationnel!
Good morning, good afternoon Bonjour
Goodbye Au revoir
Good evening Bonsoir
Good night Bonne nuit
Good health! Santé!
Good luck! Bonne chance!
Happy birthday! Bon anniversaire!
Happy Christmas! Joyeux Noël!
Happy New Year! Bonne Année!
Hello! Salut!
Help! Au secours!
How are you? Comment allez-vous? Comment vas-tu? Ça va?
Have a good trip! Bon voyage!
Have a good meal! Bon appétit!
Look out! Attention!
to make someone's acquaintance faire la connaissance de quelqu'un
meeting (*appointment*) le rendez-vous
It's a pity! C'est dommage!
Really? Sans blague? Vraiment?
See you soon A bientôt, A tout à l'heure
So long A bientôt, Au revoir
Sleep well Dors bien, Dormez bien
Stop thief! Au voleur!
thank you merci
thank you very much merci beaucoup, merci bien
That's it! C'est ça!
till next week à la semaine prochaine
till this evening à ce soir
till tomorrow à demain
too bad! tant pis!
What! Comment!

willingly volontiers
Will you repeat the question please? Plaît-il? Voulez-vous répéter la question, s'il vous plaît?

18 FAMILY LA FAMILLE
adult un(e) adulte
aunt la tante
baby le bébé
bride la nouvelle mariée
bridegroom le nouveau marié
brother le frère
cousin le (la) cousin(e)
daughter la fille
daughter-in-law la belle-fille
elder aîné(e)
father le père
father-in-law le beau-père
granddaughter la petite fille
grandfather le grand-père
grandmother la grand'mère
grandson le petit-fils
grown-ups les grandes personnes
husband le mari, l'époux (m)
kids les gosses (m & f)
mother la mère
mother-in-law la belle-mère
nephew le neveu
niece la nièce
parents les parents (mpl)
relatives les parents (mpl)
sister la sœur
sister-in-law la belle-sœur
son le fils
son-in-law le beau-fils, le gendre
uncle l'oncle (m)
widow la veuve
widower le veuf
wife la femme, l'épouse (f)
young people les jeunes gens
younger (*e.g. sister, brother*) cadet(te)

19 FARM LA FERME
barley l'orge (f)
barn la grange
cart la charrette
cattle le bétail
combine-harvester la moissonneuse-batteuse
corn le blé
cow-shed l'étable (f)
crop la récolte
dairy la laiterie
farmer le fermier
farmer's wife la fermière
farm-yard la basse-cour
fertiliser l'engrais (m)
flock le troupeau
fork la fourche
gate la barrière
harvest la moisson
hay le foin
to make hay faire les foins
henhouse le poulailler
loft le grenier
milk le lait
to milk the cows traire les vaches

mill le moulin
oats l'avoine (f)
orchard le verger
pigsty la porcherie
plough la charrue
to plough labourer
pond l'étang (m), la mare
to reap faucher
shepherd le berger
to sow semer
stable l'écurie (f)
straw la paille
tractor le tracteur
well le puits

20 FLOWERS/TREES LES FLEURS/LES ARBRES

ash le frêne
beech le hêtre
branch la branche
bush le buisson
(horse) chestnut le marronier
(sweet) chestnut le châtaignier
clover le trèfle
copse le taillis
daisy la marguerite
daffodil la jonquille
elm l'orme (m)
fir le sapin
forest la forêt
hawthorn l'aubépine (f)
hedge la haie
holly le houx
ivy le lierre
lime le tilleul
oak le chêne
pine le pin
plane-tree le platane
poplar le peuplier
rose la rose
shamrock le trèfle d'Irlande
tamarisk le tamaris
thistle le chardon
trunk le tronc
walnut le noyer
willow le saule
wood le bois
yew l'if (m)

21 FOOD/DRINK LA NOURRITURE/LES BOISSONS

bacon le bacon, le lard
beef le bœuf
beer la bière
pint of beer un demi
bread le pain
bread roll le petit pain
butter le beurre
cake le gâteau (pl: les gâteaux)
(breakfast) cereals les céréales (fpl) en flocons
champagne le champagne
cheese le fromage
chips les (pommes) frites (fpl)
crescent roll le croissant
crisps les chips (mpl), les pommes (fpl) chip
chocolate le chocolat

chop la côtelette
cider le cidre
coffee le café
cream la crème
crumb la miette
egg l'œuf (m)
fish le poisson
fruit juice le jus de fruit
ham le jambon
ice cream la glace
jam la confiture
lamb l'agneau (m)
leg of lamb le gigot d'agneau
lemonade la limonade
lemon squash le citron pressé
marmalade la confiture d'oranges
meat la viande
milk le lait
mushroom le champignon
mustard la moutarde
omelette l'omelette (f)
pancake la crêpe
pepper le poivre
pork le porc
potato la pomme de terre
roast rôti
salt le sel
sandwich le sandwich
sausage la saucisse (*large*), le saucisson (*small*)
slice la tranche
snail l'escargot (m)
soup le potage, la soupe
starter hors d'œuvre (m)
steak le bifteck
sugar le sucre
tea le thé
toast le pain grillé
trout la truite
vegetables les légumes (mpl) (*see also section 22*)
veal le veau
vinegar le vinaigre
water l'eau (f)
mineral/spa water l'eau minérale
wine le vin (rouge, blanc, rosé)
  table wine vin du pays, ordinaire
  guaranteed vintage appellation contrôlée
yoghurt le yaourt
(flavoured) yoghurt le yaourt parfumé

22 FRUIT/VEGETABLES LES FRUITS/LES LÉGUMES

apple la pomme
apricot l'abricot (m)
artichoke l'artichaut (m)
asparagus les asperges (fpl)
banana la banane
bean le haricot
runner bean le haricot vert
beetroot la betterave
blackberry la mûre
Brussels sprouts les choux (mpl) de Bruxelles
cabbage le chou
carrot la carotte
cauliflower le chou-fleur
celery le céleri

cherry la cerise
cress le cresson
cucumber le concombre
(red)currant la groseille
date la datte
garlic l'ail (m)
gooseberry la groseille à maquereau
grapefruit le pamplemousse
grapes les raisins (mpl); du raisin
leek le poireau
lemon le citron
lettuce la laitue
melon le melon
onion l'oignon (m)
orange l'orange (f)
parsley le persil
parsnip le panais
peas les petits pois
peach la pêche
pear la poire
pineapple l'ananas (m)
plum la prune
potato la pomme de terre
radish le radis
raspberry la framboise
rhubarb la rhubarbe
salad la salade
spinach les épinards (mpl)
sweetcorn le maïs
strawberry la fraise
tomato la tomate
turnip le navet

23 GARDEN LE JARDIN

bench le banc
broom le balai
to dig bêcher
flower la fleur
flower-bed la plate-bande, le parterre
foliage le feuillage
fork la fourche
grass l'herbe (f)
greenhouse la serre
to grow pousser (*intransitive*); cultiver (*transitive*)
hedge la haie
kitchen garden le jardin potager
ladder l'échelle (f)
lawn la pelouse, le gazon
lawn-mower la tondeuse
leaf la feuille
path l'allée (f)
plant la plante
rake le rateau
seed la graine
see-saw la balançoire
spade la bêche
sun-dial le cadran solaire
(child's) swing l'escarpolette (f)
trowel la truelle
tree l'arbre (m)
turf le gazon
weed la mauvaise herbe
wheelbarrow la brouette

24 HEALTH/ILLNESS LA SANTÉ/LES MALADIES

ambulance l'ambulance (f)
aspirin l'aspirine (f)
bandage/dressing le pansement
to be better aller mieux
to be cold avoir froid
to be hot avoir chaud
to be hungry avoir faim
to be thirsty avoir soif
blind aveugle
blindness la cécité
blood le sang
capsule (*tablet*) le cachet
the chemist le pharmacien
the chemist's shop la pharmacie
chicken-pox la varicelle
a cold un rhume
to catch cold prendre froid; attraper un rhume, s'enrhumer
to have a cold être enrhumé
cough la toux
to cough tousser
to cure, heal guérir
deaf sourd(e)
deafness la surdité
doctor le médecin
dumb muet(te)
dumbness (*physical*) le mutisme
to faint s'évanouir
to fall ill tomber malade
to feel ill se sentir souffrant
'flu la grippe
German measles la rubéole
harm/injury le mal
health la santé
to be in bad health se porter mal
to be in good health se porter bien
headache le mal de tête
to have a headache avoir mal à la tête
help l'aide (f), le secours
to help aider
to have hiccups avoir le hoquet
to hurt oneself se blesser
ill malade
to be ill être malade
illness la maladie
to look after soigner
measles la rougeole
medicine le médicament
misfortune le malheur
mumps les oreillons (mpl)
nurse l'infirmier (m), l'infirmière (f)
pain la douleur
prescription l'ordonnance (f)
to recover se remettre, (se) récupérer
tablet le comprimé
to take (one's) pulse tâter le pouls
to be sick avoir mal au cœur
to be air sick avoir le mal de l'air
to be sea sick avoir le mal de mer
serious grave
to sneeze éternuer
spots les boutons (mpl)
sticking plaster le sparadrap
to suffer souffrir
suffering la souffrance
sunstroke le coup de soleil

tablet le comprimé
to have a temperature avoir de la fièvre
bad tooth la dent gâtée
a wound une blessure
to wound blesser

N.B. also 'to hurt' in various parts of the body:
    avoir mal à . . .
e.g. avoir mal au bras *to have a pain in the arm*
      avoir mal aux dents *to have toothache*
      avoir mal au dos *to have backache*
      avoir mal à l'oreille *to have earache, etc.*

25 HOUSE/ROOMS LA MAISON/LES PIÈCES

attic le grenier
basement le sous-sol
bathroom la salle de bains
bedroom la chambre à coucher
bell la sonnette
block of flats l'immeuble (m)
bolt le verrou
bungalow une maison sans étage, un pavillon
caretaker le (la) concierge
ceiling le plafond
cellar la cave
central heating le chauffage central
to clean nettoyer
corridor le couloir
cupboard l'armoire (f), le placard
curtains les rideaux (mpl)
dining-room la salle à manger
door la porte
entrance-hall le vestibule
flat l'appartement (m)
council flat H.L.M. (Habitation à Loyer Modéré)
floor le plancher
floor (*i.e. storey*) l'étage (m)
front door la porte d'entrée
furniture les meubles (mpl)
garage le garage
gate la grille, la porte
ground floor le rez-de-chaussée
guest room la chambre d'amis
household le ménage
housewife la ménagère
kitchen la cuisine
key la clé, la clef
landing le palier
lavatory le cabinet de toilette
lift l'ascenseur (m)
living-room le séjour
lock la serrure
lounge le salon
to overlook donner sur
rent le loyer
to rent louer
roof le toit
room la pièce, la salle
shutter le contrevent, le volet
stairs l'escalier (m)
study le cabinet de travail
tenant le (la) locataire
threshold le seuil
to tidy (away) ranger
villa une villa

wall le mur
window la fenêtre
window-sill le rebord de la fenêtre
yard la cour

Bathroom La salle de bains
bath la baignoire
to bathe se baigner
razor-point la prise de rasoir
shower la douche
soap lc savon
sponge une éponge
tap le robinet
toothbrush la brosse à dents
toothpaste le dentifrice
towel la serviette (de toilette)
washbowl le lavabo

Bedroom La chambre (à coucher)
alarm clock le réveil, le réveille-matin
bed le lit
bedside table le chevet
bedside lamp la lampe de chevet
blanket la couverture
bolster le traversin
chest of drawers la commode
comb le peigne
drawer le tiroir
dressing-table la table de toilette
eiderdown l'édredon (m), le duvet
hairbrush la brosse à cheveux
hand-mirror la glace à main
to make one's bed faire son lit
mattress le matelas
mirror le miroir, la glace
pillow l'oreiller (m)
rug la descente du lit
sheet le drap
shelf le rayon
wardrobe l'armoire (f), la garde-robe

Dining-room La salle à manger
chair la chaise
cup la tasse
fork la fourchette
glass le verre
knife le couteau
to lay the table mettre le couvert
mustard la moutarde
napkin la serviette
oil l'huile (f)
pepper le poivre
place-setting le couvert
plate l'assiette (f)
salt le sel
saucer la soucoupe
sideboard le buffet
silver (*adj.*) d'argent, en argent
spoon la cuiller
stainless steel (*adj.*) d'acier inoxydable, en acier inoxydable
table la table
tablecloth la nappe
tray le plateau
vinegar le vinaigre

Kitchen La cuisine
broom le balai
bucket le seau

coffee pot la cafetière
cooker la cuisinière
dishwasher la machine à laver la vaisselle, la lave-vaisselle
duster le torchon
electric mixer le batteur (électrique)
freezer le congélateur
fridge le frigo, le réfrigérateur
frying-pan la poêle
iron le fer à repasser
to iron repasser
to do the ironing faire le repassage
jug la cruche (*large*), le cruchon (*small*), le pot
kettle la bouilloire
oven le four
pressure-cooker l'auto-cuiseur (m)
saucepan la casserole
sink l'évier (m)
spin-dryer l'essoreuse (f)
stew-pan la marmite
stool le tabouret
stove le poêle, le fourneau
tap le robinet
teapot la théière
vacuum-cleaner l'aspirateur (m)
to do the washing faire la lessive
washing-machine la machine à laver
to do the washing-up faire la vaisselle

Living room/lounge Le séjour/le salon
armchair le fauteuil
bookcase la bibliothèque
carpet le tapis
clock la pendule
curtains les rideaux (mpl)
cushion le coussin
hi-fi le système hi-fi
occasional table la petite table de salon
picture le tableau
radio la radio
(transistor) radio le transistor
record-player l'électrophone (m), le tourne-disque(s) (m)
settee le canapé
shelf le rayon
standard lamp le lampadaire
tape-recorder le magnétophone
TV le poste de télévision, le téléviseur
video tape-recorder le magnétoscope

26 HUMAN BODY LE CORPS HUMAIN

ankle la cheville
arm le bras
back le dos
beard la barbe
blood le sang
bone l'os (m)
breath l'haleine (f), le souffle
out of breath hors d'haleine
cheek la joue
chest la poitrine
chin le menton
complexion le teint
ear l'oreille (f)
elbow le coude
eye l'œil (m) (pl: les yeux)
eyebrow le sourcil
eyelash le cil

eyelid la paupière
face la figure, le visage
finger le doigt
fist le poing
flesh la chair
foot le pied
forehead le front
hair les cheveux (mpl)
hand la main
head la tête
heart le cœur
heel le talon
hip la hanche
knee le genou (pl: les genoux)
leg la jambe
lip la lèvre
lung le poumon
mouth la bouche
moustache la (les) moustache(s) (fpl)
nail l'ongle (m)
neck le cou
nose le nez
shoulder l'épaule (f)
sigh le soupir
skin la peau
stomach l'estomac (m), le ventre
thigh la cuisse
throat la gorge
thumb le pouce
tongue la langue
tooth la dent
toe l'orteil (m), le doigt de pied
voice la voix
waist la taille
wrinkle la ride
wrist le poignet

N.B. Remember to use the definite article in French, instead of the possessive adjective, for expressions such as:
Elle se brosse **les** dents. *She brushes her teeth.*
Il a **les** cheveux noirs. *He has black hair.*
Je me suis foulé **le** poignet. *I have sprained my wrist.*

27 INSECTS LES INSECTES

ant la fourmi
bee l'abeille (f)
bug la punaise
butterfly le papillon
cicada la cigale
fly la mouche
grasshopper la sauterelle
mosquito le moustique
spider l'araignée (f)
to sting piquer
wasp la guêpe

28 JOBS/PROFESSIONS LES MÉTIERS/ LES PROFESSIONS

accountant le (la) comptable
air-hostess l'hôtesse (f) de l'air
antique-dealer l'antiquaire (m)
apprentice l'apprenti(e)
auctioneer le directeur de la vente
auctioneer-valuer le commissaire-priseur
baker le boulanger

barrister l'avocat (m)
blacksmith le forgeron
bookseller le (la) libraire
bricklayer le maçon en briques
builder le constructeur
businessman le commerçant, l'homme (m) d'affaires
butcher le boucher
caretaker le (la) concierge
carpenter le charpentier, le menuisier
cashier le caissier, la caissière
chemist (*medical*) le pharmacien
chemist (*industrial*) le chimiste
civil servant le fonctionnaire
conductor le receveur
conductress la receveuse
cook la cuisinière
(head) cook le chef de cuisine
commercial traveller le commis-voyageur
computer operator le (la) mécanographe
customs officer le douanier
daily help la femme de ménage, la femme de journée
dentist le (la) dentiste
doctor le médecin
(woman) doctor la femme médecin
driver le chauffeur
dustman le boueur
electrician l'électricien (m)
engineer l'ingénieur (m)
farmer le fermier
farmer's wife la fermière
fireman le sapeur-pompier
fisherman le pêcheur
foreman le chef d'équipe, le contre-maître
gardener le jardinier
garage-owner le garagiste
grocer l'épicier (m)
greengrocer le marchand de légumes
hairdresser le coiffeur, la coiffeuse
hotel-keeper l'hôtelier (m)
housekeeper la femme de charge
housewife la ménagère
interpreter l'interprète (m & f)
journalist le (la) journaliste
judge le juge
librarian le (la) bibliothécaire
lorry-driver le routier
maid la bonne
manager le gérant
mason le maçon
mayor le maire
mechanic le mécanicien
MP le Député (*France*); le Membre de la Chambre des Communes (*England*)
miner le mineur
musician le musicien
nurse l'infirmier (m), l'infirmière (f)
painter le peintre
painter/decorator le peintre-décorateur
photographer le (la) photographe
pilot le pilote
plumber le plombier
poet le poète
poetess la femme poète
policeman l'agent (m) de police (*town*); le gendarme (*country*); le policier
policewoman la femme-agent

politician l'homme (m) politique, la femme politique
postman le facteur
priest le prêtre
Prime Minister le Premier Ministre
railway worker le cheminot
receptionist la (le) réceptionniste
redundant en surnombre
representative le représentant
to be retired être à la retraite
sailor le marin, le matelot
sales-assistant le commis, le vendeur, la vendeuse
second-hand dealer le brocanteur, la brocanteuse
second-hand book dealer le (la) bouquiniste
secretary le (la) secrétaire
servant le (la) domestique
shoe-mender le cordonnier
shop-keeper le (la) marchand(e)
soldier le soldat
solicitor l'avoué (m); le notaire
tailor le tailleur
teacher le professeur
junior school teacher l'instituteur (m), l'institutrice (f)
telephonist le (la) standardiste
trade unionist le syndicaliste
typist le (la) dactylo
unemployed person le chômeur, la chômeuse
usherette l'ouvreuse (f)
vicar le curé
waiter le garçon
waitress la serveuse
worker l'ouvrier (m), l'ouvrière (f)
writer l'écrivain (m)

29 LETTERS LES LETTRES

The following material is frequently required for writing letters in the free composition section of O-level and CSE examinations.

My name is . . .   Je m'appelle . . .
I am . . . years old. J'ai . . . ans.
I live at (in) . . .   J'habite . . .

I have	blue	eyes.	J'ai les yeux	bleus.
	brown			bruns.
	green			verts.
	grey			gris.

I have	dark	hair.	J'ai les cheveux	bruns/noirs.
	blond			blonds.
	red			roux.

I am	big	for my age.	Je suis	grand(e)	pour mon âge.
	small			petit(e)	

I have . . . brothers. J'ai . . . frères.
I have . . . sisters. J'ai . . . sœurs.

I have a	cat	called . . .	J'ai un	chat	qui s'appelle . . .
	dog			chien	
	rabbit			lapin	

I like	swimming	J'aime	nager.
	horse-riding.		monter à cheval.
	playing tennis.		jouer au tennis.
	playing football.		jouer au football.

To begin a letter to a friend: Mon cher . . .
                              Ma chère . . .

To begin a letter to your parents: Mes chers parents,

To begin a letter to a stranger: Monsieur,
                                                        Madame,
To end a letter to a friend: Bien amicalement,

To end a letter to your parents: Gros baisers,

To end a letter to a stranger: Veuillez agréer, Monsieur
   (Madame), l'expression de mes sentiments distingués.

Expressions of quantity

Remember to use **de** or **d'** after expressions of quantity:
beaucoup **de** pommes
un kilo **de** poires
une bouteille **de** vin
une boîte **d'**ananas

30 NUMBER/QUANTITY   LES NOMBRES/LES QUANTITÉS

1	un	32	trente-deux, etc.
2	deux	40	quarante
3	trois	41	quarante et un
4	quatre	42	quarante-deux, etc.
5	cinq	50	cinquante
6	six	51	cinquante et un
7	sept	52	cinquante-deux, etc.
8	huit	60	soixante
9	neuf	61	soixante et un
10	dix	62	soixante-deux, etc.
11	onze	70	soixante-dix
12	douze	71	soixante et onze
13	treize	72	soixante-douze, etc.
14	quatorze	80	quatre-vingts
15	quinze	81	quatre-vingt-un, etc.
16	seize	90	quatre-vingt-dix
17	dix-sept	91	quatre-vingt-onze, etc.
18	dix-huit	99	quatre-vingt-dix-neuf
19	dix-neuf	100	cent
20	vingt	200	deux cents
21	vingt et un	300	trois cents
22	vingt-deux, etc.	301	trois cent un
30	trente	450	quatre cent cinquante
31	trente et un		

N.B. the 's' is omitted in the plural hundreds when another number follows.

1000 mille
3000 trois mille
N.B. An 's' is never added to **mille** (= thousand).
Milles = miles.

1,000,000 un million

about 10 une dizaine (de)
about 20 une vingtaine (de)
about 100 une centaine (de)
a dozen une douzaine (de)

a quarter un quart
a half une moitié
half demi(e)
three-quarters trois-quarts
a third un tiers
two-thirds deux tiers
a fifth un cinquième, etc.

1 kilo = 1000g = 2.2 lb
1 litre = 1¾ pints

first premier, première
second second, deuxième
third troisième, etc.

Note particularly the spelling of **cinquième** and **neuvième**.

When expressing the date, remember to use:
   le premier avril *the first of April*
   le trois décembre *the third of December*
   le vingt-trois février *the twenty-third of February, etc.*

31 PASTIMES   LES PASSE-TEMPS

amusement le divertissement, la distraction
athletics l'athlétisme (m)
badminton le badminton
ballet le ballet
to play basketball jouer au basket-ball
to play billiards jouer au billard
boating le canotage
boxing la boxe
camera l'appareil (m) photographique
cine-camera la camera
carpentry la menuiserie
to go camping faire du camping
to play cards jouer aux cartes
to play chess jouer aux échecs
to play cricket jouer au cricket
crosswords les mots croisés
cycling le cyclisme
dance le bal
detective story le roman policier
disco la discothèque, le dancing
do-it-yourself le bricolage
draughts le jeu de dames
to enjoy oneself s'amuser
to fish pêcher
game le jeu (*e.g. cards*); la partie (*e.g. a game (hand) of cards*); le sport (*outdoor game*); le match (*a competitive game*)
girl guide l'éclaireuse (f)
golf le golf
hockey le hockey
horse-race la course de chevaux
horse-riding l'équitation (f)
to go horse-riding monter à cheval
jogging le jogging
kite le cerf-volant
to knit tricoter
to listen to the radio écouter la radio
magazine la revue
model-making faire des maquettes
mountaineering l'alpinisme (m)
netball le netball
painting la peinture
party la (sur)boum, la soirée
a play une pièce de théâtre
to play a musical instrument jouer de . . .
e.g. **cello** jouer du violoncelle
   clarinet jouer de la clarinette
   drums jouer de la batterie
   flute jouer de la flûte
   guitar jouer de la guitare
   oboe jouer du hautbois
   organ jouer de l'orgue (f)
   piano jouer du piano
   trumpet jouer de la trompette
   violin jouer du violon

to take photos prendre des photographies
'pop' music la musique pop, la musique disco
programme l'émission (f) (*broadcast*); le programme
race la course
racket la raquette
record le disque
record-player l'électrophone (m), le tourne-disque(s)
to read a novel lire un roman
to ride a bicycle monter à vélo, à bicyclette
to ride a horse monter à cheval
riding l'équitation (f)
rugby le rugby
scouting le scoutisme
to sew coudre
sewing-machine la machine à coudre
skating le patinage
to skate patiner
snooker (une sorte de) jeu de billard
squash le squash
stadium le stade
to collect stamps collectionner les timbres
swimming la natation
to swim nager
swimming pool la piscine
to play table-football jouer au baby-foot
to play table-tennis jouer au ping-pong
tape-recorder le magnétophone
tape (*for recording*) la bande (magnétique)
team l'équipe (f)
tennis le tennis
theatre le théâtre
toboggan la luge, le toboggan
to toboggan faire du toboggan
toy le jouet
track (*e.g. running*) la piste
training l'entraînement (m)
transistor radio le transistor
TV la télévision
TV set le poste de télévision, le téléviseur
to go for a walk faire une promenade, se promener
to take the dog for a walk promener le chien
volleyball le volleyball
wrestling la lutte
Youth Club le Club des Jeunes, la Maison des Jeunes

32 PLACE/POSITION LES ENDROITS/ LES SITUATIONS

before devant
behind derrière
bottom le bas, le fond
centre le centre
in the distance au loin
elsewhere ailleurs
end le bout, l'extrémité (f)
everywhere partout
far loin
here and there çà et là
inside dedans, à l'intérieur (m)
middle le centre, le milieu
nearby tout près
nowhere nulle part
on sur
outside dehors, à l'extérieur (m)
over dessus, par-dessus

place l'endroit (m); le lieu (un bel endroit; son lieu de naissance)
side le côté
space l'espace (m)
together ensemble
top le haut
under sous, au-dessous de

33 POST OFFICE LE BUREAU DE POSTE

address l'adresse (f)
airmail la poste aérienne
card la carte
counter le guichet
envelope l'enveloppe (f)
form la fiche, le formulaire, la formule
letter la lettre
letter-box la boîte aux lettres
mail le courrier
packet le paquet
parcel le colis
to post a letter mettre une lettre à la poste
postal order le mandat (postal)
postbag la sacoche
postman le facteur
registered recommandé
stamp le timbre(-poste)
telegram le télégramme
telephone le téléphone
to telephone téléphoner à

34 RAILWAY LE CHEMIN DE FER

arrival l'arrivée (f)
booking-office le guichet
compartment le compartiment
first-class compartment un compartiment de première classe
second-class compartment un compartiment de seconde classe
non-smoking compartment un compartiment non-fumeur
smoking compartment un compartiment pour fumeurs
departure le départ
dining-car le wagon-restaurant
door la portière
engine la locomotive
entrance l'entrée (f)
exit la sortie
guard le chef de train
information bureau le bureau de renseignements
journey le voyage
(short) journey le trajet
left-luggage office la consigne
level-crossing le passage à niveau
line la voie
luggage les bagages (mpl)
luggage-rack le filet à bagages, le porte-bagages
luggage-van le fourgon à bagages
passenger le voyageur
platform le quai
porter le porteur, l'employé
railway station la gare
refreshment-room le buffet
sleeping-car le wagon-lit
station master le chef de gare
suitcase la valise
ticket le billet

single ticket le billet d'aller
return ticket le billet d'aller et retour
ticket collector le contrôleur
timetable (board) l'indicateur (m)
train le train
express train le rapide
goods train le train de marchandises
non-stop train le train direct
stopping train le train omnibus
trolley le chariot (à bagages)
trunk la malle
waiting room la salle d'attente

35 SEASIDE AU BORD DE LA MER

anchor l'ancre (m)
to bathe se baigner
bay la baie
beach la plage
(shingle) beach la plage de galets
boat le bateau
bucket le seau
cliff la falaise
coast la côte
crab le crabe
crossing la traversée
deckchair le transatlantique, le transa(t)
dinghy le canot
to disembark débarquer
to dive plonger
to drown (se) noyer
to embark s'embarquer
to fish pêcher
fisherman le pêcheur
fishing-boat la barque (de pêcheur)
fishing-rod la canne à pêche
holiday-maker l'estivant (m), le vacancier
jetty, pier la jetée
life-buoy la bouée de sauvetage
lighthouse le phare
mast le mât
to moor amarrer
navy la marine
oar l'aviron (m)
paddle la pagaie
to paddle pagayer (*e.g. a canoe*); patauger (*= to wade*)
passenger le passager
passenger-boat le paquebot
rock le rocher, la roche
rowing-boat le bateau à rames
sailing la voile
to go sailing faire de la voile
sailing-boat le voilier, le bateau à voiles, le canot à voile
sailor le marin, le matelot
sand le sable
sand castle le château de sable
seagull la mouette
ship le navire
shipwreck le naufrage
to be shipwrecked faire naufrage
shrimp la crevette
spade la pelle
steamer le vapeur
to sunbathe prendre des bains de soleil
surfing le surfing
to swim nager

swimming costume le maillot de bain
swimming trunks le caleçon de bain
tide la marée
at high tide à marée haute
at low tide à marée basse
water-skiing le ski nautique
to go water-skiing faire du ski nautique
to go wind-surfing faire de la planche à voile

36 SCHOOL L'ÉCOLE

headmaster le directeur (*primary school*); le proviseur (*secondary school*)
deputy head (*pastoral*) le censeur
supervisor le 'pion' (*in class*), le surveillant (*outside the classroom*)

Subjects Les matières

art le dessin
biology la biologie, l'histoire naturelle
chemistry la chimie
civics l'instruction civique
commercial studies les cours commerciaux
computer studies la mécanographie
craft les travaux pratiques
domestic science les arts ménagers
economics l'économie politique
English l'anglais
French le français
geography la géographie
geology la géologie
German l'allemand
Greek le grec
gymnastics la gymnastique
history l'histoire (f)
home economics les cours ménagers
Latin le latin
Italian l'italien
maths les mathématiques (mpl)
metalwork le travail des métaux
music la musique
physics la physique
PE l'éducation physique
pottery la poterie
Russian le russe
scripture les études religieuses, la religion
sewing la couture
social sciences les sciences humaines
Spanish l'espagnol
technical drawing le dessin industriel
Welsh le gallois
woodwork le travail du bois
workshop practice les cours d'atelier

37 SHOPPING LES ACHATS

bank note le billet (de banque)
basket le panier
to buy acheter
(loose) change la monnaie
cheap bon marché
cheque le chèque
cheque book le carnet de chèques
to cash a cheque toucher un chèque
(traveller's) cheque le chèque de voyage
to cost coûter

counter le comptoir
customer le client, la cliente
dear cher
groceries les provisions (fpl)
how much C'est combien? Ça fait combien?
money l'argent (m)
to owe devoir
to pay payer
pound (*weight and money*) la livre
pound (*weight only*) le demi-kilo
price le prix
purse le porte-monnaie
sales les soldes (mpl)
to save épargner
savings bank la caisse d'épargne
scales la balance
to sell vendre
shelf le rayon
shop assistant le vendeur, la vendeuse
to go shopping faire des achats, faire des courses,
    faire des emplettes
size l'encolure (f) (*shirts*); la pointure (*shoes*);
    la taille (*clothes*)
to spend dépenser
stall l'étalage (m)
till la caisse
trade le commerce
trolley le chariot
wallet le portefeuille
to weigh peser
weight le poids
to go window-shopping faire du lèche-vitrine
to wrap emballer, envelopper

38 TIME L'HEURE/LE TEMPS
after après
at first d'abord
at last enfin
again de nouveau, encore une fois
ago il y a
already déjà
always toujours
at once aussitôt, tout de suite
before avant
to begin commencer
beginning le commencement, le début
century le siècle
clock la pendule (*house*); l'horloge (f) (*public building*)
day le jour, la journée
day before la veille
day before yesterday avant-hier
early de bonne heure
end la fin
to end finir, terminer
eve la veille
evening le soir, la soirée
formerly jadis
fortnight quinze jours, une quinzaine
from time to time de temps en temps
future l'avenir
in the future à l'avenir
half an hour une demi-heure
hour l'heure (f)
immediately immédiatement, tout de suite

to last durer
late tard, en retard
later plus tard
midday midi (m)
midnight minuit (m)
minute la minute
moment le moment, l'instant (m)
month le mois
morning le matin, la matinée
next prochain (*adj.*); ensuite (*adv.*)
never ne . . . jamais
night la nuit
at nightfall à la nuit tombante, à la tombée de la nuit
now de nos jours; maintenant
often souvent
once une fois
to pass (*of time*) s'écouler
in the past autrefois
period (*of time*) l'époque (f)
precisely (à cinq heures) précises
at present à présent, actuellement
presently tout à l'heure
previously auparavant
a quarter of an hour un quart d'heure
quickly vite
rarely rarement
to remain rester
second la seconde
since depuis
soon bientôt
so soon si tôt
a stay un séjour
still encore, toujours
straightaway immédiatement, tout de suite
suddenly tout à coup
time (*by the clock*) l'heure (f)
time (*occasion*) la fois
a long time longtemps
during this time pendant ce temps
in time à temps
then puis
today aujourd'hui
tomorrow demain
up till now jusqu'ici
usually d'habitude
week la semaine
weekend le weekend
when quand, lorsque
year l'an (m), l'année (f)
yesterday hier
yesterday morning hier matin
yesterday evening hier soir
every day tous les jours
every afternoon tous les après-midi
every evening tous les soirs
every morning tous les matins
every month tous les mois
every week toutes les semaines
every year tous les ans
the next day le lendemain
the next morning le lendemain matin
next week la semaine prochaine
next month le mois prochain
last month le mois dernier
last week la semaine dernière

39 TOWN LA VILLE

avenue l'avenue (f), le boulevard
baker's la boulangerie
bank la banque
branch (*of bank*) la succursale
bookshop la librairie
building le bâtiment
bus station la gare routière
busy (*e.g. street*) animé(e)
butcher's la boucherie
cake-shop la pâtisserie
car park le parking
cathedral la cathédrale
church l'église (f)
chemist's la pharmacie
cinema le cinéma
civic centre le centre civique
clothes shop la boutique, le magasin de vêtements
concert hall la salle des concerts
crossroads le carrefour, le croisement
dairy la crémerie, la laiterie
district le quartier
draper's le magasin de nouveautés, la mercerie
dry cleaner's le pressing
drug store la droguerie
factory l'usine (f)
fire station la caserne des sapeurs-pompiers
greengrocer's le marchand de légumes
grocer's l'épicerie (f)
hospital l'hôpital (m)
information centre le syndicat d'initiative
ironmonger's la quincaillerie
jeweller's la bijouterie
launderette la blanchisserie automatique, la laverie
law court le tribunal, le palais de justice
lost property office le bureau des objets trouvés
market le marché
museum le musée
newspaper stand le kiosque (à journaux)
outskirts les environs (mpl)
park le jardin public
pavement le trottoir
pedestrian le piéton
pedestrian crossing le passage clouté
police station le commissariat de police, la gendarmerie, le poste de police
pork butcher's la charcuterie
railway station la gare
recreation centre le centre sportif
rush hour les heures (fpl) d'affluence
shop window la vitrine
shoe shop le magasin de chaussures
square la place
sports ground le terrain de sport
sports stadium le stade
stationer's la papeterie
street la rue
streetlamp le réverbère
suburbs la banlieue, les faubourgs (mpl)
supermarket le supermarché
sweetshop la confiserie
theatre le théâtre
tobacconist's le débit de tabac
town clock l'horloge (f)
town hall l'Hôtel de Ville (*large town*), la Mairie (*small town*)

traffic la circulation
traffic jam, l'embouteillage (m)
traffic lights les feux (mpl)
underground (railway) le métro
watchmaker's l'horlogerie (f)
workshop l'atelier (m)
Youth centre le Centre des Jeunes

40 TRAVEL/TRANSPORT LES VOYAGES/LE TRANSPORT

Check the different sections connected with travel, e.g. airport, railway, etc.

abroad à l'étranger
bicycle la bicyclette, le vélo
bus l'autobus (m)
bus stop l'arrêt (m) d'autobus
coach le car
English Channel la Manche
ferry le ferry
frontier la frontière
to hitch-hike faire de l'auto-stop
hovercraft l'aéroglisseur (m), le hovercraft
identity card la carte d'identité
motorway l'autoroute (f)
to park garer, stationner
passport le passeport
to set off se mettre en route
taxi le taxi
ticket le billet, le ticket
travel agency l'agence (f) de voyages
youth hostel l'auberge (f) de jeunesse

41 WEATHER LE TEMPS

What's the weather like? Quel temps fait-il?
It's cold. Il fait froid.
It's dark. Il fait nuit.
It's foggy. Il fait du brouillard.
It's freezing. Il gèle.
It's thawing. Il dégèle.
It's hot. Il fait très chaud.
It's light. Il fait jour.
It's raining. Il pleut.
It's pouring with rain. Il pleut à verse.
It's snowing. Il neige.
It's sunny. Il fait du soleil.
It's thundering. Il tonne.
It's warm. Il fait chaud.
It's windy. Il fait du vent.
The weather is bad. Il fait mauvais temps.
breeze la brise
climate le climat
cloud le nuage
cold froid
cool frais, fraîche
dawn l'aube (f), le point du jour
dew la rosée
heat la chaleur
ice la glace
lightning les éclairs (mpl), la foudre
to melt fondre
mist la brume
moon la lune
moonlight le clair de lune
rain la pluie
to rain pleuvoir

shower of rain l'averse (f)	**snow** la neige
rainbow l'arc-en-ciel (m)	**star** l'étoile (f)
seasons les saisons (fpl)	**storm** la tempête
spring le printemps	**sunrise** le lever du soleil
summer l'été (m)	**sunset** le coucher du soleil
autumn l'automne (m or f)	**thunder** le tonnerre
winter l'hiver (m)	**thunderstorm** l'orage (m)
in spring au printemps	**clap of thunder** le coup de tonnerre
in summer en été	**twilight** le crépuscule
in autumn en automne	**weather forecast** la météo
in winter en hiver	

3 Background knowledge

The Examination Boards which set questions on background knowledge have different methods of testing. You should check the relevant section of your Examination Board's syllabus to find out which topics you should cover and which of the following types of test you will have to do.

(a) Incomplete statements in English (usually about 50). The candidate is asked to complete a certain number of these statements (e.g. 30) by the addition of one relevant fact.

(b) Questions in English to be answered in English. You may have a choice of e.g. 30, and have to answer e.g. 10.

(c) Multiple-choice questions in English. This type of test is often answered by giving letter/ number references or by ticking the correct answer.

(d) Short paragraphs to be written in English giving e.g. five facts about certain topics.

1 THE ALPS

(a) The Alps form a natural frontier between France and Italy.
(b) The highest mountain in the Alps is **Mont Blanc.**
(c) The Alps are snow-capped all the year round.
(d) The area is famous for winter sports (e.g. skiing) in places such as Chamonix and Val d'Isère.
(e) The Alps produce half the hydro-electricity of France. One of the most famous dams is the Serre-Ponçon dam.

2 ALSACE-LORRAINE

(a) Alsace and Lorraine are the border-lands on the frontier with Germany. These lands have been fought over by the French and the Germans throughout history.

1871: Franco-Prussian War   1914–18: First World War   1939–45: Second World War

(b) This is an area of fertile plains and wooded hills, bordered by the river Rhine in the east.

(c) Agriculture is very important in this region: wheat, fruit, wine, beer, timber.

(d) There are also important iron and coal mines here. These give rise to other industries: chemicals, glass, steel.

(e) The **Vosges** mountains, covered with pine forests, divide Alsace from Lorraine.

(f) **Strasbourg** is the capital of Alsace. **Nancy** is the ancient capital of Lorraine.

(g) Climate: cold, snowy winters/hot summers.

(h) Joan of Arc was born in this region (see also section 36) at Domrémy.

(i) In 1792 the French National Anthem, 'La Marseillaise', was composed in Strasbourg by Rouget de Lisle.

3 MAP OF FRANCE: MOUNTAINS, RIVERS, TOWNS

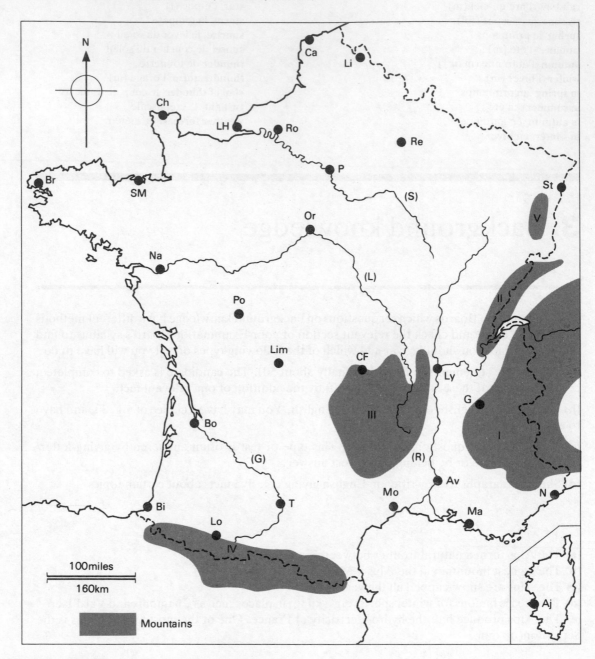

Look at the map of France and check that you know the positions of:

Mountains		**Rivers**
I	Alps	(G)	The Garonne
II	Jura	(L)	The Loire
III	Massif Central	(S)	The Seine
IV	Pyrenees	(R)	The Rhône
V	Vosges		

Towns

Aj	Ajaccio	LH	Le Havre	O	Orléans
Av	Avignon	Li	Lille	P	Paris
Bi	Biarritz	Lim	Limoges	Po	Poitiers
Bo	Bordeaux	Lo	Lourdes	Re	Reims
Br	Brest	Ly	Lyon	Ro	Rouen
Ca	Calais	Ma	Marseille	SM	St Malo
CF	Clermont-Ferrand	Mo	Montpellier	St	Strasbourg
Ch	Cherbourg	Na	Nantes	T	Toulouse
G	Grenoble	Ni	Nice		

4 The regions of France

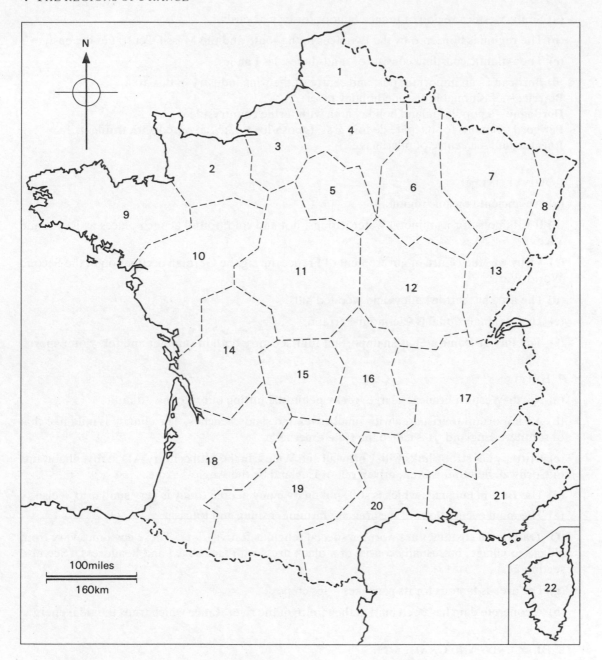

Check that you know how to spell these regions as well as where they are located.

1 Nord	9 Bretagne	16 Auvergne
2 Basse-Normandie	10 Pays de la Loire	17 Rhône-Alpes
3 Haute-Normandie	11 Centre	18 Aquitaine
4 Picardie	12 Bourgogne	19 Midi-Pyrénées
5 Région Parisienne	13 Franche-Comté	20 Languedoc-Roussillon
6 Champagne-Ardennes	14 Poitou-Charentes	21 Provence-Côte d'Azur
7 Lorraine	15 Limousin	22 Corse
8 Alsace		

5 AQUITAINE

(a) South-western region of France famous for its vineyards.

(b) The region is bordered by the Pyrenees in the south and the Massif Central in the east.

(c) The Atlantic coastline consists of sand-dunes: **les Landes.**

(d) Bordeaux – an important port and centre of the wine industry in this area.
Biarritz – a fashionable seaside/holiday resort.
Dordogne – a popular inland holiday area with fertile countryside.
Périgord – famous for its 'pâté de foie gras' (goose-liver pâté flavoured with truffles).
Rocamadour – a centre of pilgrimage.

6 AUVERGNE

(a) An ancient volcanic region.

(b) It is famous for its mineral-water springs, hot and cold, found at such places as Royat and Vichy.

(c) Vichy was the centre of government of France during the German occupation of the Second World War.

(d) The area has fertile valleys and wooded hills.

(e) The regional capital is Clermont-Ferrand.

(f) The **Puy de Dôme** area is an important tourist centre both in summer and for winter sports.

7 BRITTANY

(a) North-Western France: a large, rocky peninsula jutting out into the Atlantic.

(b) An important tourist area with small coves and sandy beaches. The climate is mild like that of southern England. It is called the **Côte Emeraude.**

(c) Brittany has strong links with Cornwall and Wales. In the fifth century AD many inhabitants of Cornwall fled to this area, driven out of England by the Anglo-Saxons.

(d) The Breton language which is still spoken by many people today is very similar to Welsh.

(e) The main occupations of the area are farming, fishing and tourism.

(f) Traditional costumes are worn on special religious festival days. These costumes vary from village to village, but usually consist of a black dress with lace shawl and headdress. (See also section 22.)

(g) The area is famous for its pancakes – 'les crêpes'.

(h) A concrete dam has been built at the mouth of the river **Rance** which traps the tidal energy.

8 BURGUNDY AND CHAMPAGNE

(a) Burgundy is a rich grape-growing region in the Saône valley.

(b) The architecture of the region is noteworthy: ornate roofs, covered with shining coloured tiles in intricate patterns, mostly in black, green and gold.

(c) Champagne is an agricultural region east of Paris. It is part of the Parisian Basin. It is a region of plains and plateaux.

(d) Reims is the old, provincial capital.

(e) The Champagne region is famous for the sparkling wine named after it.

9 CORSICA

(a) Corsica is a mediterranean island between France and Italy.

(b) The country is mountainous and is covered with vast areas of 'maquis' – bushes of aromatic herbs such as rosemary.

(c) This type of countryside has always been ideal for hiding bandits. Even today, the independent spirit of the Corsicans is still in evidence.

(d) Napoleon was born in the capital – Ajaccio.

10 LANGUEDOC

(a) This is the Mediterranean coastal area between the Rhône delta and the Pyrenees.

(b) The area is being developed as a major tourist centre.

(c) Good climate and beaches.

(d) Wine-producing area.

11 LIMOUSIN

(a) Shoe-making centre of France.

(b) **Limoges** is famous for porcelain.

(c) Poor soil. Granite rock.

(d) Some sheep-rearing.

12 LOIRE VALLEY

(a) Region south-west of Paris famous for its castles built along the Loire river and its tributaries.

(b) In the 16th and 17th centuries the Kings of France came here to relax and get away from Paris. They built 'hunting lodges' which are the castles we see today, e.g. Chambord, Chenonceau, Amboise, Azay-le-Rideau.

(c) The Loire is the longest river in France.

(d) The region produces early fruit and vegetables.

(e) It is also an important wine-producing area.

13 NORMANDY

(a) Northern coastal region.

(b) Famous seaside resorts, e.g. Deauville, Trouville.

(c) **Le Mont-Saint-Michel** is a well-known tourist spot. It is an island off the Normandy coast with a medieval abbey at the top. At low tide the water retreats for about seven miles.

(d) The capital of Normandy is **Caen.**

(e) **Rouen** is another famous town. Joan of Arc was burnt at the stake here.

(f) The famous invasion of Normandy by the Allied Forces – 'Operation Overlord' – took place in 1944.

(g) Normandy was the birthplace of William the Conqueror. There is a famous tapestry about his exploits at **Bayeux.**

(h) Around the Seine estuary there are orchards and dairy farms.

(i) Famous products include: apples, cider, butter, cheeses (e.g. Camembert, Pont-l'Évêque) and 'Calvados', a liqueur made from apples.

14 PICARDY

(a) Northernmost area of France.

(b) An industrial area near the frontier with Belgium. The industries include mining, metallurgy, chemicals, glassworks, sugar refineries and breweries.

(c) The landscape is flat with mile after mile of fields of wheat and sugar-beet.

(d) **Dunkerque** – famous scene of the rearguard action by Allied troops in May 1940.

15 POITOU-CHARENTES

(a) Mid-Western area of France with an Atlantic climate.

(b) This is a rich agricultural area.

(c) There are several important towns:
Cognac – brandy is made here.
Poitiers is an old University town.

Royan is a popular holiday resort which has been rebuilt after being almost completely destroyed in 1945.

Saintes has some important Roman remains.

16 PROVENCE AND RHÔNE VALLEY

(a) South-eastern part of France.

(b) **La Côte d'Azur** is a famous tourist area, on the Mediterranean coast, e.g. Cannes, St Tropez.

(c) **Marseille** is the main port. There are also important oil refineries here.

(d) **La Camargue** is a flat delta at the mouth of the river Rhône. This area is famous for its rice, horses and cowboys.

(e) Climate is hot and dry in summer and mild in winter.

(f) The Rhône valley produces early fruit and vegetables. It is famous for its production of grapes (it is an important wine-producing area), citrus fruits, olives, lavender and flowers.

(g) **Grasse** is the centre of the perfume-manufacturing industry.

(h) **Donzère-Mondragon** is an important hydro-electricity station in the Rhône valley.

(i) The **Mistral** is the cold north wind which sometimes blows down the Rhône valley.

(j) **Bauxite** is found in the hills of Provence at **Les Baux.** It is used in the manufacture of aluminium.

(k) Provençal specialities include 'bouillabaisse' – a fish soup, and 'ratatouille' – a vegetable stew made from courgettes and aubergines.

(l) Roman remains are found in many places, e.g. Arles, Nîmes, Orange.

(m) Provence has inspired many artists, e.g. Cézanne, Picasso, Van Gogh.

17 PYRENEES

(a) These are the mountains between France and Spain.

(b) The inhabitants of this region are called the **Basques.** They have strong ties with the Basques on the Spanish side of the Pyrenees.

(c) **Lourdes** is a famous centre of pilgrimage, especially for invalids.

(d) **Lacq** is a very important area for the extraction of natural gas.

(e) The **Pic du Midi** observatory is one of the best equipped in the world.

18 PARIS

(a) Capital city of France, on the river **Seine**.

(b) Chief tourist centre of France. Some of the main places of interest are: the Eiffel Tower, the Cathedral of Notre Dame, the Sacré-Cœur, the Louvre Museum, and Les Invalides which contains Napoleon's tomb.

(c) Paris is famous for its pavement cafés and bright night-life, and is the fashion centre of the world.

(d) The river Seine divides Paris into two sections:
(i) the Right Bank – the main shopping area, e.g. Les Galeries Lafayette, Le Printemps; also the Opéra and theatres.
(ii) the Left Bank – the student quarter: 'Le Quartier Latin'.

(e) The two islands in the centre of Paris are the Ile de la Cité and the Ile St Louis. They are the sites of the earliest settlements.

(f) Paris was originally called 'Lutetia', and inhabited by the Gauls.

(g) In the nineteenth century Paris changed radically. Broad, new avenues replaced the cramped streets, in the areas we know today. **Haussmann** was the man who designed and carried out these major changes. There is a famous **boulevard** (avenue) named after him. The Champs Elysées is the great avenue which stretches from the Place de la Concorde to the Place Charles de Gaulle (formerly called the Place de l'Étoile). Twelve avenues radiate from the Place Charles de Gaulle in whose centre is the Arc de Triomphe.

(h) Paris is the political, industrial and administrative centre of France.

(i) The Élysée Palace is the official residence of the French President (see also section 26).

(j) **La Bourse** is the French Stock Exchange.

(k) The **Louvre** Museum and Art Gallery house the Mona Lisa and the Vénus de Milo.

(l) **Montmartre** is in the north of the city. This is the traditional centre for artists, but nowadays it is more of a tourist centre. It has a sophisticated night-life.

(m) The Métro is the Paris underground railway.

(n) **Versailles** lies 20 miles south-west of Paris. Louis XIV built the famous château here in the 17th century.

19 THE COMMON MARKET/EEC (EUROPEAN ECONOMIC COMMUNITY)

(a) There are at present ten members of the Common Market:
Belgium, Denmark, France, Great Britain, Greece, Italy, Ireland, Luxembourg, The Netherlands and West Germany.

(b) These member countries still have their own separate parliaments, laws, systems of social security, etc., but their aims are to introduce free trade, to abolish customs duties (tariffs) and quotas (limits on goods which are to be imported), and to allow the free movement of workers between member countries.

(c) The main stages in the development of the Common Market were:
1951 Treaty of Paris Formation of the European Coal and Steel Union between Belgium, France, Germany, Italy, Luxembourg and the Netherlands.
1957 Treaty of Rome These six countries founded the EEC (European Economic Community).
1957 Euratom The European Atomic Energy Community was set up to develop peaceful uses of atomic energy.
1973 Denmark, Great Britain and Ireland joined the EEC.
1981 Greece became a member country.

(d) **The Commission** (which proposes rules) and the **Council** (which decides the rules) meet in Brussels.

(e) The **European Parliament** discusses the proposals and meets in Strasbourg and in Luxemburg.

(f) The **Court of Justice** hears cases which concern the Community. It sits in Luxembourg.

(g) Half the farmers of Europe are French and a third of the farmland of the EEC is French, therefore the French have a special interest in the EEC's agricultural policy (**CAP** – Common Agricultural Policy).

20 AGRICULTURE/WINE-GROWING

(a) France is an important agricultural country.

(b) She grows sufficient wheat on the northern plains to meet her own requirements.

(c) She has a variety of crops: barley, rye, oats, sugar beet, potatoes, fruit.

(d) France is also important for beef and dairy cattle, especially in the North.

(e) Self-sufficiency has always been the ideal of the French peasant. This results in a variety of crops on the farm.

(f) 'Coopératives' are becoming more numerous as farmers begin to share the cost of machinery and production. The wine industry especially is seeing an increase in the use of coopératives by local wine-growers.

(g) A 'vignoble' is a vineyard.

(h) A 'vigneron' is a wine-grower.

(i) Almost all regions of France grow grapes and make wine.

(j) The main wine-producing areas are:

Bordeaux – 'clarets', e.g. Saint-Émilion	Champagne
Burgundy, e.g. Beaujolais	Charentes – brandy, e.g. Cognac
Côtes du Rhône, e.g. Châteauneuf du Pape	Languedoc – 'vin ordinaire'

21 INDUSTRIAL AREAS/FUEL AND MINERAL RESOURCES

(a) Coal: North-East France and also St. Étienne, near Lyon.

(b) Electricity, 'La Houille blanche': Savoy and the Rhône Valley – hydro-electric power.

(c) Natural gas and its by-products (chemicals, fertilizers, sulphur): Lacq, S.W. France.

(d) Nuclear reactors: Rhône Valley, Marcoule, Pierrelatte, and also Grenoble.

(e) Iron ore: Lorraine.

(f) Car-manufacturing: Paris.

(g) Silk: Lyon.

(h) Wool/cotton industries: Lille, Rouen.

22 FOLKLORE AND FESTIVALS

(a) In France as in other European countries there are national festivals and local festivals. The local festivals are almost always connected with a local saint whose anniversary (e.g. of birth or canonisation) is celebrated with processions where the local people wear the traditional costume. For example, in Britanny there are special religious festivals called 'Pardons' where the local people, wearing traditional dress, walk in procession through the streets (symbolising a pilgrimage to ask for forgiveness of sins) to the local church. After a service in church there is usually a festival of dancing.

(b) Christmas – Noël
This begins with midnight mass followed by the 'réveillon', the Christmas meal. Children traditionally put out shoes to receive presents.

(c) New Year – Le Nouvel An
The French send cards for the New Year rather than for Christmas. This is the time for presents to be given.

(d) 6 janvier
This day is celebrated in France with a special flat cake containing a bean. The cake is called 'la Galette des Rois'. The person who finds the bean is King or Queen for the day and chooses a 'consort'. This festival is linked with Epiphany and the Magi.

(e) Shrove Tuesday – Mardi gras
This is celebrated with carnivals in certain towns. The Battle of Flowers in Nice is the most famous.

(f) 14 July – La Fête Nationale
This national holiday celebrates the beginning of the French Revolution in 1789. It is sometimes called 'Bastille Day' as this was the day when the people of Paris forced their way into the Bastille prison in Paris and released the prisoners.

(g) All Saints' Day (1 November) – La Toussaint
This day is a national holiday in France.

Marriages
In France a civil ceremony is compulsory to legalise a marriage. This ceremony takes place in the town hall (**la mairie** in a small town, **l'hôtel de ville** in a large town). A church ceremony is optional and does not replace the civil ceremony. It is the mayor who officiates at the ceremony.

23 FOOD AND DRINK

(a) France is said to have the highest standard of cooking in the world. 'Cordon bleu' = high-class cooking.

(b) The meals in France are:

Le petit déjeuner – breakfast
This usually consists of a large cup ('un bol') of coffee or hot chocolate for the children and bread ('croissants' and 'brioche' on Sundays or special occasions) with butter and jam or honey.

Le déjeuner – lunch

This is usually the largest meal of the day and except in large towns most people return home for lunch. Lunch normally begins at midday and most people do not return to work or school until 2 p.m. Lunch normally consists of: hors d'œuvres, meat course, vegetable course, salad (not in every home), cheese, dessert or fruit.

Le goûter – tea

This is for younger children returning home from school at about 4–4.30 p.m. It is really a snack, e.g. 'pain-chocolat', a roll with chocolate inside, biscuits and fruit.

Le dîner/le souper – the evening meal

This is usually taken between 7.30 and 9 p.m. although, especially in the south of France, the family meal may last until 10-10.30 p.m., having begun at about 8-8.30 p.m. This meal is similar in content to the midday meal but soup, 'le potage', replaces the hors d'œuvres, and fruit is taken instead of a dessert.

(c) Almost all French families drink red wine, 'vin ordinaire', with their two main daily meals. Better-quality wine is drunk on special occasions. Most Frenchmen pride themselves on their knowledge of French wines. Young children often drink a glass of wine diluted with water.

(d) Below are some of the different categories of wine:

Vin ordinaire – everyday wine which is relatively cheap to buy.

Vin du pays – like 'Vin ordinaire' but this is a local wine.

Vin de qualité supérieure (VDQS) – a better-quality wine.

Vin d'appellation contrôlée – a wine whose strength is guaranteed and which is only made from certain types of grape in certain regions.

Domaine and **Château** wines – the grapes are grown and the wine is bottled on the same estate. These are the 'grandes marques', the famous names in wine-producing.

24 FRENCH EDUCATION

(a) Schooling is compulsory in France between the ages of 6 and 16.

(b) Secondary-school children usually begin school at 8 a.m. Primary-school children begin between 8.30 and 9 a.m.

(c) The lunch break is often two hours long, from 11.30 to 1.30 p.m. for primary-school children and from 12 noon to 2 p.m. for secondary-school children.

(d) Classes normally end at 4 p.m. for primary-school children and at 5 p.m. for secondary-school pupils.

(e) Children go to school on Saturday mornings but Wednesday and Saturday afternoons are normally free.

(f) There are many religious festivals during the year when French children have a day's holiday. At Christmas and at Easter there is normally a fortnight's holiday. In the summer, school normally closes at the end of June and the new school year begins in the middle of September.

(g) All schools in France teach the same subjects, have the same number of lessons in each subject each week, have the same syllabus, and normally use the same text-books in each subject.

(h) Nursery education, **l'école maternelle,** is optional for children between the ages of 2 and 6. There are many state nursery schools in France. Primary education, **l'école primaire,** is for children between the ages of 6 and 11.

(i) **L'orientation scolaire** – In the last year of primary school, pupils are assessed and allocated to a particular type of secondary school:

  (i) **Lycée** – Grammar school

 (ii) **CES** (Collège d'Enseignement Secondaire) – Comprehensive School

(iii) **CEG** (Collège d'Enseignement Général) – Secondary Modern School

'Le premier cycle' is the name for the first four years of secondary school. At the end of these four years there is another 'orientation scolaire'. Having been assessed, pupils then follow the 'second cycle' courses at one of the above three types of school or at a **CET** (Collège d'Enseignement Technique). These courses last for two years.

The **brevet** examination is the school-leaving certificate taken at the age of sixteen.

The **baccalauréat** examination is taken by Lycée pupils at the age of 18. A pass in this examination will allow them to continue their studies at university.

For the baccalauréat, which is taken at the same age as British pupils take A levels, French pupils study more subjects than their British counterparts. There are certain basic subjects which all pupils must take, e.g. French, Maths and a foreign language. The other subjects taken will depend on whether they are 'Arts', 'Science' or 'Technical' students. The baccalauréat also includes a gymnastics or swimming test.

(j) Sport, especially team games, does not play an important part in school life but 'classes de neige' and 'classes de mer' are arranged by many French schools. During the school term French schools take classes to ski-resorts in winter and to seaside resorts in the summer. The teachers accompany the pupils who have lessons in the morning and then go skiing or swimming in the afternoon.

25 HIGHER EDUCATION

(a) After passing the baccalauréat, the most able pupils go on to a further two years' study to prepare for the entrance examination to the 'Grandes Écoles'. The 'Grandes Écoles' have tremendous prestige attached to them and success at a 'Grande École' usually brings with it entry to the top posts in all professions.

Three of the most well-known 'Grandes Écoles' are:
L'École Normale Supérieure – for humanities and sciences.
L'École Polytechnique – for the army, civil service, engineering and government service.
L'École Nationale d'Administration – for postgraduates in economics, politics and sociology and especially for those who wish to go into the Civil Service.

(b) University. A university course normally lasts for four years. The various courses can lead to:

Licence – a first degree.

CAPES (Certificat d'Aptitude au Professorat de l'Enseignement Secondaire) – a teaching diploma.

Maîtrise – a second degree.

Agrégation – a competitive (and difficult) exam. The holders of the Agrégation usually proceed to the more senior posts in schools.

Doctorat – a research degree awarded after many years' work.

26 FRENCH INSTITUTIONS

(a) Since France is a Republic, the Head of State is the President. The rules for governing the country are laid down in a written constitution.

(b) The Fifth Republic has been in existence since 1958.

(c) The President of the Republic is Président Mitterrand. He was elected in 1981.

(d) The French flag has three vertical, equal bands of blue, white and red. It is called the **Tricolore.**

(e) The French National Anthem is called 'La Marseillaise'.

(f) The Republican motto is 'Liberté, Égalité, Fraternité' (Liberty, Equality, Fraternity).

The President

The President of France is elected by universal suffrage. He holds office for seven years. He is the Head of Government as well as the Head of State.

Parliament

There are two 'houses' of parliament in France:
  (i) **L'Assemblée Nationale** – The National Assembly. The members of the National Assembly are called 'Députés'. They are elected by the people to serve for five years.

(ii) **Le Sénat** – The Senate. The senators are elected for nine years by delegates from local councils and National Assembly deputies.

The President chooses the Prime Minister.

Local government

(i) The **Conseil Général** is the French equivalent of the British county council.

(ii) The **Conseil Municipal** is the equivalent of the British town council.

(iii) A **Président du Conseil,** elected by the council itself now administers the 'département' instead of the government-appointed **préfect.**

Law courts

Present French law is based on the Code Napoléon. During the French Revolution an attempt was made to create a uniform system of laws. Before this, French law had consisted of a mixture of regional and local laws which favoured the Church and the nobles.

There are different types of court for different crimes: commercial courts, industrial courts, juvenile courts, etc.

The Press

Some of the major national newspapers are:
   Le Figaro, Le Monde, France-Soir, La Croix (Catholic newspaper), l'Humanité (official Communist party newspaper).

There are also many regional newspapers with a wide circulation, such as:
   Ouest-France, Le Progrès (Lyon), etc.

Some of the major periodicals are:
   Paris-Match, Le Canard Enchaîné, l'Express, Le Nouvel Observateur.

Radio/TV

The state broadcasting corporation is called the ORTF (Office de Radiodiffusion-Télévision Française).
   There are three TV Channels (Chaînes):
   Première Chaîne: TF 1   Deuxième Chaîne: A2   Troisième Chaîne: FR 3

The main radio channels are:
   France-Culture   France-Musique   France-Inter   Europe 1

27 MODERN DISCOVERIES IN SCIENCE AND INDUSTRY

(a) Aircraft Blériot was the first man to cross the English Channel by plane, in 1909.

(b) Ballooning The Montgolfier brothers invented the hot-air balloon.

(c) Braille invented the alphabet for the blind which bears his name.

(d) Cinema The Lumière brothers were pioneers of the cinema.

(e) Modern chemistry The father of modern chemistry was Lavoisier.

(f) The pioneer of fingerprints for identification was Bertillon.

(g) Pasteurisation Louis Pasteur discovered that micro-organisms are destroyed by heat. He also discovered a serum to combat rabies.

(h) Photography Daguerre was a pioneer of photography in France.

(i) Radium Pierre and Marie Curie discovered radium.

(j) Telegraph Ampère's researches led to the invention of the telegraph system.

28 LIFE OF THE ORDINARY PEOPLE

(a) In towns, most ordinary people live in flats. Each block of flats is looked after by a 'concierge' (caretaker). The equivalent of council flats in Britain is the **HLM** (Habitation à Loyer Modéré).

(b) In the country, you find isolated houses and farms, and also villages. Houses in the country usually have gardens.

(c) The style of the houses varies from region to region. In the south of France the roofs are made of red tiles. There are often stones on the roofs as protection against the Mistral wind. In Brittany the roofs are often made of granite.

(d) In towns there is almost always a weekly market, and large towns have a daily market. Local farmers, especially in rural areas, bring their produce to these markets. French markets begin early in the morning and are usually over by midday.

(e) Cafés are important in both town and village life. They are the local meeting places for young and old alike.

29 BEST-KNOWN PRODUCTS

(a) **Cars** e.g. Citroën, Peugeot, Renault, Simca.

(b) **Cheese** There are about 350 different sorts of cheese in France. Some of the most famous are: Camembert, Brie, Pont L'Évêque, Roquefort.

(c) **'Haute Couture'** France is the centre of the fashion world. The names of some of the most famous dress-designers are: Cardin, Chanel, Dior, Yves St. Laurent.

(d) **Perfume** The centre of the French perfume industry is Grasse in the south of France.

(e) **Wine** See section 23.

30 SPORT

(a) Many of the sports played in France are also found in other European countries (e.g. tennis, football), but there are some sports which are special to France.

(b) **Boules** The French game of 'boules' has certain similarities with English bowls but one of the major differences is that French 'boules' is played on a hard soil surface. The object of the game is to get your 'boule' as near the 'cochonnet' (small ball) as possible. The 'boules' may be thrown instead of being rolled.

(c) **Cycling** Although cycling is not confined to France alone, it is nevertheless a very important sport in France. 'Le Tour de France' is one of the most well-known of all cycle races. The 'maillot jaune' is the yellow tee-shirt worn by the previous day's 'stage' winner.

(d) **Pelote** is a Basque game. It is played with a crescent-shaped basket. This is used to catch a ball, which is then flung against a wall.

(e) **Pétanque** is a southern version of 'boules'.

31 TRANSPORT

(a) **Air**
France has air-links with all major and most minor countries of the world. 'Concorde' was built as a joint British/French venture.

(b) **Rail**
Most of the French railway network is electrified.
A **rapide** is an express train.
An **omnibus** is a suburban train.
The **Mistral** is the famous express train (named after the wind) which goes from Paris to the south of France.
The **métro** is the French underground railway in Paris. N.B. it is not a car! A 'carnet' is a book of tickets (10) for the métro. It can also be used for buses in Paris. It is cheaper to buy a 'carnet' than 10 individual tickets.

(c) **Road**
There are several motorways (**autoroutes**) in France. Drivers using the motorway pay according to the distance travelled.
'N' stands for Route Nationale. This indicates a main road, for example, 'N.7' is the main road (except for the motorway) from Paris to the south of France.

(d) **Sea**
France has sea on three sides: the Atlantic to the west, the Channel to the north and the Mediterranean to the south. France has sea access to all parts of the world.

32 PRINCIPAL HISTORICAL DATES

(a) Rulers of France

481–751	Merovingians	1774–1792	Louis XVI
751–987	Carolingians (Charlemagne, the most famous of the Carolingians, was crowned on Christmas Day 800)	1792–1814	Napoleon Bonaparte (First Republic)
987–1328	Capetians	1814–1848	Restoration of the Monarchy Louis XVIII 1814–1824 Charles X 1824-1830 Louis-Philippe 1830-1848
1328–1589	Valois (1428: Joan of Arc led the the French armies against the English)	1848–1870	Louis Napoleon (Second Republic)
1589–1610	Henri IV	1871–1940	Third Republic
1610–1643	Louis XIII	1940–1944	German Occupation
1643–1715	Louis XIV	1944–1958	Fourth Republic
1715–1774	Louis XV	1958–	Fifth Republic

(b) Principal historical events since the 18th century

1789 The storming of the Bastille prison marked the beginning of the French Revolution.

1793 Execution of Louis XVI. First Republic proclaimed.

1804 Napoleon Bonaparte proclaimed Emperor.

1815 Napoleon Bonaparte and the French defeated at Waterloo. The Monarchy restored.

1830 Revolution. Louis-Philippe proclaimed King.

1848 Revolution. Louis Napoleon became Head of State. (He was Napoleon Bonaparte's nephew.)

1851 Louis Napoleon seized power in a Coup d'État.

1852 Louis Napoleon proclaimed Emperor.

1870 The French army defeated by the Prussians.

1914 Germany declared war on France.

1919 Treaty of Versailles between Allies and Germany.

1940 France invaded by the Germans. The government of unoccupied France moved to Vichy.

1944 France liberated by the Allies.

1958 Algerian Crisis.

1961 Referendum on Algeria endorsed De Gaulle's policy.

1968 Anti-government riots by students in Paris and throughout France.

33 THE FRENCH REVOLUTION

(a) The French Revolution lasted for ten years, 1789-1799. The demands of the revolutionaries were moderate at the beginning but quickly got out of control.

(b) 1789 Louis XVI was on the throne of France.

The 'Tennis Court Oath' – certain members of the Estates-General (parliament) met in an indoor tennis court to propose a new constitution whereby France would be governed by an 'Assemblée Nationale'.

Organised bands of citizens began to take over the government of France by force.

(c) 14th July 1789. The people of Paris stormed the Bastille prison. This was the beginning of the French Revolution. The 'Assemblée Nationale' took over the running of the country. The property of the church and of the nobles was confiscated. Many nobles, including Louis XVI and his queen, Marie-Antoinette, were executed during the French Revolution.

(d) There were different revolutionary groups. The most well-known are:

The **Jacobins:** These were extremists led by Danton and Marat.

The **Girondins:** These were middle-class citizens originally from the Bordeaux area. They were opposed to the Jacobins.

(e) Robespierre

Robespierre was a lawyer who wanted the Revolution to change French society completely. He was responsible for the 'Reign of Terror' in which anyone who opposed Robespierre was executed. The 'Reign of Terror' ended with the execution of Robespierre himself.

34 OCCUPATION AND RESISTANCE

(a) In May 1940 the German army, sent by Hitler, invaded Holland, Belgium and France. English soldiers in France could not retaliate and were forced to retreat to Dunkirk and then across the English Channel in the famous rescue operation.

(b) In June 1940 Paris surrendered to the Germans, and signed a peace treaty with them. A 'puppet' government was set up at Vichy, under Marshal Pétain.

(c) Resistance to the Vichy government was strong, especially in Paris. A resistance network was established by means of small groups throughout France. Attacks were made on the occupying forces.

35 FAMOUS FRENCH PEOPLE

(a) Writers

17th century

Corneille ⎫
Racine ⎭ Tragedies

Molière Comedies (See section 38.)
La Fontaine Animal fables
Mme de Sévigné Letters

Descartes ⎫
Pascal ⎭ Philosophers

La Bruyère ⎫
La Rochefoucauld ⎭ Moralists

18th century

Rousseau – believed that man is happiest in his natural state.
Voltaire – wrote in favour of equality, freedom and tolerance.

19th century

Balzac ⎫
Dumas ⎪
Flaubert ⎬ Novelists
Stendhal ⎪
Zola ⎭

Maupassant Short stories
Victor Hugo (See section 43)
Baudelaire ⎫
Verlaine ⎭ Poets
Valéry (also 20th century) Poet and philosopher

20th century

Gide ⎫
Mauriac ⎬ Novelists
Proust ⎭

Camus ⎫
Sartre ⎭ Existentialist philosophers, novelists

(b) Painters

17th century
Boucher
Poussin

18th century
Fragonard
Watteau

19th century
David
Delacroix
Cézanne
Degas
Manet

Monet (See section 44.)
Renoir
Seurat
Van Gogh
Rodin (Sculpture)

20th century
Chagalle
Gaugin
Matisse
Picasso

(c) Musicians

19th/20th century
Berlioz
Bizet
Chopin
Debussy
Ravel
Fauré
Gounod
Massenet
Messiaen
Poulenc
Saint-Saëns

(d) Film directors

René Clair   Chabrol
Cocteau   Renais
Renoir   Truffaut
Vadim

(e) Actors and actresses

Barrault   Brigitte Bardot
Fernandel   Catherine Deneuve
Gabin   Jeanne Moreau
Jouvet   Michèle Morgan
Tati   Romy Schneider

36 JOAN OF ARC (1412–1431)

(a) Born in Domrémy in Lorraine, of peasant parents. In her teens she had visions which told her that she must leave home, go to the King and lead the French army to victory against the English. She was also told to see that the Dauphin Charles was crowned King at Rheims.

(b) She obeyed her 'voices' and achieved all of these things, in spite of many difficulties. She inspired confidence in Charles and in the hearts of the ordinary soldiers, but many of the leaders were jealous of her and helped to bring about her downfall.

(c) She was eventually captured by the English and handed over to her French enemies. She was tried for witchcraft and burnt at the stake in Rouen in 1431.

37 LOUIS XIV (1643–1715)

(a) Louis XIV is often referred to as the 'Sun King'. His emblem was a sun's face.

(b) He built the palace of Versailles which is about 20 miles south-west of Paris.

(c) He was an absolute monarch who is reputed to have said: 'L'État c'est moi.'

(d) Life at his court was full of ritual, the most famous being:
Le Petit Lever/Le Petit Coucher
Le Grand Lever/Le Grand Coucher
These rituals were centred on the King getting up and going to bed surrounded and helped by his courtiers who thought that it was a great honour to be present.

(e) Louis XIV was a great patron of the Arts and Sciences. He founded the Académie Française and the Académie des Sciences.

38 MOLIÈRE (1622-1673)

(a) Molière was born Jean-Baptiste Poquelin in Paris.

(b) His father was the Royal Upholsterer to Louis XIV.

(c) Although he studied law he joined the Béjart family theatrical company.

(d) He spent twelve years touring the provinces with this group and then returned with them to Paris where they were befriended by the Royal family.

(e) He performed in many plays at court including his own plays which became famous, e.g. 'L'Avare' and 'Tartuffe'.

(f) During a performance of 'Le Malade Imaginaire' Molière collapsed and later died.

39 LOUIS XVI (1754-1793)

(a) Louis became King in 1774. He wanted to be a wise king but he proved to be a weak monarch.

(b) His wife, Marie-Antoinette, was unpopular as she was Austrian and appeared to be frivolous and extravagant, while most French people at that time lived in great poverty.

(c) The people of Paris were very discontented. There was little money left in the Treasury. Louis XVI became increasingly powerless, and eventually the people formed a National Assembly to govern the country.

(d) The storming of the Bastille marked the beginning of the French Revolution.

(e) With the declaration of France as a Republic, Louis XVI and his wife were sentenced to death.

40 NAPOLEON (1769-1821)

(a) Napoleon was born in Ajaccio in Corsica.

(b) He was a brilliant soldier and was appointed in 1799 as one of the three consuls to rule France.

(c) In 1804 he crowned himself Emperor.

(d) He was responsible for many innovations in French life, including the introduction of the metric system and a new legal system (the **Code Napoléon**).

(e) In 1812 Napoleon's army was defeated in its attempt to capture Moscow. He lost half his army through the bleak winter conditions for which they were not prepared.

(f) In 1814 Napoleon abdicated and went into exile on the Island of Elba.

(g) In 1815 Napoleon escaped from Elba, returned to Paris and reformed his army. They were defeated at Waterloo, and Napoleon was banished to the Island of St. Helena, where he died in 1821.

41 PASTEUR (1822–1895)

(a) Pasteur discovered that disease is caused by microbes.

(b) His early research led him to examine the fermentation of such liquids as milk and beer. He discovered that fermentation was due to living organisms (bacteria). He found that these organisms could be destroyed by heat. The process now used to destroy bacteria in milk is named after him (pasteurisation).

(c) He also discovered that certain diseases, e.g. rabies, could be prevented by innoculation with small amounts of bacteria.

42 BIZET (1838–1875)

(a) Bizet was born in Paris.

(b) He won a prize for operetta at the age of 19.

(c) His most famous opera was 'Carmen', which was first performed in 1875.

(d) He also wrote music for the operas 'L'Arlésienne' and 'The Pearlfishers'.

43 VICTOR HUGO (1802–1885)

(a) Victor Hugo was born at Besançon. His father was a major in Napoleon's army.

(b) He married his childhood sweetheart, Adèle Foucher.

(c) He was a most prolific writer of poems, plays, novels and political pamphlets.

(d) His favourite daughter Léopoldine was drowned at the age of 19. He never fully recovered from this loss.

(e) He spent 19 years in exile, mainly in Jersey and Guernsey, as he opposed the government of Louis Napoleon.

(f) In 1870 he returned to Paris.

(g) He died in 1885.

(h) His most famous novel is 'Notre-Dame de Paris' (The Hunchback of Notre-Dame).

44 MONET (1840–1926)

(a) Monet was born in Paris of a family of grocers, but he spent most of his childhood in Le Havre.

(b) He showed an early talent for drawing, but rebelled against school discipline.

(c) He broke away from the traditional views of established artists.

(d) He believed that only by working in the open air could he capture nature as he wanted. Light and shade were very important to him. He studied light and colour from a technical point of view. He would paint the same subject at different times of day and in different lights in order to capture all its various aspects. His paintings of Rouen Cathedral are examples of this.

(e) Gradually he became more and more interested in the impression a painting gave rather than in precise details. This led to the 'Impressionist' movement in art.

(f) Some of his most famous paintings are: 'Le Déjeuner sur l'herbe', 'Gare St. Lazare', and the paintings of Rouen Cathedral and of water-lilies.

45 DE GAULLE (1890–1970)

(a) De Gaulle was born in Lille. He entered the military school at St Cyr in 1910.

(b) 1914 He was captured during the First World War. He made five attempts to escape. He was released in 1918.

(c) 1940 De Gaulle left occupied France in order to lead the Free French Army from England.

(d) 1944 When France was liberated, De Gaulle returned triumphantly to Paris.

(e) 1946 De Gaulle retired from public life but was recalled during the Algerian crisis in 1958, and became President of France.

(f) 1969 De Gaulle retired from public life, after the failure of his referendum on decentralisation.

(g) 1970 Death of De Gaulle.

Part II Test Yourself

1 Grammar

Answers to these tests are given on pages 71–72. When you have done each test, check your answers. If you are not satisfied with your performance, check the relevant Grammar Revision sections again, and then test yourself again.

TEST 1: NOUNS, ADJECTIVES, ADVERBS

1 Give the feminine singular form of 'fou'.
2 Give the feminine singular form of 'doux'.
3 Give the feminine singular form of 'vieux'.
4 Translate: such a man.
5 Translate: several books.
6 Give the French for 'quickly'.
7 Give the French for 'truly'.
8 Give the French for 'evidently'.
9 Give the French for 'nicely'.
10 Give the French for 'badly'.
11 Translate: the owls.
12 Translate: the jewels.
13 Translate: the newspapers.
14 Give the plural of 'madame'.
15 Give the plural of 'mademoiselle'.
16 Give the plural of 'monsieur'.
17 Translate: the new pupil (m).
18 Translate: the handsome man.
19 Translate: the old bus.
20 Translate: my story.

TEST 2: PRONOUNS
Translate:

1 I have given the books to them.
2 Give me some.
3 These books are yours.
4 Who saw that?
5 Someone rang the bell.
6 Everyone is in the dining-room.
7 We are going to her house.
8 Whose pen is this? It's mine.
9 Who saw it? They (did).
10 It's us.
11 Which dress do you prefer? This one.
12 Behind him. In front of me.
13 Look at this.
14 Don't eat any.
15 I'll eat anything.
16 Where are my pencils? Here are yours.
17 Do you have everything you need?
18 Each of these apples is bad.
19 Have you found what you were looking for?
20 *I* did it.

TEST 3: CONJUNCTIONS AND PREPOSITIONS
Translate:

1 We shall stay until ten o'clock.
2 She looked out of the window.
3 Come on Sunday.
4 You are out of breath.
5 I have been learning French for four years.
6 Leave before six o'clock.

7 The telephone rang while he was having lunch.
8 Talk to me about the holidays.
9 He was walking along the street.
10 We can go there on foot.
11 She will stay in London for three weeks.
12 They ran into the house for it had begun to rain.
13 He lives in France.
14 I walked in the rain.
15 Those dresses are in fashion.
16 One in ten failed.
17 We worked in Paris for two months.
18 She spoke in a soft voice.
19 I will go out as soon as I have finished this letter.
20 You are among friends.

TEST 4: THE PRESENT TENSE

Give the correct form of the following verbs in the present tense, *without* looking back at the verb lists:

1 Il (finir).
2 Nous (manger).
3 Vous (appeler).
4 Je (venir).
5 Elles (aller).
6 Tu (jeter).
7 Elle (vouloir).
8 Nous (commencer).
9 Ils (être).
10 Elles (avoir).
11 Vous (faire).
12 Il (écrire).
13 Tu (savoir).
14 Vous (dire).
15 Nous (se coucher).
16 Je (recevoir).
17 Elles (s'asseoir).
18 Elle (devoir).
19 Ils (connaître).
20 Vous (prendre).

Translate:
21 We are leaving.
22 He is looking.
23 I do like.
24 They are sleeping.

Now check your answers on page 71. If you scored 10-15, re-check those verbs which you had wrong and then do the test again. If you scored less than 10, you should revise *all* the present tense section again before re-testing yourself.

TEST 5: THE FUTURE TENSE

Give the correct form of the following verbs in the future tense:

1 Il (avoir).
2 Je (pouvoir).
3 Elle (s'asseoir).
4 Vous (venir).
5 Tu (vouloir).
6 Ils (appeler).
7 Nous (faire).
8 Il (falloir).
9 Tu (être).
10 Elles (recevoir).
11 Je (courir).
12 Elle (devoir).
13 Vous (envoyer).
14 Tu (finir).
15 Il (pleuvoir).
16 Elles (répéter).
17 Je (savoir).
18 Nous (apercevoir).
19 Tu (tenir).
20 Nous (cueillir).

TEST 6: THE IMPERFECT TENSE

Translate:

1 I used to be.
2 He was finishing.
3 They would come on Wednesdays.
4 She was.
5 You (*singular*) were going.
6 We were.
7 They were arriving.
8 You (*plural*) used to buy.
9 I would leave early on Tuesdays.
10 She was hurrying.

TEST 7: THE PERFECT TENSE

Give the correct form of the following verbs in the perfect tense:

1 Il (devoir).
2 Elle (s'asseoir).
3 Vous (mettre).
4 Je (suivre).
5 Tu (se taire).
6 Nous (descendre).
7 Elles (voir).
8 Il (prendre).
9 Je (devenir).
10 Nous (vivre).
11 Il (se souvenir).
12 Vous (ouvrir).
13 Tu (connaître).
14 Ils (recevoir).
15 Nous (vouloir).
16 Je (rentrer).
17 Elles (avoir).
18 Elle (craindre).
19 Vous (être).
20 Il (pouvoir).

TEST 8: THE PAST HISTORIC TENSE

Translate into English:

1 Ils mirent.
2 Je dus.
3 Nous prîmes.
4 Ils eurent.
5 Elle sut.
6 Ils virent.
7 Elles vinrent.
8 Il fut.
9 Il fit.
10 Elle but.
11 Je lus.
12 Nous crûmes.
13 Il fallut.
14 Ils s'assirent.
15 Elles furent.
16 Ils purent.
17 Il vint.
18 Ils plaignirent.
19 Elles parurent.
20 Elle revint.

As indicated by the above test, remember that you are unlikely to meet the past historic tense in the second person (i.e. **tu/vous**) forms.

TEST 9: THE IMPERATIVE

Translate:

1 Go. (*Singular*)
2 Go there. (*Singular*)
3 Have. (*Singular or plural*)
4 Be. (*Singular or plural*)
5 Know. (*Use 'savoir' singular or plural*)
6 Let us go.
7 Don't talk. (*Singular*)
8 Don't let us bathe. (**se baigner**)
9 Don't smoke. (*Plural*)
10 Let us leave.

TEST 10: PARTICIPLES AND INFINITIVES

Give the present participle of:
être, finir, avoir, écouter, prendre, aller, savoir, vouloir.

Translate:
1 She fell while coming downstairs.
2 On opening the door, I saw the headmaster.
3 They were going out.
4 After arriving at the campsite, we put up the tent.
5 I saw some girls playing tennis.
6 She left without saying 'Goodbye'.
7 After resting for half an hour, we went down to the beach.
8 I will tell the boys to come in.
9 We have a lot to do.
10 He promised to come.
11 He will be happy to come.
12 You look like your father.
13 I am going to borrow some books from your brother.
14 That man stole a record-player from my sister.
15 I have forgotten to bring my umbrella.

16 There will be a football match on Saturday.
17 We have 200 francs left.
18 If it had been fine, we would have gone out.
19 They have just finished.
20 It isn't a question of money.

TEST 11: NEGATIVES, QUESTION FORMS, INVERSION

Translate:

1 Whom did you see?
2 What children?

3 Will your sister come with you?
4 We never see anyone.
5 She's French, isn't she?
6 We only like chips.
7 He scarcely speaks about her.
8 He has worked hard, hasn't he?
9 Nothing happened.
10 'Come in,' she said.

2 Vocabulary

Can you give ten key-words for each of the following topics?

1 The seaside
2 Camping
3 Travel
4 School
5 The countryside
6 Accidents and injuries
7 Shopping
8 The family
9 The weather
10 The house
11 The farm
12 The garden
13 The town
14 Pastimes
15 Direction and distance
16 Clothes
17 The railway
18 The airport
19 Health and illness
20 Jobs

To check your answers, look in the relevant Vocabulary Topic sections.

3 Background knowledge

TEST 1

1 With which region of France do you associate Camembert cheese?
2 In which region of France is Lacq?
3 What is the English equivalent of a Collège d'Enseignement Secondaire?
4 What was the 'Maquis'?
5 Who was Victor Hugo?
6 For which product is Grasse famous?
7 To which movement of French painting did Monet belong?
8 Which is the highest mountain in France?
9 For what is Marie Curie famous?

10 What are 'Le Monde' and 'Le Figaro'?
11 Where was Joan of Arc burnt at the stake?
12 What does 'VDQS' mean on a bottle of wine?
13 What is the date of France's national holiday?
14 Which is the longest river in France?
15 In what town is the European Commission to be found?
16 What is at the centre of the Place Charles De Gaulle in Paris?
17 Who was Robespierre?
18 Who was the 'Sun King'?
19 In which French town did Marshal Pétain set up government during the Second World War?
20 What do the letters 'HLM' mean?

TEST 2

Write a short paragraph in English about each of the following topics:

1 Education in France
2 Napoleon
3 Brittany
4 The Common Market
5 Louis Pasteur
6 Paris
7 The French Parliament
8 The French Revolution
9 Food and drink in France
10 Joan of Arc

TEST 3

1 Where in France is the 'Côte d'Azur'?
2 In France who administers a 'département'?
3 What is the English equivalent of 'Mardi Gras'?
4 In which region of France is 'pelote' a popular sport?
5 Who is entitled to wear 'le maillot jaune'?
6 What is 'Paris-Match'?
7 What is grown in a 'vignoble'?
8 What is 'une crêpe'?
9 What examination do French pupils take at the age of 18?
10 Who introduced the Metric System in France?
11 Name the French wind that has given its name to a French train.
12 Which Frenchman discovered a serum to combat rabies?
13 In which part of France is the 'Côte Emeraude'?
14 Which mountains separate France from Spain?
15 Which northern port was the scene of a rearguard action by Allied troops in May 1940?
16 Where do marriages take place, legally, in France?
17 What is 'un goûter'?
18 What is 'Le Louvre'?
19 In which part of Paris would you expect to find artists?
20 Which seventeenth century French writer wrote animal fables?

TEST 4

(Selected from ALSEB)

1 Which one of the following is *not* a Channel port?
  A Dieppe
  B Bordeaux
  C Boulogne
  D Dunkirk

2 Which mountains separate France from Switzerland?
  A Alps
  B Pyrenees
  C Massif Central
  D Ardennes

3 Which French ruler ordered the building of the Arc de Triomphe?
  A Louis XIV
  B Napoleon
  C De Gaulle
  D Henri IV

4 What happened on 14th July 1789?
  A The French revolution ended
  B The King escaped from Paris
  C The people invaded the Bastille
  D Louis XVI was executed

5 What is the name of the French island in the Mediterranean?
  A Corsica
  B Ile-de-France
  C Guernsey
  D Sardinia

6 Which of the following founded a famous fashion house?
  A Yves Saint-Martin
  B Escoffier
  C Cartier
  D Dior

7 What was Renoir?
  A A composer
  B A writer
  C An actor
  D A painter

8 Which of the following jobs does a French mayor have to do?
  A Collect income tax
  B Check school attendance
  C Conduct weddings
  D Appoint local councillors

9 To which of the following regions would you go if you wanted a holiday in the mountains?
  A Savoy
  B Côte d'Azur
  C Normandy
  D Brittany

10 Which group of people is associated with the Latin quarter?
  A Fashion designers
  B Dancers
  C Students
  D Italian chefs

11 What is the French equivalent of the House of Commons?
  A Palais de l'Élysée
  B Assemblée Nationale
  C Conseil d'État
  D Sénat

12 Which is the main city of Alsace-Lorraine?
  A Grenoble
  B Strasbourg
  C Rouen
  D Toulouse

13 What is the Sacré-Cœur in Paris?
  A Art gallery
  B Night club
  C Hospital
  D Church

14 What is the name of the French National Anthem?
  A L'Internationale
  B Ma Normandie
  C Vive la France
  D La Marseillaise

15 In which part of Paris is the cathedral of Notre-Dame?
  A Montmartre
  B Rive Gauche
  C Ile-de-la-Cité
  D Passy

Answers

Test 1 (p. 67)

1 folle
2 douce
3 vieille
4 un tel homme
5 plusieurs livres
6 vite
7 vraiment
8 évidemment
9 gentiment
10 mal
11 les hiboux
12 les bijoux
13 les journaux
14 mesdames
15 mesdemoiselles
16 messieurs
17 le nouvel élève
18 le bel homme
19 le vieil autobus
20 mon histoire

Test 2 (p. 67)

1 Je leur ai donné les livres.
2 Donnez-m'en.
3 Ces livres sont à vous (les tiens, les vôtres).
4 Qui a vu cela?
5 Quelqu'un a sonné.
6 Tout le monde est dans la salle à manger.
7 Nous allons chez elle.
8 A qui est ce stylo? C'est le mien. (Il est à moi.)
9 Qui l'a vu? Eux.
10 C'est nous.
11 Quelle robe préférez-vous? Celle-ci.
12 Derrière lui. Devant moi.
13 Regardez ceci.
14 N'en mangez pas.
15 Je mangerai n'importe quoi.
16 Où sont mes crayons? Voici les tiens.
17 Avez-vous tout ce dont vous avez besoin?
18 Chacune de ces pommes est mauvaise.
19 As-tu trouvé ce que tu cherchais?
20 Moi, je l'ai fait.

Test 3 (p. 67)

1 Nous resterons jusqu'à dix heures.
2 Elle a regardé par la fenêtre.
3 Venez (viens) dimanche.
4 Vous êtes (tu es) hors d'haleine.
5 J'apprends le français depuis quatre ans.
6 Partez (pars) avant six heures.
7 Le téléphone a sonné pendant qu'il déjeunait.
8 Parle(z)-moi au sujet des vacances.
9 Il marchait le long de la rue.
10 Nous pouvons y aller à pied.
11 Elle restera à Londres pour trois semaines.
12 Ils sont entrés dans la maison en courant car il avait commencé à pleuvoir.
13 Il habite en France.
14 J'ai marché sous la pluie.
15 Ces robes-là sont à la mode.
16 Un sur dix a échoué.
17 Nous avons travaillé à Paris pendant deux semaines.
18 Elle a parlé d'une voix douce.
19 Je sortirai dès que j'aurai fini cette lettre.
20 Vous êtes (tu es) entre amis.

Test 4 (p. 68)

1 Il finit.
2 Nous mangeons.
3 Vous appelez.
4 Je viens.
5 Elles vont.
6 Tu jettes.
7 Elle veut.
8 Nous commençons.
9 Ils sont.
10 Elles ont.
11 Vous faites.
12 Il écrit.
13 Tu sais.
14 Vous dites.
15 Nous nous couchons.
16 Je reçois.
17 Elles s'asseyent.
18 Elle doit.
19 Ils connaissent.
20 Vous prenez.
21 Nous partons.
22 Il regarde.
23 J'aime.
24 Ils dorment.

Test 5 (p. 68)

1 Il aura.
2 Je pourrai.
3 Elle s'assiéra.
4 Vous viendrez.
5 Tu voudras.
6 Ils appelleront.
7 Nous ferons.
8 Il faudra.
9 Tu seras.
10 Elles recevront.
11 Je courrai.
12 Elle devra.
13 Vous enverrez.
14 Tu finiras.
15 Il pleuvra.
16 Elles répéteront.
17 Je saurai.
18 Nous apercevrons.
19 Tu tiendras.
20 Nous cueillerons.

Test 6 (p. 68)

1 J'étais.
2 Il finissait.
3 Ils venaient le mercredi.
4 Elle était.
5 Tu allais.
6 Nous étions.
7 Ils arrivaient.
8 Vous achetiez.
9 Je partais de bonne heure le mardi.
10 Elle se dépêchait.

Test 7 (p. 68)

1 Il a dû.
2 Elle s'est assise.
3 Vous avez mis.
4 J'ai suivi.
5 Tu t'es tu(e).
6 Nous sommes descendu(e)s.
7 Elles ont vu.
8 Il a pris.
9 Je suis devenu(e).
10 Nous avons vécu.
11 Il s'est souvenu.
12 Vous avez ouvert.
13 Tu as connu.
14 Ils ont reçu.
15 Nous avons voulu.
16 Je suis rentré(e).
17 Elles ont eu.
18 Elle a craint.
19 Vous avez été.
20 Il a pu.

Test 8 (p. 68)

1 They put.
2 I owed, I had to.
3 We took.
4 They had.
5 She knew.
6 They saw.

7 They came.
8 He was.
9 He did, he made.
10 She drank.
11 I read.
12 We believed.
13 It was necessary.
14 They sat down.
15 They were.
16 They were able.
17 He came.
18 They pitied.
19 They appeared.
20 She came back.

Test 9 (p. 68)

1 Va.
2 Vas-y.
3 Aie/ayez.
4 Sois/soyez.
5 Sache/sachez.
6 Allons.
7 Ne parle pas.
8 Ne nous baignons pas.
9 Ne fumez pas.
10 Partons.

Test 10 (p. 68)

Present participles:

étant, finissant, ayant, écoutant, prenant, allant, sachant, voulant.

1 Elle est tombée en descendant l'escalier.
2 En ouvrant la porte, j'ai vu le directeur.
3 Ils sortaient.
4 Après être arrivés au camping, nous avons dressé la tente.
5 J'ai vu des jeunes filles qui jouaient au tennis.
6 Elle est partie sans dire 'au revoir'.
7 Après nous être reposés pendant une demi-heure, nous sommes descendus à la plage.
8 Je dirai aux garçons d'entrer.
9 Nous avons beaucoup à faire.
10 Il a promis de venir.
11 Il sera content de venir.
12 Tu (vous) ressembles (ressemblez) à ton (votre) père.
13 Je vais emprunter des livres à ton (votre) frère.
14 Cet homme-là a volé un électrophone à ma sœur.
15 J'ai oublié d'apporter mon parapluie.
16 Il y aura un match de football samedi.
17 Il nous reste 200 francs.
18 S'il avait fait beau, nous serions sortis.
19 Ils viennent de finir.
20 Il ne s'agit pas d'argent.

Test 11 (p. 69)

1 Qui avez-vous (as-tu) vu?
2 Quels enfants?
3 Votre (ta) sœur, viendra-t-elle avec vous (toi)?
  Est-ce que votre (ta) sœur viendra avec vous (toi)?
4 Nous ne voyons jamais personne.
5 Elle est Française, n'est-ce pas?
6 Nous n'aimons que les frites.
7 Il ne parle guère d'elle.
8 Il a travaillé dur, n'est-ce pas?
9 Rien n'est arrivé.
10 'Entrez,' a-t-elle dit.

BACKGROUND KNOWLEDGE

Test 1 (p. 69)

1 Normandy
2 Pyrenees
3 A comprehensive school
4 French Resistance workers
5 A famous 19th century French writer
6 Perfume
7 Impressionist movement
8 Mont Blanc
9 She discovered radium
10 French newspapers
11 Rouen
12 Vin de Qualité Supérieure – a fine wine
13 14th July
14 Loire
15 Brussels
16 Arc de Triomphe
17 A French Revolutionary leader
18 Louis XIV
19 Vichy
20 Habitation à Loyer Modéré – a council flat

Test 3 (p. 70)

1 The Mediterranean coast
2 The 'Préfet'
3 Shrove Tuesday
4 The Basque region
5 The leader in the 'Tour de France' cycle race
6 A French weekly magazine
7 Grapes
8 A pancake
9 The 'baccalauréat'
10 Napoleon
11 The 'Mistral'
12 Louis Pasteur
13 The West coast of Brittany
14 The Pyrenees
15 Dunkirk
16 In the town hall
17 (Afternoon) tea
18 A museum and art gallery in Paris
19 Montmartre
20 La Fontaine

Test 4 (p. 70)

1 B Bordeaux
2 A Alps
3 B Napoleon
4 C The people invaded the Bastille
5 A Corsica
6 D Dior
7 D A painter
8 C Conduct weddings
9 A Savoy
10 C Students
11 B Assemblée Nationale
12 B Strasbourg
13 D Church
14 D La Marseillaise
15 C Ile-de-la-Cité

Part III Examination Practice

1 Reading

Most Examination Boards, both O-level and CSE, set a reading test. This test consists of an unseen passage of French to be read aloud to the examiner. The candidate is given about five minutes in which to prepare the reading.

PROCEDURE

Preparation

Always read the passage through several times. During the first reading you should concentrate especially on the meaning of the passage. Do not worry about the pronunciation of individual words at this stage. Once you have understood the main idea(s) of the passage, you should then look more carefully at phrasing and obvious 'test' words.

Reading

During the reading test, the examiner will be looking for the following:

(a) an obvious understanding of the passage
(b) correct pronunciation
(c) correct intonation
(d) overall 'Frenchness'

To gain a high mark in the reading test, you must practise all of these points. Try to listen to French people speaking as often as possible. You should be able to tune in to at least one French radio station. Check the wavelengths and try to listen to some French each day, especially in the weeks prior to the examination. It is also a good idea to tape-record yourself reading a passage of French and then to listen critically, applying the above criteria to your recording.

Useful hints

1 After you have read through the passage for its meaning, you should then check each sentence to see if there are any commas. Remember that in French the voice should rise at a comma and fall at a full-stop:

Un instant après, en voyant son ami, il a traversé la rue.
Similarly check to see if there are any question marks. Remember that the voice should rise at the question mark:

Etes-vous là?
Try to make your reading as meaningful as possible by giving the correct intonation and phrasing.

2 Check carefully the pronunciation of individual words, especially ones which you know need careful attention. Above all avoid anglicising words such as **autobus, important,** etc. If the words have obvious English equivalents, check carefully to see where the 'stress' comes in French.

As a general rule, the 'stress' in French occurs on the last syllable:

e.g. auto**bus,** ciné**ma,** impor**tant,** amu**sant,** etc.

3 One of the most important points to remember when reading French is that you should not pronounce the final consonant at the end of a word unless the following word in the same sentence begins with a vowel or 'h', and providing that there is no comma in between.

Les garçons – here the final 's' on both words should *not* be pronounced.

Les hommes – the 's' of 'les' should be pronounced, but that of 'hommes' should not.
(Remember that no 'h' is pronounced in French.)

Nos amis sont arrivés lundi dernier.

In the above sentence, only the consonants in dark type are pronounced at the end of the words. The other final consonants are not pronounced. This 'linking on' of final consonant sounds is called *liaison*.

Once you have read your examination reading passage, paying attention to meaning, pronunciation and intonation, you should then check carefully for liaisons.

4 (a) In order to achieve 'Frenchness' in your reading, you should also practise the 'u' and 'r' sounds.

In order to achieve an authentic 'u' sound, place the tip of the tongue near the top of your lower teeth and make your mouth into a perfect closed 'o' shape; do not move the lips whilst producing the 'u' sound.

To pronounce the French 'r', imagine that you are gargling at the back of your throat. (Do not over-practise this in the early stages or you will hurt your throat!)

(b) Nasal vowel sounds are also important in achieving 'Frenchness' in your reading. Practise holding your nose to say 'on, en' etc. Then try to achieve a similar sound without holding your nose.

Practice is needed if you are to achieve all of the above in the five minutes available at the beginning of the examination.

Read the passages below and prepare them for reading aloud following the outline given.

PASSAGES FOR READING ALOUD

Reading passage 1 (SEB)

Quand Alice a paru, Jean était là. Il lui a dit:
– Je venais t'inviter à aller au cinéma ce soir.
– Merci, Jean, tu es bien aimable. Mais j'ai du travail pour demain, et je rentre me coucher.
– Voilà une idée! a-t-il dit. On joue 'Le Mystère de la Tour Eiffel' au Tivoli.
Depuis longtemps, Alice n'avait pas été au cinéma.
– Le Tivoli? a-t-elle dit. C'est loin.
– Loin? On prendra un taxi!
Elle hésitait. Après tout, c'était une occasion de porter ses vêtements neufs.
– Attends-moi. Le temps que je m'habille.

(a) Meaning
John is trying to persuade his friend Alice to go to the cinema with him.

(b) Pronunciation
Points to remember:
Quand Alice – the 'd' should be pronounced as a 't' here.
travail – do not pronounce the 'l'.
Eiffel – Check the pronunciation of this word carefully. It should sound like 'F L'.
longtemps – do not pronounce the 'ps'.
loin – do not anglicise.
hésitait – do not pronounce the 'h'.
occasion – do not anglicise.
Attends – do not pronounce the 'ds'.
temps – do not pronounce the 'ps'.
habille – do not pronounce the 'h'.

(c) Intonation
The voice should be raised at the commas and when there is a question.

(d) Liaison
Care is needed with such words as:
pas été, était une, etc.

(e) Frenchness
Remember to pay attention to the vowels and especially the 'u' sound, e.g. paru, tu, du, une. Care must also be taken with nasal sounds.

Reading passage 2 (NIEC)

Deux mois après, comme il passait rue des Martyrs, Henri lut sur une porte: Dufour, épicier.

    Il entra.

    La grosse dame se trouvait au comptoir. On se reconnut aussitôt, et, après mille politesses, il demanda des nouvelles. 'Et mademoiselle Henriette, comment va-t-elle?'

    – Très bien, merci: elle est mariée.

    – Ah! . , .

    Une émotion l'étreignit; il ajouta:

    – Et . . . avec qui?

    – Mais avec le jeune homme qui nous accompagnait, vous savez bien; c'est lui qui prend la suite.

    – Oh! parfaitement.

    Il s'en alla fort triste, sans trop savoir pourquoi. Mme Dufour le rappela.

    – Et votre ami? dit-elle timidement.

    – Mais il va bien.

    – Faites-lui nos compliments, n'est-ce pas; et quand il passera, dites-lui donc de venir nous voir.

(a) Meaning

Henri renews his acquaintance with Mme Dufour and enquires about Henriette. The news that she is married saddens him. Before he leaves, Mme Dufour asks him how his friend is.

(b) Pronunciation

Points to remember:

Henri   ⎫
Henriette ⎬   the 'H' should not be pronounced in French.
         ⎭

Deux – the 'x' should not be pronounced.

Martyrs – do not anglicise, but you should stress the 'y' sound. Do not pronounce the final 's'.

com**p**toir – do not pronounce the 'p'.

politess**es** – do not pronounce the final 'es'.

mad**e**moiselle – do not pronounce the first 'e' in this word.

très bien, merci – beware! Remember that the vowel 'è' is short, and that the 's' is not pronounced. Do not anglicise 'merci'.

mari**ée** – this accented vowel *must* be pronounced.

ét**reig**nit – this is not as difficult as it looks. Treat the two vowels 'ei' as one sound and do not try to pronounce the 'g' as a separate sound.

accompa**g**nait – as above, the 'g' is not pronounced separately.

tro**p** – remember that this word has a long vowel sound and that the final consonant 'p' is not pronounced.

'ss' should be pronounced as a 'hissing' sound, e.g. politesses, passait, grosse.

compliment**s** – do not anglicise and do not pronounce the final 'ts'.

faite**s** – do not pronounce the final 's'.

dite**s** – do not pronounce the final 's'.

(c) Intonation

There are commas in most sentences which will require the voice to be raised.

There are also two questions which must be intoned accurately.

(d) Liaison

Care is needed with such words as:

    Il‿entra, trouvait‿au, elle‿est, il‿ajouta, mais‿avec, jeune‿homme, nous‿accompagnait, s'en‿allait, votre‿ami, dit-‿elle, quand‿il, etc.

Remember that before a vowel the 'd' of **quand** is pronounced as a 't'.

(e) Frenchness

Attention must be paid to vowel sounds, e.g. the 'u' in such words as 'r**u**e', 'l**u**t', D**u**four', 'reconn**u**t, '**u**ne', 'l**u**i'.

The 'r' in such words as 'rue', 'Henri', 'entra', etc., must be practised.

Reading passage 3 (Oxford)

Quand il emergea du métro, le brouillard s'était épaissi, et le commissaire en reconnut la saveur sur ses lèvres. Il ne vit personne sur le boulevard, entendit seulement des pas au loin et, dans la même direction, un train qui sifflait en quittant la gare. Un certain nombre de fenêtres étaient encore éclairées et, dans la brume, donnaient une impression de paix, de sécurité. Ces maisons ni riches ni pauvres, ni neuves ni vieilles, aux appartements à peu près pareils, étaient surtout habitées par des gens de classe moyenne, des professeurs, des fonctionnaires, des employés qui prenaient leur métro ou leur autobus à la même heure chaque matin. Il appuya sur le bouton et, quand la porte s'ouvrit, se dirigea vers l'ascenseur.

(a) Meaning

This is a descriptive passage about a middle-class district of Paris one foggy day. It is seen through the eyes of a policeman who is returning home.

(b) Pronunciation

Points to remember:

Quan**d** il – this 'd' should be pronounced as a 't'.

le broui**ll**ard – 'ill' here should be pronounced like the 'y' in 'yellow'.

épai**ss**i – 'ss' should be hissed.

reconnu**t** – do not pronounce the 't'.

vi**t** – do not pronounce the 't'.

boulevar**d** – do not pronounce the 'd'.

entendi**t** – do not pronounce the 't'.

dan**s** – do not pronounce the 's'.

pai**x** – do not pronounce the 'x'.

habitées – do not pronounce the 'h'.

heure – do not pronounce the 'h'.

diri**g**ea – 'g': soft pronunciation.

(c) Intonation

There are commas in each sentence which require the voice to be lifted.

(d) Liaison

Care is needed with such words as:

    Quand‿il, s'était‿épaissi, fenêtres‿étaient‿encore‿éclairées, donnaient‿une, aux‿appartements, des‿employés, leur‿autobus, il‿appuya, etc.

(e) Frenchness

Care must be taken with vowel and nasal sounds, e.g. d**u**, reconn**u**t, br**u**me, autob**u**s, app**u**ya, etc.

Reading passage 4 (SEREB)

Jean allait retrouver son amie Marie à la terrasse du café vers midi et quart. C'est lui qui est arrivé le premier. Malheureusement, les tables étaient toutes occupées. Mais au bout de cinq minutes, un monsieur est parti et Jean a pris sa place. Il a commandé un vin blanc qu'il a bu lentement, en lisant son journal. Enfin Marie est arrivée.

    – Salut! a-t-elle dit, en l'embrassant. Tu m'as attendue longtemps?

    – Oh non, a répondu Jean d'un air résigné. Une demi-heure, comme d'habitude. Qu'est-ce que tu prends?

    – Une citronnade bien fraîche. Il fait tellement chaud aujourd'hui.

(a) Meaning

Jean is going to meet his friend Marie at the café. After finding an empty seat, Jean has a drink whilst waiting for Marie who is late.

(b) Pronunciation

Points to remember:

terrasse ⎫
          ⎬   remember that 'ss' in French is pronounced in a 'hissing' manner.
embrassant ⎭

lisant ⎫
        ⎬   one 's' in the middle of a word sounds like 'z'.
résigné ⎭

quar**t** – do not anglicise; do not pronounce the 't'. This word is pronounced like the French word 'car'.

prem**ier** – this is the masculine form, therefore the ending sounds like 'yé'.

mal**h**eureusemen**t** – do not pronounce the 'h' or the 't'.

blan**c** – do not pronounce the 'c'.

salu**t** – do not pronounce the 't'. Be careful with the 'u' vowel sound.

lon**g**tem**ps** – do not pronounce the 'g' or the 'ps'.

pren**ds** – do not pronounce the 'ds'.

chau**d** – do not pronounce the 'd'.

en**fin** – care must be taken in the pronunciation of this word to avoid making it sound like 'en**fant**'.

There are also several 'u' vowel sounds: e.g. d**u**, occ**u**pées, b**u**, t**u**, attend**u**e, répond**u**, **u**ne.

(c) Intonation

There are several sentences with commas and there are two questions. All of these must have the correct intonation.

(d) Liaison

Care is needed with such words as:

son amie, est arrivé, est arrivée, mais au bout (but there is *no* liaison with 'mais oui'), d'un air résigné.

(e) Frenchness

Attention to vowels, nasal sounds and the 'r', as always.

READING CONTINUATION QUESTIONS

At the end of the oral reading test, certain Examination Boards ask the candidate to provide a sequel to the passage by imagining that they are one of the people (the character will be specified) from the passage. This is a form of role-playing. The candidate might be asked:

– Imaginez que vous êtes . . . Qu'est-ce que vous avez fait après?

In the answer, the candidate should use the perfect tense (check this in Grammar Revision section 23 if you are unsure).

e.g. J'ai decidé de . . .
Je suis allé voir . . .
Je suis rentré à la maison, etc.

Normally, you will be expected to complete your answer in about four or five sentences.

2 Conversation

All O-level and CSE Examination Boards set a test in French conversation. The test varies according to the different Boards' emphasis on prepared or general conversation. You should check the syllabus requirements of your particular Examination Board to find out which type of conversation test they set.

The conversation test consists normally of one or more of the following:

(a) A selection of questions (e.g. 10) chosen from a larger list (e.g. 100) which the candidate has already prepared during the year. The candidate will not be allowed to look at the questions in the examination since this is an oral examination.

(b) A short talk on a chosen topic, e.g. a region of France which has been studied, or a particular interest. This will not be a monologue by the candidate, but will take the form of a discussion.

(c) Conversation on previously specified topics, e.g. family, holidays, hobbies, etc.

(d) General conversation on everyday matters similar to (c), but without specified topics.

PREPARATION

(a) Preparation for this type of test will depend on the questions which are listed in the syllabus of your Examination Board. Check the questions given below under Conversation Topics to see which are listed by your Examination Board.

(b) Your preparation will depend on the topic chosen, but imagine that *you* are going to ask someone about your particular topic and practise the answers to these questions in French. Find out as much as possible about your topic so that you can make your talk interesting, but at the same time keep your information simple since you must speak about it in French.

(c) Given below are specimen questions and answers under topic headings.

(d) Prepare as for (c); specimen questions and answers are given below.
For both O-level and CSE the questions which you will be asked in the general conversation section of the examination will be mainly about yourself, your school, family, home, hobbies, interests, travels, etc. You should prepare a few sentences on each of these topics which you could use in a conversation with a stranger.

Make sure that you can answer the questions listed below but also be prepared to add extra information. In a conversation examination, many questions will depend on what you have already said and will follow on naturally from your previous statements.

The Vocabulary Topics should help you in your preparation for this part of the examination. Learn as much vocabulary as possible on the topics below and practise answering the questions, remembering that it is not an exhaustive list but a representation of the different types of question asked in both O-level and CSE examinations. The questions are not divided into O-level questions and CSE questions, since many are to be found in both examinations. The answers given are suggestions only; you should fill in the details relevant to you.

In almost all conversation tests you will be asked the following two questions:
– Comment vous appelez-vous?
– Quel âge avez-vous?

You will answer these using:
– Je m'appelle . . .
– J'ai . . . ans.

Always use 'monsieur' or 'madame' when speaking to the examiner, especially at the beginning and end of the examination.
– Bonjour, monsieur (madame).
– Au revoir, monsieur (madame), et merci.

If you do not understand a question then ask the examiner to repeat it:
– Voulez-vous répéter la question, s'il vous plaît, monsieur (madame)?
However, do not use this as a ploy to stall for time. There is a limit to the number of times you can ask the examiner to repeat a question!

CONVERSATION TOPICS

1 L'ÂGE

– Quel âge avez-vous?
  – J'ai (seize) ans.

– Quel âge a votre frère?
  – Il a . . . ans.

– Quel âge a votre sœur?
  – Elle a . . . ans.

– En quelle année êtes-vous né(e)?
  – Je suis né(e) en . . . (dix-neuf cent soixante-six).

2 L'HEURE

– A quelle heure vous levez-vous le samedi?
  – Le samedi je me lève à (neuf heures).

– A quelle heure vous levez-vous le dimanche?
  – Le dimanche je me lève à . . .

– A quelle heure vous couchez-vous le samedi?
– Le samedi je me couche à . . .

– A quelle heure vous couchez-vous le dimanche?
– Le dimanche je me couche à . . .

– A quelle heure vous êtes-vous levé aujourd'hui?
– Aujourd'hui je me suis levé à (huit heures).

– A quelle heure vous êtes-vous couché hier?
– Hier je me suis couché à . . .

– A quelle heure vous êtes-vous levé samedi dernier?
– Samedi dernier je me suis levé à . . .

– A quelle heure vous êtes-vous couché samedi dernier?
– Samedi dernier je me suis couché à . . .

– A quelle heure vous êtes-vous levé dimanche dernier?
– Dimanche dernier je me suis levé à . . .

– A quelle heure vous êtes-vous couché dimanche dernier?
– Dimanche dernier je me suis couché à . . .

In the above questions you must distinguish carefully between those questions where the present tense is required and those questions which are in the perfect tense. In the examination you must listen to the question carefully as this will indicate to you which tense is required in your answer.

– Quelle heure est-il maintenant?
– Il est . . . (dix heures et demie).

– A quelle heure quittez-vous la maison le matin?
– Le matin je quitte la maison à . . .

– A quelle heure avez-vous quitté la maison ce matin?
– Ce matin j'ai quitté la maison à . . .

– A quelle heure arriverez-vous à la maison ce soir?
– J'arriverai à la maison ce soir à . . .

(Note the use of the future tense in both question and answer.)

– Si vous sortez le soir avec des amis, à quelle heure devez-vous rentrer?
– Si je sors le soir avec des amis je dois rentrer à . . . (onze heures).

La date

– Quel jour sommes-nous aujourd'hui?
– Aujourd'hui nous sommes . . . (e.g. mercredi).

– Quelle est la date aujourd'hui?
– Aujourd'hui c'est . . . (le dix juin).

– Quelle est la date de votre anniversaire?
– La date de mon anniversaire est . . . (le seize février).

3 L'ÉCOLE

– Aimez-vous l'école? Pourquoi?
– J'aime l'école parce que j'aime travailler.
– Je n'aime pas l'école parce que je n'aime pas travailler.

– Quelle est votre matière préférée à l'école?
– Je préfère . . . (l'histoire, le dessin, etc.).

– Quelles sont les matières que vous étudiez à l'école?
– J'étudie . . . (le français, le dessin, etc.) (See Vocabulary Topic 36.)

– Habitez-vous loin de l'école?
– Oui, j'habite à . . . (dix kilomètres de l'école).
– Non, j'habite tout près de l'école.

– A quelle heure arrivez-vous à l'école le matin?
– J'arrive à l'école à . . . (neuf heures moins le quart).

– A quelle heure quittez-vous l'école?
– Je quitte l'école à . . . (quatre heures moins le quart).

– Quand avez-vous l'intention de quitter l'école?
– J'ai l'intention de quitter l'école cette année/dans deux ans.

– Qu'avez-vous l'intention de faire quand vous quitterez l'école?
– J'ai l'intention de continuer mes études à l'université de . . .
– J'ai l'intention de devenir . . . (See Vocabulary Topic 28.)

– Quels jours de la semaine venez-vous en classe?
– Je viens en classe le lundi, mardi, mercredi, jeudi et vendredi.

– Allez-vous continuer vos études l'année prochaine?
– Oui, je vais continuer mes études l'année prochaine.
– Non, je vais quitter l'école.

– Depuis combien de temps êtes-vous dans cette école?
– Je suis dans cette école depuis . . . (cinq ans).

– Depuis combien de temps apprenez-vous le français?
– J'apprends le français depuis . . . (cinq ans).

– Combien d'élèves y a-t-il dans votre classe?
– Il y en a . . . (trente).

– Combien de cours avez-vous le matin à l'école?
– J'en ai . . . (cinq).

– Combien de cours avez-vous l'après-midi à l'école?
– J'en ai . . . (quatre).

– Etes-vous venu seul à l'école ou avec un ami?
– Je suis venu seul à l'école.
– Je suis venu avec un ami.

4 La famille

– Combien de personnes y a-t-il dans votre famille?
– Il y en a . . . (quatre).

– Que font vos parents?
– Mon père est . . .; ma mère est . . . (See Vocabulary Topic 28.)

– Avez-vous des frères ou des sœurs?
– Oui, j'ai . . . (deux frères).
– Non, je suis enfant unique.

– Qui se lève le premier chez vous?
– (Mon père) se lève le premier chez moi.

– Avez-vous des animaux à la maison?
– Oui, nous avons un chat et un chien.

– Est-ce que vous aidez vos parents à la maison?
– Oui, je fais la vaisselle, je range ma chambre, et je travaille dans le jardin.

– Passez-vous des vacances en famille ou avec des amis?
– Je passe des vacances en famille.
– Je passe des vacances avec des amis.

5 La maison

– Préférez-vous habiter une maison ou un appartement?
– Je préfère habiter . . .

– Combien de pièces y a-t-il dans votre maison?
– Il y en a . . . (huit).

– Quelles sont les différentes pièces dans votre maison?
– Il y a la cuisine, le salon . . . (See Vocabulary Topic 25.)

– Décrivez votre maison.
– Ma maison est grande (petite). Il y a (huit) pièces. Nous avons un grand (petit) jardin derrière la maison. Dans le jardin il y a un arbre, de jolies fleurs et des légumes.

– Quels meubles avez-vous dans votre chambre?
– Dans ma chambre il y a (un lit, un chevet, une chaise, etc.). (See Vocabulary Topic 25.)

– A quelle distance de l'école se trouve votre maison?
– Ma maison se trouve à . . . (deux kilomètres de l'école).

– Dans quelle pièce se trouve votre poste de télévision?
– Notre poste de télévision se trouve dans le salon.

– Avez-vous une chambre particulière (à vous seul)?
– Oui, j'ai une chambre particulière (à moi).
– Non, je n'ai pas de chambre à moi seul.

– Décrivez votre chambre.
– Ma chambre est grande (petite). Les murs sont . . . (bleus). Les rideaux sont . . . (bleus aussi). J'ai (un lit, une armoire, etc).

6 VOTRE VILLE/VILLAGE

– Décrivez votre ville/village.
– Ma ville est grande (petite). Il y a un (deux, etc.) cinéma(s) et beaucoup d'églises. Il y a une rivière et un terrain de sports. Au centre de la ville il y a beaucoup de magasins et deux grands supermarchés.
– Mon village est petit et il n'y a pas beaucoup de maisons. Il y a quelques fermes aux environs. Il y a une église et une épicerie. Mon village est tranquille.

(Remember that these are only suggestions and that you should fill in your own details and practise them beforehand.)

– Quels magasins y a-t-il près de chez vous?
– Près de chez moi il y a une épicerie.

– Qu'est-ce qu'une charcuterie?
– C'est un magasin où on achète du jambon et des saucissons.

– Où allez-vous pour acheter des cachets d'aspirine?
– Je vais à la pharmacie.

– Où allez-vous pour acheter de la viande?
– Je vais à la boucherie.

– Où allez-vous pour acheter de l'essence? (*petrol*)
– Je vais à la station-service.

– Où allez-vous pour acheter des timbres?
– Je vais au bureau de poste.

– Où allez-vous pour acheter des livres?
– Je vais à la librairie. (*bookshop*)

– Où va-t-on pour demander des renseignements dans une ville française?
– On va au Syndicat d'Initiative.

– Comment un Syndicat d'Initiative peut-il vous être utile?
– Il nous donne des renseignements sur la ville.

7 LES PASSE-TEMPS/LES LOISIRS

– Comment occupez-vous vos moments de loisir?
– J'aime lire, regarder la télévision, écouter les disques, etc.

– Quel est votre passe-temps favori?
– J'aime jouer au tennis.
– J'aime monter à cheval.
– J'aime jouer au football.
– J'aime regarder la télévision.

– Quel genre de livres préférez-vous?
– Je préfère les livres d'aventures (les romans, les romans policiers, la poésie, les westerns, etc.).

– Quel genre de musique préférez-vous?
– Je préfère la musique moderne (classique).

– Quel genre de films préférez-vous?
  – Je préfère les comédies (les westerns, les films policiers, les films d'horreur).

– Allez-vous souvent au cinéma?
  – Je vais au cinéma une fois par semaine.

– Avez-vous un vélo (un cheval)?
  – Oui, j'ai un vélo (un cheval).
  – Non, je n'ai pas de vélo (de cheval).

– Où allez-vous à vélo (à cheval)?
  – Je me promène à la campagne à vélo (à cheval).

– Savez-vous nager (danser)?
  – Oui, je sais nager (danser).
  – Non, je ne sais pas nager (danser).

– Où nagez-vous?
  – Je nage à la mer (à la piscine).

– Jouez-vous d'un instrument de musique?
  – Oui, je joue du piano (du violon, de la guitare, de la flûte, du hautbois, etc.).

– Est-ce que vous collectionnez quelque chose?
  – Oui, je collectionne les timbres-poste (les cartes postales, etc.).

– Etes-vous membre d'un Club des Jeunes?
  – Oui, je suis membre d'un Club des Jeunes.

– Aimez-vous mieux lire, écouter la radio ou regarder la télévision?
  – Je préfère regarder la télévision.

– Que faites-vous le soir après avoir fini vos devoirs?
  – J'écoute mes disques après avoir fini mes devoirs.

– Quel est votre sport préféré?
  – Je préfère le football (le rugby, le tennis, etc.).

– Quels sports est-ce qu'on joue en été?
  – En été on joue au cricket et au tennis.

– Quels sports pratiquez-vous à l'école?
  – Je pratique le football (le hockey, le basketball, etc.).

8 LES REPAS

– Qu'est-ce que vous avez mangé pour le petit déjeuner aujourd'hui?
  – J'ai mangé du pain grillé. (*toast*)
  – J'ai mangé un œuf à la coque. (*boiled egg*)
  – J'ai mangé du bacon et un œuf.
  – Je n'ai rien mangé pour le petit déjeuner.

– Qu'est-ce que vous avez bu au petit déjeuner aujourd'hui?
  – J'ai bu du café (du thé) au petit déjeuner.

– Qui a préparé votre petit déjeuner ce matin?
  – Ma mère a préparé le petit déjeuner ce matin.
  – J'ai préparé le petit déjeuner ce matin.

– Est-ce que vous mangez souvent dans un restaurant?
  – Oui, je mange souvent dans un restaurant.
  – Non, je ne mange pas souvent dans un restaurant.

– Quels sont les repas que vous prenez chaque jour, et à quelle heure?
  – Je prends le petit déjeuner à . . . (huit heures).
  – Je prends le déjeuner à . . . (midi).
  – Je prends le goûter à . . . (quatre heures).
  – Je prends le dîner (le souper) à . . . (huit heures).

– Quels fruits aimez-vous?
  – J'aime . . . (les oranges).

– Quels légumes n'aimez-vous pas?
  – Je n'aime pas (les haricots verts).

– Est-ce que vous rentrez à la maison pour déjeuner?
  – Oui, je rentre à la maison pour déjeuner.
  – Non, je reste à l'école pour déjeuner.

– Aimez-vous les repas français?
  – Oui, j'aime les repas français.
  – Non, je n'aime pas les repas français.
  – Je n'en ai jamais mangé.

– Qu'est-ce qu'on mange en France pour le petit déjeuner?
  – En France on mange du pain, du beurre, de la confiture et quelquefois des croissants pour le petit déjeuner.

9 LE TEMPS

– Quel temps fait-il aujourd'hui?
  – Aujourd'hui il pleut.
  – Aujourd'hui il fait beau.
(See Vocabulary Topic 41.)

– Quel temps a-t-il fait hier?
  – Hier il a plu.
  – Hier il a fait beau temps.

10 LES VACANCES/LES VOYAGES

– Aimez-vous voyager? Pourquoi?
  – Oui, j'aime voyager. J'aime visiter les endroits intéressants.

– Où êtes-vous allé en vacances l'année dernière?
  – Je suis allé . . . (en France, en Espagne) l'année dernière.
  – Je suis resté à la maison.

– Qu'est-ce que vous avez fait l'été dernier?
  – Je suis allé à l'étranger (*abroad*).
  – Je suis allé en Écosse.

– Etes-vous jamais allé en France?
  – Oui, je suis allé en France il y a deux ans.
  – Non, je ne suis jamais allé en France.

– Où irez-vous passer les vacances cet été?
  – J'irai en Italie cet été.
  – Je resterai à la maison.

– Préférez-vous passer les vacances au bord de la mer ou à la campagne? Pourquoi?
  – Je préfère passer les vacances au bord de la mer parce que j'aime nager à la mer.
  – Je préfère passer les vacances à la campagne parce que j'aime me promener à la campagne.

– Quel pays étranger voudriez-vous visiter et pourquoi?
  – Je voudrais visiter . . . (la France, parce qu'on me dit que c'est un beau pays).

– Quels pays avez-vous visité?
  – J'ai visité (le Pays de Galles, l'Irlande, le Portugal, etc.).

– Aimez-vous faire du camping?
  – Oui, j'aime faire du camping.
  – Non, je n'aime pas faire du camping.

– Où avez-vous fait du camping?
  – J'ai fait du camping . . . (en France, en Grèce, etc.).

– Combien de semaines de vacances avez-vous par an?
  – J'ai (dix) semaines de vacances par an.

– Avez-vous fait des vacances avec un groupe de l'école? Où êtes-vous allé?
  – Je suis allé en Belgique avec un groupe de l'école.

– Comment peut-on traverser la Manche? (*English Channel*)
  – On peut traverser la Manche en bateau, en avion ou en hovercraft.

– Avez-vous voyagé en avion? Où êtes-vous allé?
  – Je suis allé en Autriche en avion.

– Préférez-vous voyager en avion, en train, ou en voiture?
– Je préfère voyager en . . .

– Que faites-vous généralement pendant les vacances de Noël (de Pâques)?
– Je reste à la maison avec ma famille.

11 VOUS-MÊME

– Quelle est la date de votre anniversaire?
– Mon anniversaire est . . . (le dix mars).

– Où habitez-vous?
– J'habite . . . (Londres).

– Qu'est-ce que vous espérez faire l'année prochaine?
– L'année prochaine j'espère trouver un emploi.
– L'année prochaine j'espère rester à l'école pour continuer mes études.

– Qu'est-ce que vous espérez faire après avoir quitté l'école?
– J'espère devenir . . . (See Vocabulary Topic 28.)

– Qu'est-ce que vous avez fait hier soir?
– Hier soir j'ai fait mes devoirs.

– Qu'est-ce que vous avez fait samedi dernier?
– Je suis allé en ville samedi dernier.

– Qu'est-ce que vous avez fait dimanche dernier?
– Dimanche dernier je suis allé à l'église et j'ai rendu visite à ma grand'mère.

– Qu'est-ce que vous ferez samedi prochain?
– Samedi prochain j'irai en ville.

– Qu'est-ce que vous ferez dimanche prochain?
– Dimanche prochain je resterai à la maison.

– Que faites-vous quand vous êtes malade?
– J'appelle le médecin quand je suis malade.

– Que faites-vous quand vous avez soif?
– Je bois de l'eau quand j'ai soif.

– Que faites-vous quand vous avez faim?
– Je mange des biscuits quand j'ai faim.

– Que faites-vous quand vous êtes fatigué?
– Je me repose quand je suis fatigué.

– Préférez-vous regarder la télévision ou aller au cinéma?
– Je préfère regarder la télévision.

– Qu'est-ce que vous allez faire demain?
– Je travaillerai à l'école demain.

– De quelle couleur sont vos cheveux?
– Mes cheveux sont bruns (blonds, roux).

– Où faites-vous vos devoirs?
– Je fais mes devoirs dans ma chambre.

– Est-ce qu'on vous donne de l'argent de poche?
– Oui, on me donne de l'argent de poche.

– Comment dépensez-vous votre argent de poche?
– J'achète des disques et des livres.
– Je l'économise. (*save it*)

– Combien de devoirs avez-vous chaque soir?
– J'ai beaucoup de devoirs chaque soir.

– Qu'est-ce que vous faites après vous être levé le matin?
– Après m'être levé le matin je prends le petit déjeuner.

– Que faites-vous généralement le week-end?
– Le week-end je fais mes devoirs et je sors avec mes amis.

– Qu'est-ce que vous avez fait ce matin avant de venir à l'école?
  – Ce matin je me suis levé à huit heures, puis j'ai pris le petit déjeuner.

– Comment s'appelle votre meilleur(e) ami(e)?
  – Il (elle) s'appelle . . .

– Décrivez les vêtements que vous portez en ce moment.
  – Je porte une chemise (un pantalon, une jupe, une cravate, un blazer, etc.).

12   LA FRANCE

– Où se trouvent les plus beaux châteaux de la France?
  – Ils se trouvent dans la région de la Loire.

– En quels pays parle-t-on français?
  – On parle français en France, en Belgique, et au Canada.

– Où se trouve la Côte d'Azur?
  – Elle se trouve dans le Midi de la France.

– Comment est le drapeau national de la France?
  – Il est bleu, blanc et rouge.

– Quand est-ce qu'on célèbre la fête nationale en France?
  – On célèbre la fête nationale le quatorze juillet.

– Qu'est-ce qu'on produit en Normandie?
  – On y produit du fromage et du cidre.

– Qui résidait dans le Palais de Versailles?
  – Louis Quatorze résidait dans le Palais de Versailles.
  – Les rois de France résidaient dans le Palais de Versailles.

– Comment s'appelle le fleuve qui traverse Paris?
  – Le fleuve s'appelle la Seine.

TEST YOURSELF

The following is a list of questions for you to try answering orally. If you are unsure of any of the answers, check back to the relevant Conversation Topic and then test yourself again.

A   In the present tense:

1 Comment vous appelez-vous?
2 Comment t'appelles-tu?
3 Quel âge avez-vous?
4 Quel âge as-tu?
5 Où habitez-vous?
6 Avez-vous des sœurs?
7 Avez-vous des frères?
8 Que fait votre père?
9 Que fait votre mère?
10 Quelles sont les matières que vous étudiez à l'école?
11 Allez-vous continuer vos études l'année prochaine?
12 A quelle heure vous levez-vous le samedi?
13 A quelle heure vous couchez-vous le samedi?
14 Que faites-vous généralement le dimanche?
15 Allez-vous souvent au cinéma?
16 Quel genre de programmes de télévision préférez-vous?
17 Décrivez les vêtements que vous portez en ce moment.
18 Que portez-vous quand il fait très froid?
19 Est-ce que vous aimez les sports? Lesquels?
20 Quel est votre passe-temps favori?

B   In the perfect tense:

1 A quelle heure vous êtes-vous levé(e) ce matin?
2 A quelle heure vous êtes-vous couché(e) hier soir?
3 Comment êtes-vous venu(e) en classe aujourd'hui?
4 Qu'est-ce que vous avez mangé au petit déjeuner ce matin?
5 Qu'est-ce que vous avez mangé hier soir?
6 Etes-vous allé(e) à l'étranger?
7 Etes-vous déjà allé(e) en France?
8 Où avez-vous passé vos vacances l'année dernière?
9 Qu'est-ce que vous avez fait pendant les vacances de Noël?
10 Comment avez-vous fêté votre anniversaire?

C   In the future tense:

1 Que ferez-vous ce soir?
2 Où irez-vous samedi prochain?
3 Que ferez-vous dimanche prochain?
4 Où irez-vous en vacances cette année?
5 Quand aurez-vous dix-huit ans?
6 A quelle heure arriverez-vous à la maison ce soir?
7 A quelle heure quitterez-vous l'école aujourd'hui?
8 Irez-vous au cinéma samedi prochain?
9 A quelle heure vous coucherez-vous ce soir?
10 Où serez-vous dans deux heures?

3 Oral composition

PICTURE NARRATIVE

Oral narrative composition based on a series of connected pictures is tested by several O-level and CSE Examination Boards. The test normally consists of a set of four or six pictures which relate an incident. The candidate has to tell the story, usually in the third person, to the examiner. The choice of tense (present tense or perfect tense) is often left to the discretion of the candidate, but consistency in tense usage is expected.

This type of test is similar to the written picture composition test. However, in the oral examination, candidates are not allowed to write anything down. Candidates are normally given five minutes in which to prepare their oral composition. This time must be used wisely to prepare *all* the pictures and not just the beginning of the composition. Always prepare a good ending as well as a good beginning since the ending will be fresh in the examiner's mind when awarding you a mark.

You should prepare about three or four sentences on each picture, using linking phrases between the pictures in order to produce a continuous narrative and avoid a disjointed effect. Always remember that you are telling a story and should therefore *not* say 'Dans la première image nous voyons . . .' etc.

Keep the French simple and above all be accurate in your use of verbs. Do not work out the story in English and then try to put it into French. Candidates who try to do this often 'dry up' searching for words or phrases in French. Think in French at all times. Accurate simple French will earn you more marks than complicated but incomplete or inaccurate sentences.

Although you will not know beforehand the topic for oral composition, it is possible for you to do some preparation in the weeks before the examination. The topic chosen for narrative composition often includes an accident or theft, and police, firemen, or doctors are often involved. Check that you are sure of the vocabulary for these topic areas. Check also words to do with losing one's way (s'égarer, perdre le chemin), breaking a leg (se casser la jambe), telephoning the police (téléphoner à la police), taking someone to hospital (emmener quelqu'un à l'hôpital), etc.

The topic areas which you should revise include the following:
Accident/injury   Café/hotel/restaurant   Camping   Countryside   Farm   House
Railway   Seaside   School   Shopping   Town   Travel   Weather

You should also prepare some of the following elements for inclusion in your oral narrative:

(a) a season of the year, e.g.
pendant les grandes vacances
au mois de janvier
l'année dernière (in this case, remember that you would then have to use the past tenses for your narrative)

(b) a day of the week, e.g.
lundi matin
samedi dernier (N.B. past tenses would be required)

(c) a time of day, e.g.
à dix heures et demie
à trois heures de l'après-midi

(d) a reference to the weather where relevant, e.g.
par un beau jour d'été
par un mauvais jour d'hiver

(e) French names for your characters, e.g.
Pierre, Marc, Louise, Eve-Marie, Monsieur et Madame Duval

(f) a French location, e.g.
à Paris, à Biarritz, à Avignon

(g) 'link' words to be used in your narrative for linking the pictures together, e.g.
   puis, quelques minutes plus tard, au bout d'une demi-heure, bientôt

   Look at the following sets of pictures and prepare them for oral composition. Time yourself
to complete your preparation in five minutes.

1

2

3

4

SET QUESTIONS ON PICTURES

Several Examination Boards use set questions based on a picture (or pictures) which are to be answered orally. When this type of test is used you must not only study the picture(s) carefully but also pay careful attention to the questions. There will often be a useful piece of information given in the question, usually in the form of the verb. The specific questions will vary according to the picture, but there are several types of question which can apply to almost any picture:

Quel temps fait-il?	What is the weather like?
Quelle heure est-il?	What time is it?
Comment est . . . ?	What is . . . like?
Comment sont . . . ?	What are . . . like?
Combien de . . . ?	How many (much) . . . ?
Où est (sont) . . . ?	Where is (are) . . . ?
Pourquoi . . . ?	Why . . . ?
Qu'est-ce que . . . ?	What . . . ?
Que fait . . . ?	What is (someone) doing . . . ?
Que font . . . ?	What are (they) doing . . . ?
Où se passe cette scène?	Where is this scene taking place?
A qui est . . . ?	To whom does (something) belong?

Look at the pictures below and answer the questions orally, remembering that you will not see the questions in the examination itself.

1 The port

(a) Où se passe cette scène?
(b) Quel temps fait-il?
(c) Quelle heure est-il?
(d) Que vend l'homme au centre?
(e) Combien d'oiseaux voyez-vous?

(f) Que fait l'homme à droite?
(g) Combien de bateaux voyez-vous?
(h) Que fait l'homme à gauche?
(i) Où se trouve l'agence de voyages?
(j) Que font les enfants?

2 Preparing for the holidays

(a) Où est la voiture?

(b) Où est le chat?

(c) Qu'est-ce qu'il y a dans le coffre de la voiture?

(d) En quelle saison se passe cette scène?

(e) Qu'est-ce qu'il y a à droite de la maison?

(f) Combien de raquettes de tennis y a-t-il?

(g) Qu'est-ce que l'homme tient à la main droite?

(h) Qu'est-ce que la petite fille prend?

(i) Où est le garçon?

(j) Où va la famille?

3 At the swimming pool

(a) Où se passe cette scène?

(b) Quel temps fait-il?

(c) Que fait la dame à droite?

(d) Que fait la dame au premier plan?

(e) Que font les deux garçons à gauche?

(f) Que fait-on dans une piscine?

(g) Qu'est-ce qu'on porte pour nager?

(h) Sur quoi la dame s'est-elle couchée?

(i) Qu'est-ce que le garçon (A) va faire?

(j) Savez-vous nager?

4 Snowscene

(a) En quelle saison se passe cette scène?
(b) Quel temps fait-il?
(c) Que font les enfants à gauche?
(d) Que font les enfants près de l'arbre à droite?
(e) Que font les enfants sur la colline?

(f) Décrivez les vêtements de l'enfant (A).
(g) Qu'est-ce qui est arrivé à l'enfant (B)?
(h) Où se trouve la forêt?
(i) Comment vous amusez-vous dans la neige?

Sometimes you are asked to describe a picture, without any questions to prompt you. Say as much as you can about these pictures:

4 Role-play

In this type of oral test the candidate is presented with a situation which he or she would be likely to meet when visiting France. The examiner plays the role of, for example, a stallholder in a market, a petrol-pump attendant or a booking-office clerk, and the candidate is given written instructions (in English) concerning his or her role, e.g. buying fruit, petrol, railway ticket, etc.

The test will be in the form of a conversation with the examiner. You will be given several minutes before the actual examination to prepare, but part of the examination may be spontaneous, depending on the answers you give. You must be prepared to sustain a conversation in French according to the situation given.

It is very likely that the 'character' with whom you must hold a conversation will need to be addressed in the polite 'vous' form; but always check your instructions carefully in case the 'tu' form is required, i.e. for talking to a member of your family, or friend of your own age.

Remember to use the words 'monsieur' or 'madame' when addressing a stranger in French.

Check carefully Grammar Revision section 35 to make sure that you know how to form questions in French. Many of the role-playing situations require you to ask someone for information.

You may also be asked to give an order in French in certain situations, e.g. sending for the doctor or policeman. Check Grammar Revision section 28 for this.

The following phrases will be useful for many different role-play situations:

Pour aller à . . .?	How do I get to . . .?
Y a-t-il . . .?	Is (are) there . . .?
J'ai besoin de . . .	I need . . .
Il me faut . . .	I need . . .
Je dois . . .	I must . . .
Je peux . . .	I can . . .
Je ne peux pas . . .	I can't . . .
Puis-je . . .?	Can I . . .?
Pouvez-vous . . .?	Can you . . .?
Pouvez-vous me dire . . .?	Can you tell me . . .?
Pouvez-vous me dire où se trouve . . .?	Can you tell me where . . . is?

Pourriez-vous . . .?	Could you . . .?
Je voudrais . . .	I would like . . .
Je veux . . .	I want . . .
Je ne veux pas . . .	I don't want . . .
Attendez!	Wait!
D'accord!	All right!
Bien sûr.	Of course.
Entendu.	Of course.
Certainement.	Of course.
Avec plaisir.	With pleasure.
Malheureusement.	Unfortunately.
Excusez-moi.	Excuse me.
Je suis désolé.	I am sorry.
Quel dommage!	What a pity!
Quelle chance!	What luck!
Formidable!	Great!
Chouette!	Great!

De rien, monsieur (madame).
Je vous en prie, monsieur (madame).
Il n'y a pas de quoi, monsieur (madame).

} These expressions are used as a reply when you have been thanked for something. They are the equivalent of 'Don't mention it' or 'My pleasure' or 'Not at all'.

For each of the following situations a list of useful expressions is given, plus some examination role-play questions and specimen answers.

1 SEEKING ACCOMMODATION – CAMPSITE/HOTEL/YOUTH HOSTEL

Useful expressions

Camping
See Vocabulary Topic 6.

Avez-vous une place libre, monsieur, pour une tente/une caravane?
Do you have any room for a tent/caravan?
la carte d'identité *identity card*
Où sont les WC et les lavabos? *Where is the toilet and washroom block?*

Hotel
See Vocabulary Topic 5.

Est-ce que vous avez des chambres libres, monsieur? *Do you have any vacant rooms, sir?*
une chambre à deux lits (personnes) *a double room*
une chambre à une personne *a single room*
avec salle de bains *with bathroom*
avec douche *with shower*
service compris *service charge included*
le petit déjeuner compris *breakfast included*
la demi-pension *half board*
la pension complète *full board*

Youth hostel (L'auberge de jeunesse)

le père aubergiste *the warden*
Avez-vous des lits pour ce soir? *Have you any beds for tonight?*
Est-ce que je peux louer un sac de couchage et des couvertures?
May I hire a sleeping-bag and some blankets?

C'est combien la nuit?
C'est combien par nuit? } *How much is it per night?*

C'est combien par personne? *How much is it per person?*

1 Au terrain de camping (SEREB)

The examiner, who will be playing the role of the campsite warden, will speak first. This is not a translation exercise. Try to make your conversation as fluent and as natural as possible. Wait for the reply in between each part.

Full marks can be obtained in this section only if a suitable form of the verb is used in each part. You must not consult other sources of information nor write anything down.

(a) Ask if there is any room on the campsite for one night.
(b) Say that you are on your own with just a tent.
(c) Ask where the toilets and washrooms are.
(d) Ask where you will be able to buy some bread in the morning.

Specimen answers

(a) Est-ce que vous avez une place libre pour une nuit, monsieur?
(b) Je suis seul et j'ai une tente.
(c) Où sont les lavabos et les WC, s'il vous plaît?
(d) Où est-ce que je pourrai acheter du pain demain matin, monsieur?

2 A l'auberge de jeunesse

You arrive at a youth hostel. The examiner is the warden.

(a) Ask the warden if there is any room.
(b) Say that there are three of you.
(c) Say that you would like to hire sleeping-bags.
(d) Ask if the breakfast is included.

Specimen answers
(a) Est-ce que vous avez des lits, monsieur?
(b) Nous sommes trois, monsieur.
(c) Nous voudrions louer des sacs de couchage.
(d) Est-ce que le petit déjeuner est compris?

3 A l'hôtel (EAEB)

You arrive at a hotel in the evening. The examiner is the hotel proprietor.

(a) Ask if there are any rooms vacant for the night.
(b) Say you would like a single room with a bathroom.
(c) Ask the price of the room for the night, and when told ask if the breakfast is included.

Specimen answers
(a) Est-ce que vous avez des chambres libres pour cette nuit, monsieur?
(b) Je voudrais une chambre pour une personne, avec salle de bains.
(c) C'est combien la nuit? Le petit déjeuner est compris?

2 Asking for information/asking the way

Useful expressions
See Vocabulary Topic 15.

Le Syndicat d'Initiative *Tourist Information Office*
un plan de la ville *a plan of the town*
une carte de la région *a map of the region*
Pour aller à . . . s'il vous plaît? *How does one get to . . . please?*
tournez à droite *turn to the right*
tournez à gauche *turn to the left*
la première rue à droite *the first street on the right*
la première rue à gauche *the first street on the left*

allez tout droit* *go straight on*

(*You must be very careful with the pronunciation of 'droit'. The 't' should not be pronounced, unlike 'droite' where the 't' is pronounced.)

allez jusqu'à . . . *go as far as* . . .
Pouvez-vous m'aider? *Can you help me?*
au bout de . . . *at the end of* . . .
. . . minutes d'ici . . . *minutes from here*
. . . mètres d'ici . . . *metres from here*
de l'autre côté *on the other side*
tout près *quite near*

---

1 At the Information Bureau (LREB)

You have just arrived with your family in a small French town where you have rented a cottage for a fortnight. You go to the Syndicat d'Initiative. The examiner will play the part of the person on duty.

(a) Ask if the shops are open every day of the week.
(b) Ask what there is to see in and around the town.
(c) Say that you are very interested in castles and ask if there is one nearby.
(d) Ask how you can get to it.

Specimen answers
(a) Est-ce que les magasins sont ouverts tous les jours de la semaine?
(b) Qu'est-ce qu'il y a à voir en ville et aux environs?
(c) Je m'intéresse beaucoup aux châteaux. Est-ce qu'il y en a un près d'ici?
(d) Et pour y aller, monsieur?

---

2 Dans la rue (EAEB)

You are in the street and trying to get to your hotel. The examiner is a passer-by.

(a) Ask the passer-by if he/she can help you.
(b) Ask him/her to tell you the way to the Hôtel Moderne.
(c) Ask if you have to catch a bus to get there.

Specimen answers
(a) Pardon, monsieur (madame), pouvez-vous m'aider s'il vous plaît?
(b) Pour aller à l'Hôtel Moderne, s'il vous plaît?
(c) Est-ce qu'il faut prendre l'autobus?

---

3 MEETING PEOPLE/INVITATIONS

Useful expressions

présenter *to introduce*
heureux (heureuse) de faire votre connaissance *pleased to meet you*
enchanté *delighted (to meet you)*
Salut! *Hello!*

'Bonjour/au revoir' should always be accompanied by the person's name or 'monsieur/madame'.

(a) Comment allez-vous? ⎫
(b) Comment vas-tu? ⎬ *How are you?*
(c) Ça va? ⎭

(a) Polite form used when addressing an adult.
(b) For a person of your own age, or younger.
(c) Colloquial form.

A bientôt. ⎫
A tout à l'heure. ⎭ *See you soon.*

A ce soir. *Till this evening.*
A demain. *Till tomorrow*

inviter *to invite*

Voulez-vous . . .? ⎫
Veux tu . . .? ⎭ *Will you?*

Voudriez-vous . . .? *Would you like . . .?*
Je voudrais . . . *I would like* . . .

1 (EAEB)

Imagine you have just arrived at the home of your pen-friend in France. His/her mother/ father is there to welcome you. Your teacher will play the part of your pen-friend's mother/father.

(a) Say you are pleased to meet her/him. (d) Say you are not very hungry.
(b) Say you have two suitcases. (e) Thank her/him and say you are very tired.
(c) Say you would like lemonade.

Specimen answers

(a) Je suis heureux (heureuse) de faire votre connaissance, monsieur (madame).
(b) J'ai deux valises.
(c) Je voudrais une limonade, s'il vous plaît.
(d) Je n'ai pas grand'faim.
(e) Merci, monsieur (madame), je suis très fatigué.

2 (EAEB)

A French friend invites you to go to a party in the evening. The examiner is the friend.

(a) Thank your friend for the invitation and say you would like to go.
(b) Ask your friend at what time the party begins.
(c) Ask him/her where you should meet before the party.

Specimen answers

(a) Merci pour l'invitation. Oui, je veux bien y aller.
(b) A quelle heure la boum commence-t-elle?
(c) Où est-ce qu'on se rencontre avant la boum?

4 Illness/injury

Useful expressions
See Vocabulary Topics 1, 24 and 26.

N.B. especially 'J'ai mal à . . .' *I have a pain* . . .
    e.g. J'ai mal à la tête. *I have a headache.*   J'ai mal aux dents. *I have toothache, etc.*

1 (EAEB)

You are staying with your French correspondent and wake up in the morning with toothache. The examiner is your correspondent's mother/father.

(a) Tell your correspondent's mother/father that you do not feel well and that you have toothache.
(b) Tell him/her that you had to take some aspirins during the night.
(c) Ask him/her to telephone the dentist.

Specimen answers

(a) Je ne vais pas très bien, j'ai mal aux dents.
(b) J'ai dû prendre de l'aspirine pendant la nuit.
(c) Voulez-vous téléphoner au dentiste, s'il vous plaît, monsieur (madame)?

2 (EAEB)

Imagine you are taken ill on holiday in France. The doctor comes to see you. Your teacher will play the part of the doctor.

(a) You return the doctor's greeting.
(b) Say you have a headache.
(c) Say you are not eating.
(d) When the doctor prescribes tablets, ask when you take them.
(e) Thank the doctor for the prescription and say goodbye.

Specimen answers

(a) Bonjour, monsieur

(b) J'ai mal à la tête.

(c) Je ne peux rien manger.

(d) Quand faut-il les prendre?

(e) Merci pour l'ordonnance et au revoir, monsieur.

5 GARAGE

Useful expressions
See Vocabulary Topic 7.

> **1 A la station-service** (SEREB)
>
> The examiner, who will be playing the role of the petrol-pump attendant, will speak first.
>
> (a) Ask the assistant to fill up the tank.
>
> (b) Ask how much you owe.
>
> (c) Ask if they also sell maps.
>
> (d) Say that you want one of the North of France.

Specimen answers

(a) Voulez-vous faire le plein d'essence, monsieur?

(b) Ça fait combien, monsieur?

(c) Est-ce que vous vendez des cartes routières?

(d) Je voudrais une carte du Nord de la France, s'il vous plaît.

> **2** (EAEB)
>
> Imagine you have just arrived at a garage to say your father's car has broken down on the road. Your teacher will play the part of the person at the garage.
>
> (a) Say the car is on the Paris road.
>
> (b) Say it's three kilometres away.
>
> (c) Say it's green and black.
>
> (d) Say it's an old Ford Cortina.
>
> (e) When you are asked the registration number, say you don't know.

Specimen answers

(a) La voiture est sur la route de Paris.

(b) Elle est à trois kilomètres d'ici.

(c) Elle est verte et noire.

(d) C'est une vieille Cortina.

(e) Je le regrette, mais je ne sais pas.

6 TRAVEL

Useful expressions
See Vocabulary Topics 2, 34 and 40.

en auto *by car*
en autobus *by bus*
en avion *by plane*
en bateau *by boat*
par le train *by train*
A quelle heure arrive le train de . . .? *When does the train from . . . arrive?*
A quelle heure arrive l'avion de . . .? *When does the plane from . . . arrive?*
A quelle heure part le prochain train pour . . .? *When does the next train for . . . leave?*
Combien de temps faut-il pour aller à . . .? *How long does it take to get to . . .?*
Faut-il changer de train (d'avion)? *Does one have to change trains (planes)?*

1 A la gare (SEREB)

(a) Say that you want a single, second class ticket to Paris.
(b) Say that you only have a 100 franc note.
(c) Ask what time the train leaves.
(d) Ask where the waiting room is.

Specimen answers
(a) Un billet simple de seconde classe pour Paris, s'il vous plaît.
(b) Je n'ai qu'un billet de 100 francs.
(c) A quelle heure part le train?
(d) Où se trouve la salle d'attente, s'il vous plaît?

2 (EAEB)

Imagine you have just got on a bus in Paris with a friend and you are talking to the driver.

(a) Ask if the bus goes to Notre Dame.
(b) Ask for two tickets, please.
(c) Explain you are students.
(d) Say you haven't any change.
(e) Say you're sorry.

Specimen answers
(a) Est-ce que l'autobus va à Notre Dame?
(b) Alors deux billets s'il vous plaît.
(c) Nous sommes des étudiants.
(d) Je n'ai pas de monnaie.
(e) Je le regrette.

7 RESTAURANT/CAFÉ

Useful expressions
See Vocabulary Topics 5 and 21.

un steak-frites *steak and chips*
Qu'est-ce que vous avez comme dessert? *What is there for dessert?*
retenir une table *to reserve a table*

N.B. Use 'prendre' when you wish to say 'have' in French when speaking of food and drink:
Je prends le petit déjeuner à huit heures.
I have breakfast at eight o'clock.
Je prendrai un café-crème.
I'll have a white coffee.

1 A la terrasse d'un café (SEREB)

(a) Say that you would prefer to sit outside.
(b) Ask your friend if he/she would like some croissants.
(c) Call the waiter and order one black and one white coffee.
(d) Agree with your friend and ask how long he/she has been living there.

Specimen answers
(a) Je préfère m'asseoir à la terrasse.
(b) Est-ce que tu veux prendre des croissants?
(c) Garçon! Un café noir et un café-crème, s'il vous plaît.
(d) Oui. Depuis combien de temps habites-tu ici?

2 In a restaurant (LREB)

You enter a restaurant with three friends. Your examiner will play the part of the waiter or waitress and your friends.

(a) Ask if there is a table for four.
(b) Ask your friends what they would like to eat.
One it seems would like a salad which is not on the menu.
(c) Order the meal and ask the waiter/waitress if it is possible to have a salad.
(d) You have finished your meal. Ask the waiter/waitress for the bill and then ask if the service is included.

Specimen answers
(a) Avez-vous une table pour quatre personnes?
(b) Qu'est-ce que vous voulez prendre?
(c) Trois steak-frites, et est-ce que vous avez une salade aussi?
(d) L'addition s'il vous plaît. Est-ce que le service est compris?

8 CINEMA/THEATRE

Useful expressions
See Vocabulary Topic 8.

les comédies *comedies*
les dessins animés *cartoons*
les films d'amour *romantic films*
les films d'aventure *adventure films*
les films d'espionnage *spy films*
les films de guerre *war films*
les films d'horreur *horror films*
les films policiers *thrillers*
les westerns *cowboy films*
un film doublé *a 'dubbed' film*
un film en noir et blanc *a black and white film*
un film sous-titré *a film with subtitles*
une pièce de théâtre *a play*
une pièce de Shakespeare *a Shakespearian play*
la séance a commencé *the film/play has begun*

1 (SEREB)

The examiner, who will be playing the role of your friend, will speak first.

(a) Suggest you and your friend go to the pictures.
(b) Ask your friend to pass the paper. Then say that there is a good film on at the Rex.
(c) Say that you will have to hurry as it starts at 21h 30.
(d) Ask if your friend has enough money.

Specimen answers
(a) Nous pourrions aller au cinéma.
(b) Passe-moi le journal, s'il te plaît. Il y a un bon film au cinéma Rex.
(c) Il commence à vingt et une heures trente. Nous devons nous dépêcher.
(d) As-tu assez d'argent?

2 (EAEB)

Imagine you and your pen-friend are planning to go to the cinema. Your teacher will play the part of your pen-friend.

(a) Say you would like to go very much.
(b) Say you would like to see a French film.
(c) Ask if you are going this evening.
(d) Ask what time it begins.
(e) Say 'All right', and repeat the time.

Specimen answers

(a) Je voudrais bien y aller.

(b) Je voudrais voir un film français.

(c) On y va ce soir?

(d) A quelle heure commence-t-il?

(e) D'accord. A sept heures et demie.

9 POST OFFICE/TELEPHONING

Useful expressions

See Vocabulary Topic 33.

P et T (Postes et Télécommunications) *Post Office*

le jeton *token required when using a phone in a café*

Qui est à l'appareil? *Who is speaking?*

Allô! *Hello!* (Used when answering the phone, but not when greeting someone in the street. 'Bonjour' or 'Salut' is then used.)

Ici . . . *This is . . . speaking.*

N.B. téléphoner **à** quelqu'un *to telephone someone*

---

1 (SEREB)

The examiner, who will be playing the role of the post-office assistant, will speak first.

(a) Say you would like to telephone your friend.

(b) The number is Lisieux 62-03-24.

(c) Ask which booth to go to.

(d) Thank him/her and ask how much it costs for three minutes.

Specimen answers

(a) Je voudrais téléphoner à un ami.

(b) Son numéro est Lisieux soixante-deux, zéro trois, vingt-quatre.

(c) Quelle cabine, s'il vous plaît?

(d) Merci monsieur (madame), ça coûte combien pour trois minutes?

---

2 (EAEB)

You are at the post office in France. The examiner is the counter-clerk.

(a) Tell the clerk you would like to send a telegram to England.

(b) When asked if you have filled out a telegram form, say yes and that there are sixteen words on it.

(c) Pay the money, and ask if the telegram will arrive today.

Specimen answers

(a) Je voudrais envoyer un télégramme en Angleterre, s'il vous plaît.

(b) Oui, j'ai rempli un formulaire. Il y a seize mots en tout.

(c) Voilà monsieur (madame). Est-ce que le télégramme arrivera aujourd'hui?

10 SHOPPING

Useful expressions

See Vocabulary Topic 37.

---

1 (EAEB)

You are at a fruit and vegetable stall in the market. The examiner is the stallholder.

(a) Tell the stallholder you would like to buy half a kilo of grapes.

(b) Ask if the small peaches are good to eat.

(c) Ask if the oranges are more expensive than the peaches.

Specimen answers

(a) Je voudrais un demi-kilo de raisins, s'il vous plaît.

(b) Est-ce que les petites pêches sont bonnes à manger?

(c) Est-ce que les oranges sont plus chères que les pêches?

---

2 Chez le boulanger-pâtissier (SEREB)

The examiner, who will be playing the role of a shop assistant, will speak first.

(a) Ask the assistant to give you two large loaves.

(b) Ask how much the strawberry tarts cost.

(c) Say that they are dear, but that you will take one.

(d) Answer 'yes' to the examiner's question and say that you did not have any breakfast.

Specimen answers

(a) Deux gros pains, s'il vous plaît.

(b) Elles coûtent combien les tartes aux fraises?

(c) Elles sont chères, mais j'en prendrai une.

(d) Oui. Je n'ai pas mangé le petit déjeuner.

11 BANK/LOST PROPERTY

Useful expressions

un bureau de change *foreign exchange office*

une livre sterling ⎫
une livre anglaise ⎭ *a pound (£)*

toucher un chèque de voyage *to cash a traveller's cheque*

une récompense *a reward*

---

1 (EAEB)

You are at the bank. The examiner is the bank-clerk.

(a) Say you would like to change a traveller's cheque.

(b) Show the clerk your passport and say that the cheque is for £20.

(c) Agree to sign the form and ask where the cash desk is.

Specimen answers

(a) Je voudrais toucher un chèque de voyage, s'il vous plaît.

(b) Voilà mon passeport, monsieur (madame). C'est un chèque de vingt livres.

(c) Oui, je signerai ici. Où se trouve la caisse?

---

2 (EAEB)

You are at the Lost Property Office. Your father has lost his wallet. The examiner is the employee at the counter.

(a) Tell the employee that your father has lost his wallet.

(b) Tell the employee that your father lost it this afternoon, outside the town hall.

(c) Tell the employee that it contained 500 francs, some photos and a driving licence.

Specimen answers

(a) Mon père a perdu son portefeuille.

(b) Il l'a perdu cet après-midi devant l'Hôtel de Ville.

(c) Il y avait cinq cents francs, des photos et son permis de conduire.

5 Dictation

A dictation test is included in most O-level French examinations and in several CSE examinations. It is a test which examines several skills at the same time and therefore requires great care. There are *three* main stages to a dictation test and each one demands sustained concentration. The three main stages are:

1 Careful listening
The passage is read through once. You do not write at this stage. You must listen carefully.

2 Careful writing
The passage will then be read in short sections, each section being repeated once. You will write down each section (without the repeats) as it is read. You must think carefully about what you are writing, paying attention to spelling and grammatical constructions.

3 Careful checking
Finally, the passage will be read straight through once again. During this final reading you will be able to correct your work and you will also be given five minutes after the final reading to complete your checking.

N.B. The passage set for dictation will *make sense*. You must make sure, therefore, that what you write down also makes sense.

1 When you hear the passage read for the first time, try to follow the main events of the story, listening especially for the subject(s) of the passage. This will be important when you come to write the verbs as, in French, the sound of the third person singular is often the same as that of the third person plural (e.g. arrive, arrivent). If you have heard two names mentioned as the subject of a sentence (e.g. Pierre et Marie, les enfants) then you must remember that the verb will be plural (e.g. arrivent).

2 This emphasis on careful listening and writing is especially important when the verb is in the imperfect tense as all third person singular and plural endings will sound the same (e.g. était, étaient). Even the first person and second person singular will sound the same as the third persons singular and plural (e.g. étais, étais, était, étaient). You should not, of course, confuse these spellings when the personal pronouns 'je' and 'tu' are used, but you will need to concentrate carefully to work out which third person, singular or plural, is being used.

3 The perfect tense is easier to recognise and therefore easier to spell, as you will hear part of **avoir** or **être** with the past participle (e.g. a acheté, ont acheté). Extra care is needed, however, when the verb is conjugated with **être**, since the past participle must agree with its subject. If a personal pronoun is used (e.g. **elles**) then the agreement is obvious (e.g. elles sont arriv**ées**). If a personal pronoun is not used, care must be taken in listening to find out the gender (masculine or feminine) of the subject of the verb (e.g. les jeunes filles sont arriv**ées**).

Even greater care must be taken to check whether a verb conjugated with **avoir** has a preceding direct object.

e.g. Il a vu **la maison** qu'elle avait achet**ée**.

It is agreements like these which should be revealed in the final checking of the passage. (If you are still unsure about the rules for preceding direct object agreements, check again Grammar Revision section 23.)

Just as you must take care to spell the verb forms correctly, so you must check carefully that:
(a) You have written accents correctly where required, e.g. après, mère, écouté, etc.
(b) You have made adjectives agree with nouns, e.g. les enfants intelligent**s**.

PUNCTUATION

During the second reading of a dictation passage (i.e. when the passage is dictated phrase by phrase) the punctuation will be given in French. Check that you understand the following words:

full stop   **.**   point
comma   **,**   virgule

colon   : deux points
semi-colon ; point-virgule
open inverted commas " ouvrez les guillemets
close inverted commas " fermez les guillemets
open brackets (ouvrez les parenthèses
close brackets) fermez les parenthèses
dash   – tiret
trail dots   ... une série de points
exclamation mark ! point d'exclamation
question mark   ? point d'interrogation
new paragraph/on the next line à la ligne

DICTATION CHECK LIST

1 Remember that several different spellings may have the same sound in French. At all stages of a dictation you must ask yourself what the particular phrase or sentence which you are writing means. For example, **-é, -er, -ez, (-)ai** and **et** are all pronounced the same in French.

The first four are possible verb endings. *None* of them can be substituted for any of the others.
-é is only possible as part of a perfect tense, e.g. j'ai donn**é**.
-er is only possible as an infinitive, e.g. il va donn**er** les cahiers aux élèves.
-ez is only possible with the **vous** form of a verb, e.g. vous part**ez**.
-ai except for its use in **j'ai** (I have) is only possible as a first person (future or past historic) ending. e.g. J'arriver**ai** demain. *I shall arrive tomorrow.*
J'arriv**ai** au mois d'août. *I arrived in August.*

(The past historic tense is not often used for dictation purposes. You should check the syllabus of your own particular Examination Board to find out if the past historic tense is to be used for the dictation test.)

et on its own='and', therefore no confusion should arise.

2 Words such as **ces** and **ses** are often confused by candidates in the dictation test. You must ask yourself which one makes the most sense in the sentence you are writing.
(a) Il est sorti avec **ses** copains. *He went out with* his *friends.*
(b) Il est sorti avec **ces** copains. *He went out with* these *friends.*

Sentence (a) will normally be the correct answer unless the dictation has, prior to this sentence, specified certain friends and then wishes to stress 'these' (**ces**).

3 Accents
Check the following accents carefully. They are frequently neglected in the dictation test.
près   mère
après   père
très   frère
à (*to* or *at*)
All of these have grave accents. If you tend to make mistakes in the use of the above accents, copy them out several times for practise until you are absolutely sure of them and their position.

N.B. Do not confuse 'a', the third person singular present tense of **avoir**, which does *not* have an accent, with 'à', the preposition, which does have a grave accent.

4 Check carefully the past participles of common irregular verbs, and remember especially **dit** (past participle of **dire**) which occurs constantly in dictation tests.

5 Si and **s'y** have the same sound.
Si is often mistaken for **s'y** by candidates, but rarely vice versa. When you are writing your dictation you should check to see whether the sentence you are writing makes sense with the word 'if', or whether a reflexive verb is being used with the pronoun 'y'.
e.g. Il s'y est decidé. *He decided upon it.*

6 Bel, belle
Many candidates in dictation tests use the second of these two adjectives when the first one is required. Always check the gender of the noun being used and remember the following:
Bel (m) will describe a masculine singular noun beginning with a vowel or 'h', e.g. le bel homme.
Belle (f) will describe a feminine singular noun, e.g. la belle robe.
(N.B. the plural of **bel** is **beaux**, the plural of **belle** is **belles**.)

7 Cet, cette

These two words follow the same rule as (6) above. Beware the sound 't' before a masculine singular word beginning with a vowel or 'h':

    cet ami (m)
    cette amie (f)

8 Ma, m'a

These two sound identical but should never be confused since they are grammatically so different. Ask yourself, when writing the dictation, if they are attached to a verb or to a noun:

    ma tante (*noun*)
    m'a donné (*verb*)

9 Absolu/observer

Remember that the 'b' in words such as these will sound like a 'p', but you must use the correct spelling.

10 Quand

Similarly the 'd' of this word sounds like a 't' when followed by a vowel:

    Quand elle est arrivée . . .

11 Liaisons

When a word in French begins with a vowel, remember that the preceding word in the sentence may elide with it, e.g. ses‿amis. When listening to a dictation passage, you should bear this in mind and when writing the dictation always think of the meaning of the passage.

12 Finally, remember that many word-endings in French are silent, but you must write them accurately.

EXAMINATION DICTATION PASSAGES

O level

1 An Early Riser (AEB)

Madame Dupont avait l'habitude | de se lever toujours la première | pour préparer le café | pendant que son mari | faisait sa toilette. | Normalement elle dormait bien, | mais une nuit elle s'est réveillée, | et, | ayant mal à la tête, | elle n'a pas pu se rendormir. | Elle s'est donc levée, | elle est descendue à la cuisine, | et elle a pris de l'aspirine. |

    Monsieur Dupont, | trouvant que sa femme | n'était plus au lit, | s'est levé lui aussi. | Il s'est lavé et s'est rasé | à la salle de bains, | puis une fois habillé | il a descendu l'escalier. | Sa femme lui a demandé | ce qu'il faisait. | Le pauvre Monsieur Dupont | a regardé la pendule | et a été étonné de voir | qu'il n'était | que trois‿heures du matin!

2 A boy visits a rich friend's house (WJEC)

Les parents de *Jacques* | habitaient dans‿une belle maison | près du parc. | *Jacques* m'a fait visiter | leur appartement | qui était situé | au troisième étage. | Nous nous sommes‿arrêtés | devant de magnifiques meubles | et des tableaux splendides. | Je n'ai jamais pénétré | dans‿une telle maison. | J'ai regardé | par les fenêtres. | On n'apercevait que | des‿arbres | et, au loin, | la campagne. | J'ai songé | au cabinet de travail | de mon père, | sombre et étroit, | et au petit salon | de ma mère, | où des meubles‿anciens, | mais bien rustiques, | faisaient le plus bel ornement. | Le sentiment | de mon‿humilité | était si profond | que je ne pouvais rien dire.

3 Isabelle plays the piano (JMB)

Je vis, | à peu de distance, | le toit de la maison d'*Isabelle*. | D'un pas lent | et m'arrêtant | de temps‿à autre | comme pour admirer le paysage, | je m'approchai de sa demeure. | Sur la terrasse, | il n'y avait personne; | mais j'entendis | le son d'un piano. | Je pensai | que sa mère | lui donnait une leçon, | et j'avançai sans bruit | vers cette musique. |

    La fenêtre était ouverte: | encore un pas | et je vis le dos d'*Isabelle*. | C'était‿elle qui jouait, | et des deux mains | en même temps! |

    Parfois, | elle levait très haut | une main | qui restait suspendue | en l'air | une seconde, | puis retombait | sur plusieurs notes | à la fois. | Je ne bougeais pas plus | qu'une statue, | mais la musique s'arrêta soudain, | et *Isabelle* tourna la tête vers moi; | elle sourit et elle dit: |

– Je vous‿ai vu arriver | dans le miroir.

CSE

4 (WJEC)

'Marie,' | m'a dit mon père, | 'le facteur est déjà passé, | et il y a une lettre pour toi.' |

Ce matin-ci | j'étais descendue | plus tard que d'habitude | et les autres | avaient presque fini | leur petit déjeuner. | Je me suis approchée | de la table | et j'ai vu | près de mon assiette | une enveloppe bleue. | Maman m'a regardée avec curiosité | mais je me suis assise | sur ma chaise | sans rien dire. |

J'ai pris l'enveloppe | et je l'ai ouverte. | C'était une lettre courte. | J'ai levé les yeux | et, avec un sourire, | j'ai annoncé: |

'C'est de Pierre. | Il est enfin arrivé | chez son oncle.'

5 (LREB)

Il est midi, | il fait froid | et le soleil brille. | Tout est blanc | parce que, | pendant la nuit, | il a neigé. | Ce matin, | j'ai décidé | de faire une longue promenade | par cette belle journée. | J'ai mis mes vêtements chauds | - chapeau, | pardessus, | gants - | et je suis parti. |

C'était vraiment superbe. | Les enfants poussaient des cris de joie | en se jetant des boules de neige. | Les chiens bondissaient | et tout le monde était heureux.

6 Free composition

One of the elements common to both O-level and CSE level examinations in French is free composition. Unlike prose composition (i.e. translation from English into French), free composition demands of the candidate the ability to express his own ideas accurately and simply in French (except for 5 below).

Prose composition sets out to test certain important grammatical constructions and vocabulary. The candidate has only a limited choice of material in answering this question. He must translate the sentences, and only the sentences, which appear on the question paper. The free composition question, however, offers the candidate almost unlimited scope to show the examiner what he really knows. Thorough preparation of essay topics and of key grammatical constructions should give you a sound basis on which to construct your composition.

In almost all O-level and CSE French examinations there is a choice in the free composition section. The choice is usually between two or more of the following:

1 Letter
2 Topic (A written outline is often given on a certain topic.)
3 Picture(s)
    (a) Composition based on a series of connected pictures.
    (b) Composition based on individual pictures.
4 Continuation (following a stimulus in French)
5 Story reproduction (This type of composition differs from the other four in that the candidate is *not* asked to introduce his own ideas.)

The topics for free composition are based on familiar subjects, e.g. school, home, holidays, countryside, accidents, etc. Try to learn as many words from the Vocabulary Topics section as you can and use them, where relevant, in your free compositions.

You will not be asked to write an abstract or highly imaginative composition. The aim of this part of the examination is to test your ability to write about everyday situations accurately and simply in French. Many candidates feel that the ideas they are expressing in the free composition are too simple and they therefore try to put into French complicated ideas for which they do not have a sufficient command of the French language.

It must be emphasised also that this test is *not* a test of your ability to translate. Almost any candidate who tries to write or think out the essay in English and then tries to translate it into French is doomed to failure. Free composition is designed to test your ability to *think and write* correctly in French. The examiner does not expect the same imaginative standard as that required by the examiner in an English Language examination. The key words are *simplicity, accuracy* and *thorough preparation* for this section of the examination.

PROCEDURE

Most Examination Boards give a choice of subject matter and type of composition. If your Examination Board offers a choice of composition, do *not* decide beforehand which type of composition you will do. An arbitrary decision made during your revision programme to prepare only one type of free composition will seriously limit your chance of success. Too many candidates in the past have found to their cost that the subject matter of one type of composition, which they have prepared, occurs in another type of composition which they have not prepared. Leave your options open and prepare all types of composition which you know that your Examination Board tests.

Preparation

1 Check which examination you are taking.
2 Check which types of free composition are tested by your Examination Board.
3 Check the number of words required in your composition.
At O level the number of words required varies from 100-200.
At CSE the number of words required varies from 75-150.
4 Check which tenses are required in your composition. At O level you will almost certainly be asked to write in the past tenses. At CSE certain Examination Boards will ask you to write in the present tense, others will ask for the past tenses. You must be quite certain which tenses are required.
5 Finally check if there are any special requirements, e.g. must you include some dialogue in topic essays? Are you asked to be one of the people in the story? etc.

Once you have established which types of composition you will be required to write and the length of the composition, you should practise thoroughly during the weeks before the examination writing to the set length. Planning is essential both during practice sessions and in the examination itself. Remember that there is also a time limit in the examination and you should practise planning, writing and revising your composition within the set time.

LETTER-WRITING

The letter that you will be asked to write in both O-level and CSE examinations will be a personal one. Imagine, therefore, that you are speaking directly to the recipient(s) of the letter and use the normal forms and verb tenses of conversation.

If you are asked to write a letter to one member of your family or to a pen-friend, the **tu** (second person singular) form of the verbs will be required. Today, it is perfectly permissible for you to address a person of your own age, whom you may not have met, in the **tu** form.

If, however, you are asked to write to an adult who is not a member of your family, remember to use the polite **vous** form of the verb.

The other most-needed verb forms will be the first persons singular and plural, i.e. the **je** and **nous** forms of the verb. During your revision programme make sure that you are really familiar with these forms of the verb in all the tenses that you may possibly require, especially the present, future, imperfect and perfect tenses.

The past historic tense should *not* be used for letter-writing. This tense is a literary tense used for formal story-telling.

Look at the following different types of letter composition required at O level and CSE, and the suggested preparation and procedure. Then practise the questions which follow. Always practise this type of question under exam conditions (i.e. in the allocated time and without the use of text-books or dictionaries – this should give you greater confidence in the examination itself).

1 Write in French, using the past tenses, a letter of 180-200 words on the following subject:

Vous êtes en vacances en France et vous manquez d'argent. Écrivez à vos parents pour leur demander de vous en envoyer, expliquant pourquoi il ne vous reste plus d'argent.

Time allowed: 1 hour

Procedure

This letter is addressed to two people. The opening of the letter and the verb forms used must take account of this. Keep the content simple but include as many idiomatic constructions as possible. Think in French at all stages.

Preparation

1 (Opening)   Mes chers parents,
          or   Chers papa et maman,
2 Le voyage/l'arrivée
3 Le logement/l'hôtel
4 Les repas/affreux
5 Les visites/où?
6 Manque d'argent/à cause de 4 et 5
7 Les projets/encores des visites/magasins
8 Demande de l'argent
9 (Ending)   En attendant de vos nouvelles, je vous embrasse tous les deux. Votre fils (fille) . . .

The completed version would then be along the following lines:

Mes chers parents,

Je suis bien arrivé(e) à Paris lundi dernier. Le voyage était très agréable et nous nous sommes bien amusé(e)s surtout en faisant la traversée de la Manche en paquebot.

Malheureusement, l'hôtel est mauvais et les repas sont affreux. Nouse devons acheter alors quelque chose à manger entre les repas. J'ai dépensé beaucoup d'argent à la pâtisserie et à la confiserie. Les gâteaux sont délicieux mais ils coûtent très cher ainsi que les boissons au café.

Hier, après avoir fait la visite de la Tour Eiffel, nous sommes allé(e)s au Louvre. J'ai acheté beaucoup de cartes postales et aussi des tableaux aux bouquinistes qui se trouvent sur les quais au bord de la Seine. Il y a tant à voir et à faire ici. Je voudrais faire encore des visites et aussi courir les magasins mais je manque d'argent. Vous ne vous étonnerez donc pas si je vous demande de m'envoyer de l'argent – quinze livres si c'est possible. Tout est si cher à Paris.

En attendant de vos nouvelles, je vous embrasse tous les deux.

Votre fils (fille)

. . . . . .

2 Write in French a letter of about 100 words on the following subject:

Vous voulez passer les grandes vacances à travailler sur une ferme en France. Écrivez au fermier en parlant
  – de vous-même;
  – des dates de votre séjour;
  – du logement;
  – de l'argent que vous recevrez;
  – du temps libre.   (AEB)

Time allowed: 40 minutes

Procedure

This letter is addressed to an adult who is not a member of your family. You must therefore use the polite **vous** form of address and begin your letter with the word **Monsieur.** In a formal letter like this, you do not use the word **Cher.**

Preparation

1 (Opening) Monsieur,
2 Plan – as given in title.
3 (Ending) More formal than for a personal letter to a friend or to a member of your family:
    Veuillez agréer, Monsieur, l'assurance de mes sentiments distingués,
or Je vous prie d'agréer, Monsieur, l'expression de mes sentiments distingués.

Completed version

Monsieur,

Je vous écris parce que je voudrais passer les grandes vacances à travailler sur une ferme en France.

Je suis élève au Collège d'Enseignement Secondaire de X. J'ai dix-sept ans et j'espère continuer mes études françaises l'année prochaine. Je voudrais rester un mois en France à partir du vingt-cinq juillet.

Je vous serai reconnaissant(e) si vous pouvez me donner des renseignements sur le logement. Est-ce que je dois apporter une tente et le matériel de camping?

Je voudrais recevoir aussi des détails sur l'argent que je recevrai et les heures de travail et de temps libre.

Veuillez agréer, Monsieur, l'assurance de mes sentiments distingués,

......

Further practice

1 Vous venez de passer des vacances en France chez votre correspondant(e). Écrivez-lui pour lui remercier de votre visite et pour l'inviter à venir passer des vacances chez vous l'année prochaine.

2 Vous voulez passer des vacances en France. Écrivez une lettre au Syndicat d'Initiative de X pour demander des renseignements sur la ville et les hôtels de la région.

3 Écrivez une lettre à votre correspondant(e) pour lui raconter comment vous avez passé vos vacances de Pâques.

4 Écrivez une lettre à votre correspondant(e) pour lui raconter comment vous avez fêté votre anniversaire.

5 Écrivez une lettre à un(e) ami(e) pour l'inviter à passer quelques jours chez vous.

Certain Examination Boards may ask you to write a letter in French in reply to a letter given on the examination paper. The technique for answering this type of question is basically the same as for other letter compositions, but obviously an element of reading comprehension is necessary before you can answer the question.

Given below are two examples of this type of question.

1 Read the following letter carefully. It asks for certain pieces of information. Write a suitable reply in French supplying the information requested.

Your letter should be 100 to 130 words in length. Conventional introductory and concluding phrases forming part of the composition should not be reckoned in the total number of words.

You may choose to reply in your own name. Replies may be addressed to a male or female correspondent.   (SEB)

Time allowed: 35 minutes

Toulouse, le vingt-deux mars

Cher Douglas,

Nous étions tous très tristes de recevoir ton télégramme. Maintenant tu ne peux plus venir nous voir pendant les vacances de Pâques.

Tu t'es cassé la jambe? C'est bien bête, ça, tu sais. Comment as-tu fait cela? Est-ce que tu es resté longtemps à l'hôpital? Que fais-tu à la maison maintenant? J'espère que ta petite sœur ne t'ennuie pas trop. Quand est-ce qu'on va enlever le plâtre?

Je viens d'avoir une idée formidable! Veux-tu venir en France pendant les grandes vacances? Je serais tellement content de te montrer ma ville.

Écris-moi bientôt,

Ton copain,

Marcel

2 Vous êtes un jeune Français, et vous recevez cette lettre d'un ami anglais. Écrivez-lui une réponse. (AEB)

Time allowed: 40 minutes   Length: about 100 words

Manchester, le 6 septembre 19 . .

Mon cher Michel,

Excuse-moi, mais j'ai perdu ta dernière lettre où tu me posais beaucoup de questions sur ma vie au lycée, sur ma famille, et sur mes vacances, et j'ai oublié ce que tu voulais savoir. Je t'ai déjà dit que j'ai deux sœurs, que j'aime beaucoup mes études, et que j'ai passé quinze jours à Blackpool. Quelles étaient les autres choses que tu voulais savoir? Veux-tu me dire, toi aussi, ce que tu fais? Comment as-tu passé dimanche dernier, par exemple? On m'a dit qu'on joue au football le dimanche en France – est-ce vrai?

Écris-moi vite,
Ton ami anglais,

Peter

TOPIC COMPOSITION

This type of composition is sometimes called an 'outline' or 'structured' composition. The topic of the composition is given and the candidate is asked to write about that topic in a specified number of words. In the outline or structured composition certain ideas are given as to the information required in the composition, e.g. Quand? Où? Avec qui? etc.

Example

Tell the story outlined below, using the past tenses.   (WJEC)

Length: 180-200 words   Time allowed: 1 hour

Vous avez chez vous un certain nombre de souris blanches. Un jour, une de ces petites bêtes s'échappe.

Décrivez comment vous essayez de la reprendre et de la protéger contre le chat d'un voisin.

(a) L'évasion de la cage. Votre négligence. Vos réactions. Vos enquêtes.

(b) La chasse. Les endroits où vous la recherchez. Vos premiers efforts pour la reprendre.

(c) L'apparition du chat. Vos peurs. Redoublement d'efforts. Résultats? Le retour chez vous. L'accueil.

You may use as you wish the suggestions given and may add any relevant detail.

In this type of free composition, the basic plan is given to you and you must build your essay on this plan. The details will be your own but they must fit in with the main idea(s) already given. You may find it useful to imagine that you are telling a friend about the incident. The main tenses will be the perfect and imperfect tenses.

Suggested answer

Pour mon anniversaire mon frère m'a offert quatre souris blanches. Ma mère ne les aimait pas et m'a dit de les garder dans ma chambre. Elle m'a défendu de laisser ouverte la porte de ma chambre. Pendant quelques jours j'ai été très sage et je n'avais pas oublié de fermer la porte, mais un jour mon ami Marcel m'a téléphoné au sujet d'une boum ce soir-là chez Pierre et malheureusement j'ai oublié de fermer la porte de ma chambre.

En retournant à ma chambre je n'ai trouvé que trois souris. J'avais grand'peur et je suis allé(e) tout de suite demander à mon frère s'il avait vu ma souris. Mais tout en lui parlant j'ai vu ma souris qui descendait l'escalier. Nous nous sommes mis à la chasse mais elle est sortie par la porte de la cuisine.

A ce moment j'ai vu le chat de notre voisin dans notre jardin. Je me suis élancé par la porte et j'ai sauté sur ma souris. Je l'ai sauvée! Très content(e), je suis rentré(e) dans la maison.

Further practice

1 Un chien égaré

Vous vous promenez dans la rue – avec qui? – quand? – pourquoi?

Vous trouvez un chien égaré. Vous l'attrapez. Comment?

Que faites-vous après? Qu'est-ce qu'on dit à la maison?

2 Au voleur!

Vous passez quelques jours chez un(e) ami(e). Où? Pourquoi?

Vous voyez un cambrioleur qui entre par la fenêtre de la maison d'en face.

Que faites-vous? Comment est-ce qu'on attrape le cambrioleur?

3 Accident au bord de la mer

Vous passez des vacances au bord de la mer. Où? Avec qui?
Vous descendez à la plage. Vous voyez des enfants tomber d'un bateau.
Que faites-vous? Comment se termine l'incident?

4 Au milieu de la nuit

Vous êtes très fatigué. Pourquoi? Et vous vous couchez de bonne heure.
Au milieu de la nuit vous entendez des bruits étranges.
Vous vous levez pour voir ce qui se passe. Racontez cet incident.

5 En retard pour l'école

Un matin vous vous levez en retard. Pourquoi?
Vous vous dépêchez mais vous manquez l'autobus.
Racontez comment vous arrivez à l'école et ce que disent vos amis et vos professeurs.

PICTURE COMPOSITION TYPE 1

In this type of composition candidates are asked to tell the story suggested by a series of pictures. At CSE level questions about the pictures are sometimes asked to help you with your composition, but at O level words and phrases in French are rarely given.

Example

Write a composition in French (180-200 words) using the past tenses to tell the story illustrated in the pictures.   (WJEC)

Procedure

This type of free composition requires initially a different approach from the letter or topic composition. You should spend about five minutes looking carefully at the picture sequence in order to familiarise yourself with the story. When you feel that you understand the sequence you should begin to make notes *in French*. When you begin to write your composition you should aim to write about the same number of words for each picture where possible. As a rough guide, you should divide the total number of words required by the number of pictures. Remember, however, that this is only a rough guide and that you must use your common sense if some pictures need fewer or more words than the others. Try to use French names for people and places in your composition where suitable. Having written your composition, you must, as always, check what you have written carefully.

Preparation

You are asked to use the past tenses. For most O-level examinations this means the perfect and imperfect tenses. If you wish to use the past historic tense for this type of composition, you should check the current Syllabus and Regulations Schedule for your particular Examination Board to see if this tense is acceptable at this level.

Plan

1 Beau jour d'été – au bord de la mer – à moto.
2 Chaud – plage – maillot/caleçon – bavarder.
3 Plonger dans l'eau – deux voyous – s'emparer de la moto.
4 Plus tard – se rhabiller – chercher la moto – disparue.
5 Se fâcher – poste de police – raconter ce qui s'est passé – rentrée en autobus.
6 L'arrêt d'autobus – malheureux – rentrée.

Completed version

L'année dernière, par un beau jour d'été, Jean-Paul et Marie-Jeanne ont décidé d'aller passer la journée au bord de la mer. Jean-Paul venait d'acheter une jolie moto bleue. C'était sa première excursion à sa nouvelle moto. Ils sont allés à Deauville et se sont arrêtés près d'une falaise.

Il faisait très chaud ce jour-là. Ils sont descendus à la plage où ils ont mis leurs maillots de bain. Jean-Paul a mis un caleçon de bain rayé. Ils ont commencé à bavarder. Mais ils avaient bientôt très chaud. Ils ont décidé donc d'aller se baigner à la mer. Ils n'ont pas remarqué deux voyous près de leur moto. Dix minutes plus tard les deux voyous se sont emparés de la moto.

Quelques heures plus tard, Jean-Paul et Marie-Jeanne ont décidé de retourner en ville. Ils se sont rhabillés et ils sont allés chercher la moto. Quelle horreur! La moto avait disparu.

Ils se sont très fâchés et ont couru vite au poste de police raconter ce qui s'est passé. Ils ont trouvé un agent de police très sympathique. Après avoir noté les détails, l'agent de police leur a conseillé de rentrer en autobus. Ils sont allés donc à l'arrêt d'autobus et un car est bientôt arrivé. Malheureux, ils sont retournés en ville.

Adaptation

The number of words you have to use will vary according to your Examination Board. 200 words is the maximum required at O level for a single composition. The above plan could be used for compositions of a shorter length. The amount of detail would be reduced according to the number of words required.

Some Examination Boards may ask you to be one of the people in the story. In that case you would adapt the above composition to the first person forms (**je/nous**) of the verbs, where applicable.

CSE

Pictures similar to those above are sometimes set at CSE level. A simplified version of the above story would be required, and possibly a change of tense. The present tense is sometimes specified at this level.

Example

Write a composition in French (100-130 words) using the present tense to tell the story illustrated in the pictures.

Plan

This would be similar to the O-level plan with one or two simplifications.

Completed version

Aujourd'hui Jean et Marie décident d'aller au bord de la mer à moto. Il fait très chaud. Quand ils arrivent à la plage ils mettent leurs maillots de bain. Bientôt ils décident de se baigner parce qu'ils ont très chaud. Pendant qu'ils nagent dans la mer, deux garçons volent leur moto.

Quelques heures plus tard, ils décident de rentrer. Ils s'habillent et vont chercher la moto, mais elle n'est pas là. Ils décident donc d'aller au poste de police. Ils racontent à l'agent ce qui s'est passé. La pauvre Marie commence à pleurer. Ils doivent rentrer en autobus. Ils vont à l'arrêt d'autobus et un car arrive bientôt. Ils sont très tristes quand ils retournent à la maison.

Further practice

Look at the pictures below and use them for further free composition practice. Use the same number of words that you will have to use in the examination and practise writing the composition in the required time.

1

2

3

PICTURE COMPOSITION TYPE 2

Some Examination Boards at CSE level use individual pictures, accompanied by written questions, to test the candidate's ability to express himself in French. The pictures may or may not be connected.

Procedure

1 When answering this type of question, you must not only look carefully at the picture(s), but also read the questions carefully.

2 Always read the questions at least twice to make sure that you have understood them.

3 Pay special attention to the tense of the verb as this will be useful to you in your answer.

4 Check the subject of the verb to see if it is singular or plural.

Look at the examples below and write down your answers. Then check them with the answers on pages 156–7.

1 Café

(a) Où se passe cette scène?

(b) Combien de dames voyez-vous?

(c) Que font-elles?

(d) Que fait le garçon?

2 Countryside

(a) Que porte le monsieur?

(b) Où sont les vaches?

(c) Quel temps fait-il?

(d) Qu'est-ce qu'on va manger?

3 House

(a) Que fait l'homme?

(b) Où est-il assis?

(c) Que font les enfants?

(d) Dans quelle salle est-on?

4 By the river

(a) Où se passe cette scène?
(b) Que fait l'homme?

(c) Comment est-il habillé?
(d) Où est le chien?

5 School

(a) Où se passe cette scène?
(b) Combien d'enfants voyez-vous?

(c) Est-ce que la porte est fermée?
(d) Que fait le garçon près du professeur?

6 (SWEB)

(a) Où est-ce que le garçon arrive?
(b) Comment est-il arrivé?
(c) Pourquoi est-il venu?

7 (SWEB)

(a) Combien de personnes y a-t-il?
(b) Que fait la famille?
(c) Pourquoi est-ce que les deux enfants rient?

8 (SWEB)

(a) Où sont les deux personnes?
(b) Que fait la fillette?
(c) Qu'est-ce que la mère dira à la fillette?

9 (SWEB)

(a) Quand est-ce que cette scène se passe?
(b) Que va faire le professeur?
(c) Que faisaient les deux garçons quand il les a vus?

10 (SWEB)

(a) De quelle nationalité est le chauffeur de l'auto?
(b) Qu'est-ce que le chauffeur du camion va dire?
(c) Expliquez pourquoi il y a eu un accident.

11 (WJEC)

Look carefully at these pictures and answer *in French,* in complete sentences, the questions which are printed beneath each picture.

(a) Combien de garçons voyez-vous?
(b) Comment passent-ils leurs vacances?
(c) Pourquoi poussent-ils leurs vélos?
(d) Comment sont les garçons?

(e) Où vont-ils passer la nuit?
(f) Pourquoi est-ce que le garçon à gauche allume le feu?
(g) Pourquoi est-ce que le garçon à droite va à la ferme?
(h) Que fait le troisième garçon?

(i) Décrivez cette image. (Write your answer in 25-30 words.)

(j) Où est-ce que les garçons ont décidé de passer la nuit?
(k) Pourquoi la dame est-elle venue à la grange? (*barn*)
(l) Que fait le fermier?
(m) Comment est-ce que le fermier et sa femme sont habillés?

CONTINUATION COMPOSITION

For this type of composition, you may be given the beginning or the ending of a story in French, and you will then be asked to write your own story in French based on the opening or ending given; or, you may be given a passage to read in French and then asked to write a paragraph illustrating some incident from the passage.

Procedure

This type of composition gives great scope to the imagination. The content of the composition will be your own. You must, however, be careful to write a composition which is within your capabilities in French. Whatever you write must be grammatically accurate. Do not let your imagination run away with you, and *think in French* all the time, both during the planning stage and when actually writing the full version of the story. Avoid an over-complicated plot, but try to make your subject-matter interesting.

Once you have written your plan in French, you should then follow the procedure for the outline or structured composition.

1 Read the following passage carefully, then answer *two* of the questions which follow. (JMB)
Time allowed: 45 minutes

Paula confides in her cousin
Paula embrassa sa cousine Yvonne et s'assit dans un fauteuil:
  – Je ne peux plus travailler, dit-elle. Je suis si fatiguée.
  – Tu fais trop de travail au bureau.
  – C'est bien vrai!
  – Mais tu rentres d'un mois au bord de la mer, tu devrais te sentir en pleine forme.
Paula soupira:
  – Malheureusement ce n'est pas le cas . . .
  – Comment se sont passées les vacances?
Elle haussa les épaules:
  – Avec mon mari, les trois enfants et une maison à tenir?
  – Tu devrais partir seule de temps en temps. Cela te ferait le plus grand bien.

Choose *two* of the questions below.
In each case, write between 75 to 80 words in *French*.
To obtain high marks you must use other tenses of the verb than the present.

(a) Imaginez un incident vexant qui s'est passé pendant les vacances de Paula et de sa famille.
(b) Racontez la journée de Paula au bureau pour montrer pourquoi elle est si fatiguée.
(c) Continuez cette conversation. Imaginez ce qu'Yvonne propose à sa cousine et les réponses de Paula. Écrivez seulement les paroles des deux femmes.

2 Do not write out the following paragraph, but continue the story in French using about 150 words. (Oxford)
Time allowed: 50 minutes

En quittant le supermarché, Mme Lefèvre a vu sa propre voiture qui sortait du parking, conduite par une femme qu'elle ne connaissait pas.

DIALOGUE CONTINUATION

Certain Examination Boards will ask you to write a dialogue-continuation.
In this type of productive-writing test you must take care to use the correct forms of address, **tu** or **vous**. Look at the advice given in the letter section if you are unsure about this.
Here are some examples of dialogue questions.

1 Continue the following conversation. Write about 120 words in French. (SEB)
  – Allô! C'est toi, Jean(ne)?
  – Oui. Qui parle?
  – Ici Louis(e). Ça fait déjà huit jours que je ne t'ai pas vu(e).

2 Continue the following conversation. (100-130 words) (NIEB)
Marie-Thérèse: Bonjour, Jean-Paul. Comment vas-tu?
Jean-Paul: Pas très bien. J'ai passé une très mauvaise journée à l'école.

3 Write a conversation between a hotel guest and the manager, in which the guest is making a complaint. (50-100 words) (EMREB)

4 In the following question you are asked to complete the dialogues by supplying, in French, appropriate answers. You should use complete sentences. (SEB)
Time allowed: 30 minutes

(a) You have lost your little brother in a big store. An assistant is trying to help you to find him by asking a few questions.

(i) Vendeuse: Quel âge a-t-il, votre frère?
  . . . . . .
(ii) Vendeuse: Comment est-il?
  . . . . . .

(iii) Vendeuse: Qu'est-ce qu'il porte comme vêtements?

. . . . . .

(iv) Vendeuse: Où étiez-vous quand il a disparu?

. . . . . .

 (v) Vendeuse: Où est-ce que vous l'avez déjà cherché?

. . . . . .

(b) You are staying with your pen-friend in France. One evening you arrive back at his house later than expected from a visit to a neighbouring town. Your anxious friend asks a few questions.

 (i) Ami: Quel train devais-tu prendre?

. . . . . .

 (ii) Ami: Qu'est-ce qui s'est passé?

. . . . . .

(iii) Ami: Combien de temps as-tu attendu?

. . . . . .

(iv) Ami: Qu'est-ce que tu as fait pour passer le temps?

. . . . . .

 (v) Ami: Pourquoi n'as-tu pas téléphoné?

. . . .

All of the questions above have many possible answers as they depend on your own imagination. For specimen answers to question 4 turn to page 157.

STORY REPRODUCTION

This type of composition requires you to re-write in French, using your own words, the story read to you in French. In some ways this type of composition is similar to the outline or structured composition in that some words and phrases are given in written form to the candidates. However, you are not free to make up your own story, but must reproduce the story you will have heard, keeping to the outline given on the question paper.

Procedure

During the reading of the story you may not normally make any notes, but you may look at the written outline on the question paper. You will also be able to look at the written outline when you write the story in your own words. You must not, however, treat this composition as a dictation exercise. Naturally, your version will not be exactly word for word the same as the original story, but it must follow the same logical progression. Do not invent extra details of your own, but keep to the facts that you are given.

Example

Here is an example of the kind of story you might *hear,* but remember that you would not *see* this story.

No sense of humour (O & C)

Un jour après le déjeuner, la maîtresse annonça à la classe qu'on attendait la visite du nouvel inspecteur.

– Ce n'est pas l'ancien inspecteur que vous connaissez, dit-elle. Je vous prie d'être très sages, et surtout de ne pas rire.

On s'occupa donc à tout mettre en ordre pour faire une bonne impression sur l'inspecteur. La maîtresse demanda à Jeannette de ranger les pots de peinture qu'on avait utilisés le matin pour la leçon de dessin. Mais juste au moment où la jeune fille tenait dans sa main un pot plein de couleur, quelqu'un cria: – Voilà l'inspecteur! Elle en fut tellement surprise qu'elle renversa la peinture sur la table. Il fallait rapidement changer les tables de place, afin de cacher la grande tache de couleur. Les élèves étaient au milieu de cette confusion quand l'inspecteur entra.

– Que faites-vous là? dit-il de sa grosse voix. Asseyez-vous cet instant. Mais les tables étaient mal placées, deux élèves avaient même leur dos au tableau noir. Il leur demanda de retourner leur table et appuya ses deux mains sur la tache de couleur, qu'il n'avait pas vue. Il se mit à raconter à la classe une histoire drôle, mais quand il avait fini, pas un seul élève ne sourit. Ils n'avaient pas oublié la demande de leur maîtresse!

L'inspecteur, perplexe, s'essuya le front avec sa main. A ce moment précis, la classe éclata de rire, car l'inspecteur avait mis de la peinture partout sur son visage.

– Ça alors! dit-il, vous ne riez pas quand je raconte une histoire drôle, et puis vous éclatez de rire pour rien du tout. Vous avez donc perdu le sens de l'humour?

The story would be read aloud twice and the following instructions and outline would be given:
Write a piece of free composition in French giving the story read to you.
Write between 150 and 160 words using the past tenses.

Outline

On attend l'inspecteur – ne pas rire – on range la salle – Jeannette renverse la peinture – confusion – table mal placée – l'histoire drôle – la peinture au front.

GENERAL ADVICE

Whichever type of free composition you write, remember that when you have written the final version, you must check your work thoroughly. This is just as important as the actual writing of the composition itself and may prevent your losing important marks.

Memorise the following check list:

1 Does your composition make sense?
2 Does it have a logical progression?
3 Have you used the correct number of words?
4 Have you written your composition in the correct personal form (i.e. **tu/vous, je/nous, il/elle,** or **ils/elles**)?
5 Have you used the correct tenses?

If you can answer 'yes' to all the five questions above, then you should check the following:

1 Verb-forms:
   Do they agree with their subject?
   Are they spelt correctly?
   Do the past participles of the verbs in the perfect tense have the correct agreement (where applicable)?

2 Nouns and adjectives:
   Do they agree?
   Are they spelt correctly?
   Are the adjectives in the correct position?

3 Adverbs and prepositions:
   Are they spelt correctly?
   Are they in the correct position?
   Are they the right ones to use?

This checking of your work will take time. You should allow five to ten minutes at the end of your allocated time to check your work thoroughly. Use all the time that you are given as there will always be something that you can do to improve your composition.

7 Translation: English to French

Translation from English to French is not compulsory in the French examination of most Examination Boards. However, most GCE O-level Examination Boards do include a prose translation question as an alternative to an additional free composition. (This means that if you do not answer the prose translation question you will be required to write an extra free composition.) Some Examination Boards do have a compulsory English to French translation question.

Even if your Examination Board offers this as an alternative question, you would be well advised to prepare English to French translation in order to allow yourself a wide choice of questions. In the weeks before the examination, you should perfect your technique for answering this type of question. Practise translating using the guidelines given below.

Never attempt to translate from English to French by taking one word at a time and trying to find a French equivalent for that word.

Prose translation (English to French) is designed specifically to test certain common grammatical constructions. It is a set test and not just an arbitrary piece of English which the examiner just happens to have chosen. Try to 'detect' all the grammatical points which are being tested by the passage of English to be translated.

Use the following list as a guideline when preparing a passage for translation:

1 Read the passage through carefully.

2 If there is direct speech to be translated, decide which form of the second person (**tu** or **vous**) you must use. If the relationship between the speakers is a close one, or if the person speaking is addressing a child, or if the speakers are children speaking to each other, then you should use the **tu** form. Otherwise, for strangers or people who are not members of the same family, the **vous** form should be used.

3 Check *all* verbs and their tenses. Translate them in advance, if you wish, paying particular attention to those verbs which require **être** in the perfect tense.

Passages for translation

The first two passages include examples of the preparation required before the passages are finally translated.

1 (Oxford)   *Time allowed: 50 minutes*

Peter was angry. In summer he liked to go and see his cousins who lived in the country. There he and his sister could make plenty of noise, play by the lake and go for walks in the woods. They usually went there in August during their holidays, and enjoyed themselves very much. Another uncle had just telephoned from Paris. Peter did not know him very well. This uncle was inviting him to spend a whole month in France in order to learn to speak French like a Frenchman. Peter did not want to accept this invitation. He thought that it would be difficult and that he would not understand what people were saying. Perhaps he would not like the meals. The whole family talked about it for a long time. Finally his father said he could go by air. 'All right,' said Peter, 'buy me a ticket please.'

Grammatical analysis
Use the French form for Peter – Pierre.
Use the **tu** form in the direct speech at the end as a son is speaking to his father.
'to go *and see*' – infinitive required in French – **aller voir**.
'*in* the country' – **à** la campagne.
'*in* the woods' – **aux** bois.
'They *usually* went' – the adverb must follow the verb.
'very much' – **beaucoup.** Do not try to translate 'very'.
'had just' – imperfect tense of **venir de** required.
'did not *know him*' – 'know' refers to a person, therefore **connaître** is required.
'him' – the pronoun must be placed before the verb.
'a *whole* month' – the adjective must follow the noun.
'in France' – **en France.**
'in order to' – **pour.**
'this invitation' – feminine noun – **cette** invitation.
'understand *what*' = 'that which' (object). Use **ce que** – invert verb and subject after this.
'perhaps' – *either* **peut-être** + inverted verb and subject pronoun,
           or **peut-être que . . . .**

'The whole family' – **Toute la famille**.
'about it' – pronoun '**en**' required before the verb.
'*by* air' – **en** avion.

Verb analysis
'was angry' – imperfect tense for description – **était en colère.**
'he liked' – imperfect tense (continuous feeling) – **aimait.**
'(his cousins) who lived' – imperfect tense (description) – **qui habitaient.**
'(he and his sister) could make' – were able (repeated action) – **pouvaient faire.**

'They (usually) went' – imperfect tense (repeated action) – **ils allaient**.

'enjoyed themselves' – imperfect tense (repeated action) – **s'amusaient**.

'did not know' – imperfect tense (continuous state in past) – **connaissait**.

'was inviting' – imperfect tense – **invitait**.

'did not want' – imperfect tense (continuous) – **ne voulait pas**.

'He thought' = 'was thinking' – **croyait**.

'it would be' – conditional tense – **ce serait**.

'he would not understand' – conditional tense – **il ne comprendrait pas**.

'(people) were saying' – imperfect tense – **disaient**.

'he would not like' – conditional tense – **il n'aimerait pas**.

'The whole family talked about it' – perfect tense for completed action – **Toute la famille en a parlé**.

'his father said' – perfect tense (completed action) – **son père a dit**.

'he could go' = 'he would be able to go' – conditional tense of **pouvoir: il pourrait aller**.

'said Peter' – perfect tense – **a dit Pierre**.

'buy me' – imperative – **achète-moi**.

2 (WJEC) *Time allowed: 1 hour*

My name is Philippe. Last summer, mother and I spent several weeks in Scotland with some friends who had rented a house on the coast. We made the journey by train.

One evening, I was going for a walk on my own when I noticed two boys playing on some rocks. Suddenly, one of them slipped and fell into the sea.

I thought at first that he was going to drown, for he could not swim. Then, fortunately, a tourist who was fishing nearby succeeded in saving him with a line.

The man was soaked, but, instead of losing his temper, he turned towards the boy and told him gently: 'If you're wise, you'll learn to swim as soon as possible.'

Grammatical analysis

Direct speech at end of passage – the man would use the **tu** form when speaking to the boy.

'My name is' – use **s'appeler**, i.e. **je m'appelle**.

'Last summer' – invert noun and adjective and use 'the': **L'été dernier**.

'mother and I . . .' – remember to use the **nous** form of the verb.

'on the coast' = 'by the sea' – **au bord de la mer**.

'by train' – **par le train**.

'on my own' – one word needed, **seul**.

'playing' – use a definitive verb instead of the present participle – **qui jouaient**.

'for' – in the sense of 'because' = **car**.

'*could* not swim' = 'did not know how to' – **ne savait pas nager**.

'succeeded *in*' – **a réussi à**.

'saving him' – infinitive required after the preposition **à**, and remember to place the object pronoun before the verb.

'instead of losing' – **au lieu de** + infinitive.

'told him' – correct object pronoun **lui** (*to him*) must be placed before the verb.

'as soon as possible' – **aussitôt que possible**.

Verb analysis

'(mother and I) spent' – perfect tense for completed action – **avons passé**.

'(friends who) had rented' – pluperfect tense – **avaient loué**.

'we made (the journey)' – perfect tense for completed action – **nous avons fait le voyage**.

'I was going for a walk' – imperfect tense (description) – **je me promenais**.

'I noticed' – perfect tense (completed action) – **j'ai remarqué**.

'(one of them) slipped and fell' – Different auxiliary verbs are used here with the perfect tense: **a glissé et est tombé**.

'I thought' (next event) – perfect tense required – **J'ai pensé**.

'he was going to drown' – imperfect tense – **il allait se noyer**.

'(a tourist who) was fishing' – imperfect tense – **pêchait**.

'(The man) was soaked' – imperfect tense for description – **était trempé**.

'he turned towards' – perfect tense (next event) of reflexive verb – **Il s'est tourné vers**.

'told him' – perfect tense (next event) – **lui a dit**.

'you're wise' – present tense – **tu es sage**.

'you'll learn' – future tense – **tu apprendras**.

3 (SUJB)   *Time allowed: 1¼ hours*

It was the first time that Robert had left his hosts since his arrival in France the week before. Monsieur Deschamps had some business to do in town, and Robert's correspondent, Pierre, wanted to go to the library, so Robert accompanied them, and then went off to the fair in the park, where his friends would join him later. He wandered among the crowds, and even tried some of the attractions. Suddenly he felt a shock and nearly fell to the ground. He turned round and saw a young man with a beard, who murmured, 'Sorry, my boy,' and ran away. It was only later that he discovered that his wallet was no longer in his pocket.

When the Deschamps arrived he told them what had happened. 'Was there a lot of money in the wallet?' asked M. Deschamps. 'Only about ten francs,' he replied. 'All the same, we ought to go and see my old friend the police superintendent.'

The superintendent listened seriously to their story, and to the description that Robert gave of the young man. 'I think it must be Robert Aramis,' he said. 'He is a well-known young criminal. My men will question him. You probably won't get your money back, but we'll see.'

4 (WJEC)   *Time allowed: 1 hour*

A few days ago I had just finished breakfast when someone knocked at the door.

'It's the postman. Go and see what he's brought us, Robert,' shouted my mother who was in the kitchen.

When I opened the door, the postman, whom I knew well, gave me a parcel. 'How is your father today?' he asked, for he knew that father had been ill for several weeks.

'He is much better, thank you. He is hoping to get up soon,' I replied. On entering the kitchen I noticed that it was nearly half past eight. 'Hurry up,' said my mother. 'You won't be at school before nine o'clock.'

I live about three kilometres from school and there is no bus. I picked up my books, said goodbye and set off at once.

5 (Oxford)   *Time allowed: 50 minutes*

My uncle, who lives in the country, comes to visit us in London once a year. My sister and I always ask him to take us to the theatre. He likes to do this because he never sees a play in his little village. So everyone is happy and his visit is a great success.

This year he arrived on the day before my birthday. 'Well,' he said, 'You'll be sixteen tomorrow. I think we ought to hear an opera instead of seeing a play. Would you like that?' I replied that it would please me very much, and my sister, who plays the violin, was delighted.

'Don't pay too much attention to the story. It will probably seem a little silly to you, but art and life are two different things. Listen to the music.' It was an interesting evening. We had a marvellous meal afterwards, during which my uncle explained all that we had not understood.

6   *Time allowed: 45 minutes*

Last year, after spending two weeks in Paris, John decided to catch the midday train at the Gare du Nord. The weather was fine and the sun shone on that particular day. During his stay in Paris, John had enjoyed himself very much and was sad that he had to leave such a beautiful city.

At half past eleven he left the hotel on foot for he didn't have much luggage and he always liked walking. When he arrived at the station he bought a newspaper and a magazine. After buying them he realised that he had only five francs left, but he still had some English money which he would be able to spend on the ferry. He hoped that the crossing would be calm and that he would not be sea-sick. Next year he hoped to return to France but this time by plane.

7   *Time allowed: 45 minutes*

One winter morning, Peter and his mother, who lived in a small flat near the centre of the town, went out to do some shopping. Peter was only three years old and did not yet go to school. Louise, his elder sister who was thirteen years old, was a pupil at the comprehensive school. She liked her school very much, but always had a lot of homework to do.

Peter liked going shopping with his mother because she would buy him a bar of chocolate if he was good. His mother was anxious because the weather was so cold and Peter was often ill in winter.

'Put on your gloves and scarf, Peter,' she said, before going out. 'You must not catch cold.'

8   *Time allowed: 45 minutes*

'Get up at once!' Dad said to Annette. 'You mother is in the kitchen and breakfast is ready.'

'I have a headache and I don't want to get up,' replied Annette.

'What's the matter?' shouted mother from the kitchen.

'Annette says that she has a headache and doesn't want to get up,' said Dad.

Mrs Leclerc knew that her daughter was very lazy and was pretending to be ill. Today Annette had to help her mother to do the housework and Annette was always ill when there was work to do.

'If she has a headache, she won't have any breakfast,' replied mother.

Annette, who was always hungry, did not want to miss breakfast, so she decided to get up at once and go down to the kitchen.

8 Translation: French to English

This type of test is normally only for O-level candidates. The most important point to remember when translating a passage of French into English is that your final version must *make sense* and must be written in *normal English*. A person reading your translation should be able to understand it as he or she would understand a piece of normal English. Many candidates believe that they must translate word for word every feature of the French grammatical construction before them. A stilted non-English translation will earn you few marks.

Try to use the following procedure when translating from French into English:

1 Pay attention to the English title if there is one. It is there to help you understand the topic of the passage.

2 Read the passage several times until you are familiar with the main idea(s). Do not worry about individual vocabulary items at this stage. Concentrate on the main outline of the story.

3 Make a first translation by reading each sentence or part of a sentence (if the sentence is a long one) and translating it into normal, everyday English.

4 Read again the French sentence you have just translated in order to check that you have not left out any important information. *Do not* translate one word at a time. Languages cannot be translated satisfactorily in that way. Each language has its own way of saying things and you must find out the normal English equivalent of the French sentence in front of you.

5 Do not leave gaps, even in your first translation. The temptation is always very strong to leave a gap for a word you do not know, in the belief that the missing word will be found later. Experience has proved that gaps often remain unfilled even in a final translation. Always put in some suitable word in your first translation. Then, if you do run out of time, you will at least have something on the paper which fits, even if it is not the exact word.

6 When you have completed your first translation, read through your English version to see if it makes sense and reads like a normal piece of English. If it doesn't, work on those sections which are not quite right, always checking back to the text.

7 When you are satisfied with your English version, read the entire French passage again to make sure that you have not left anything out.

8 Finally re-write your completed version (if necessary), paying particular attention to English style and spelling. Remember to use normal English punctuation.

You should always have plenty of time for the above procedure if you concentrate hard at all stages. Thorough reading of the passage at the beginning is very important. Too many candidates begin their translation without really knowing what the passage is about. Do not rush through your translation making up your own story. You must translate what is on the paper and not what you *think* is on the paper. French to English translation requires as much care as English to French translation.

Are you a wide reader? Wide reading of *good* English will improve your fluency and cut down time wasted in the examination searching for the right word or phrase.

Now look at the example below.

Unhappy memories (AEB)

– Ne regarde pas tout le temps ta montre, Jean. Il n'y a que dix minutes que nous sommes ensemble et tu t'inquiètes déjà de l'heure! Qu'est-ce qu'il y a? A quoi penses-tu?

– C'est que j'avais promis à Daniel de lui téléphoner à huit heures. Il faut lui dire ce soir si je veux accepter la situation qu'il m'a offerte ou non. Mais toi, Marie, tu ne t'y intéresses pas, non?

– Mais si! Tu n'avais qu'à me le dire. Je ne savais pas ce qui occupait tes pensées. Je croyais que tu t'ennuyais, c'est tout. Mais dis-moi, quelle décision as-tu prise?

– Aucune. C'est difficile. Parce que si j'accepte, je dois aller vivre à Lyon, et c'est si loin de toi. Mais si je ne saisis pas cette occasion, elle ne se présentera peut-être pas deux fois. Qu'en penses-tu?

– As-tu considéré que je pourrais moi aussi aller à Lyon?

C'est ainsi, se rappela Jean, que lui et Marie s'étaient décidés à se marier. Mais quinze ans s'étaient écoulés depuis ce moment, et Marie était morte deux ans seulement après leur mariage. Jean pensait souvent à elle. Quand il rentrait le soir il s'attendait toujours à l'entendre qui préparait le dîner à la cuisine, tout en chantant une de ses chansons préférées de Brassens ou de Brel.

– Bizarre, ça, se dit Jean en entrant dans le salon. J'ai tous ces disques que Marie aimait tant, et cependant je ne les écoute jamais.

Et, sans se donner le temps de changer d'avis, il se dirigea vers l'électrophone.

1 Title – **Unhappy memories.**

2 Having read the passage (several times if necessary) we find that the outline of the story is as follows:

John is thinking of the past – fifteen years ago – when one evening he met Mary and told her that he had to make a decision about taking a job which would mean going to live in Lyons. John and Mary married and went to live in Lyons, but Mary died two years later. John remembers that he still has some records of Mary's favourite singers and he decides to listen to them.

(You will not have time in the examination to write down this outline. It should be prepared *mentally*.)

3 Your first translation will, of course, be a personal one. Concentrate on good English even at this stage.

4, 5, 6, 7 These sections will be personal too. Always work carefully and remember that English grammar and spelling are important. You will be penalised for mistakes in English as you would be in French.

8 Your final version should be on the following lines:

Translation	**Points to remember**
'Don't look at your watch all the time, John[1].	[1] John – translate well-known names.
We've only been[2] together for ten minutes	[2] **il y a . . . que** is like the **depuis** construction.
and you're already worrying about the time.[3]	[3] 'time' – **l'heure.**
What's the matter?[4] What are you thinking about?'	[4] 'matter' – **Qu'est-ce qu'il y a?**
'It's just[5] that I had	[5] 'just' – English addition for sake of style.
promised[6] Daniel that I	[6] 'promised' – do not translate 'à'.
would[7] phone him at eight o'clock.	[7] 'would' – better style than the infinitive in English.
I must[8] tell him this evening whether I wish	[8] 'must' – do not translate as 'it is necessary'.
to accept the job[9] he has offered me or not.	[9] 'job' – not 'situation'.
But you're[10] not interested in that, Mary,	[10] 'you're' – not necessary to translate every word here.
are you?'[11]	[11] 'are you' – a much better translation than the literal 'no' for **non**.

'Oh[12] yes! You only had to tell me about it. I didn't know what was preoccupying you. I thought you were bored, that's all. But tell me, what have you decided?'

'Nothing. It's difficult. Because if I accept, I'll have to go and[13] live in Lyons, and it's so far from you. But if I don't take this opportunity[14], perhaps it won't come up again.[15] What do you think about[16] it?'

'Have you considered that I could go and live in Lyons too?'

So it was[17], John remembered, that he and Mary had decided to get married. But fifteen years had passed since then[18], and Mary had died only[19] two years after their marriage. John often thought of her. When he came home in the evenings, he still[20] expected to hear her getting[21] dinner ready in the kitchen, whilst singing one of her favourite[22] songs by Brassens or[23] Brel.

'That's strange[24],' John said to himself, going into the sitting-room. 'I've all these records which Mary used to like so much, and yet I never listen to them.'

And without giving himself time[25] to change his mind, he went straight to the record-player.

[12] 'Oh' – do not translate **mais** literally here.

[13] 'and' – instead of the infinitive.

[14] 'opportunity' – not 'occasion' in English.

[15] 'again' – **deux fois.**

[16] 'about' – **penser (de)** – to have an opinion about.

[17] 'was' – the French use of **c'est** is idiomatic.

[18] 'then' – **ce moment.**

[19] 'only' – N.B. word order in English.

[20] 'still' – N.B. word order, also this meaning of **toujours.**

[21] 'getting' – the imperfect is not necessary in English here.

[22] 'favourite' – not 'preferred'.

[23] **(de)** – repetition not required in English.

[24] 'strange' – N.B. word order.

[25] 'time' – 'the' is not necessary in English.

In the above passage, there are very few really difficult problems of vocabulary. You might, perhaps, have forgotten such words as 'tu t'inquiètes', 'prise' (past participle of **prendre,** with agreement), or 's'étaient écoulés' but you could easily work out a close, if not exact, translation by considering carefully what comes just before or after.

In this passage, the problems of translation lie in finding the best English equivalent for a given word or phrase, for example:

l'heure – which is best translated in this passage as 'time';

depuis ce moment – 'since then' (rather than 'since that moment');

qui préparait – 'getting ready' (and not 'who was getting ready'), etc.

Always write a good English translation and not stilted language which has obviously been translated.

PASSAGES FOR TRANSLATION

1 Mother-in-law problems (WJEC)

Ma belle-mère, qui venait nous voir toutes les fois qu'elle s'ennuyait, arriva pendant que je donnais une leçon particulière à un élève de quatrième. Quand j'entrai au salon, après avoir raccompagné l'enfant jusqu'à la porte, elle était toujours là.

Nous échangeâmes quelques mots au sujet des vacances proches et de la chaleur qui demeurait grande. A la manière dont elle m'examinait, je suspectais qu'elle avait encore parlé de moi, de ce que je n'avais pas fait et aurais dû faire.

Je m'échappai donc au plus vite dans la pièce qui me servait de bureau. J'entendais mère et fille continuer leur conversation. La succession de questions et de réponses me faisait penser à un complot, mais je m'efforçai de ne pas lever la tête.

Lorsque ma femme Danièle vint me dire que sa mère restait à dîner, je haussai les épaules avec indifférence, ce qui n'était peut-être pas gentil, car elle soupira et me dit à l'oreille:

'Tu pourras au moins venir nous tenir compagnie . . .'

Le repas fini, je me levai de table, prétextant que mes corrections n'étaient pas terminées. Elles ne s'y trompèrent pas. Je me penchai quand même à la fenêtre et fumai plusieurs cigarettes sans penser à rien de précis.

A l'entrée des maisons, les gens prenaient le frais, assis sur des chaises. Danièle, cependant, faisait la vaisselle et un peu de sa mauvaise humeur devait passer dans ses gestes, car les assiettes se heurtaient un peu plus bruyamment que d'ordinaire.

Ma belle-mère finit par s'en aller. Du vestibule elle cria, à tue-tête:

'Ne dérange pas André, puisqu'il travaille . . .'

Danièle vint aussitôt me rejoindre. Elle dit avec reproche:

'Tu seras toujours le même . . . C'est ma mère . . .'

Puis:

'Je vais me coucher. Cette journée m'a épuisée . . .'

2 Incident at the Arc de Triomphe (Oxford)

Un groupe d'ouvriers en bleu de travail se dirigeait vers l'Arc de Triomphe. A quelques pas derrière eux suivait l'homme aux cheveux blancs.

– Le voilà, cria Kader, en tendant le doigt. Derrière ces hommes-là!

Les deux enfants se précipitèrent. Ils évitèrent facilement les véhicules, mais non l'agent de police qui les attendait.

Ils perdirent quelques minutes à discuter. Kader ne disait rien, essayant de se montrer diplomate, mais Gilles gâtait tout en affirmant que l'agent était aveugle. Heureusement pour eux, un touriste en costume allemand intervint et demanda l'autorisation de prendre une photo du groupe en train de se disputer. Tandis que l'agent s'occupait de lui, les deux amis se hâtèrent de faire le tour du monument et de mettre quelques milliers de tonnes de pierre entre eux at la Loi.

– C'est ennuyeux! se lamenta Gilles en se donnant de grandes tapes sur le front. L'homme aux cheveux blancs a dû monter!

– Il ne portait rien, dit Kader. Il redescendra pour déjeuner. On pourra sans doute nous dire à quelle heure les ouvriers s'arrêtent.

Ils trouvèrent pour se renseigner un homme excessivement bavard. Ils durent écouter toute l'histoire du monument avant d'obtenir la réponse qu'ils étaient venus chercher: midi.

3 A missing boy (Oxford)

Il était quatre heures du matin. Marcel n'était pas rentré, n'avait envoyé aucun message. Alors, à quatre heures précises, Germaine se décida à un nouvel appel téléphonique.

– Allô . . . C'est toi, Yvette? Tu dormais? Il ne faut pas te fâcher . . . Ici Germaine . . . Tu veux me rendre un grand service? Habille-toi en grande vitesse, n'importe comment. Pour gagner du temps, je vais téléphoner pour t'envoyer un taxi. A bientôt . . .

Un quart d'heure plus tard Yvette monta l'escalier. Germaine lui ouvrit la porte.

– Tu as dû être étonnée, dit-elle. Marcel n'est pas revenu. Je t'expliquerai plus tard.

– Où faut-il que je cherche Marcel? demanda Yvette.

– Tu vas rester ici. C'est moi qui dois sortir. Si on appelle, tu noteras soigneusement les messages. Si c'est Marcel, tu lui diras qui tu es. Il te connaît. Ajoute que je suis sortie, mais que je rentrerai bientôt. Et s'il revient, dis-lui la même chose, dis-lui que j'ai été inquiète, que je suis partie à sa recherche.

– Quatre heures et demie, remarqua Yvette. Ce n'est plus la peine que je me déshabille.

4 A worried man (AEB)   *Time allowed: 45 minutes*

David regarda à nouveau sa montre: six heures dix. Evidemment il s'était endormi dans le fauteuil; il avait dû dormir profondément, d'ailleurs, car les rayons du soleil pénétraient déjà dans la pièce, malgré le fait qu'il n'avait pas encore écarté les rideaux. Il se leva, et passa dans la cuisine. Les événements de la veille n'avaient pas encore commencé à le préoccuper, et, machinalement, il fit bouillir de l'eau pour faire du café. Après tout, c'était son habitude – mais bien sûr, normalement il n'était pas tout habillé à cette heure-là. Il était même sur le point de verser une tasse pour Evelyne, quand il se rendit soudain compte qu'elle n'était pas là. Il monta à la chambre pour s'assurer qu'elle n'était pas rentrée pendant qu'il dormait. Mais comme il redescendit l'escalier il se mit à réfléchir à tout ce qui s'était passé, et à tout ce qu'il pourrait faire. C'était vraiment une situation compliquée, pour ne pas dire inquiétante, et il ne fallait pas agir sans avoir longuement contemplé ses actions.

Après avoir pris sa douche il chercha du papier et s'installa à la table. Il commença par écrire les mots qu'Evelyne avait employés au téléphone. Il n'avait aucune difficulté à se les rappeler – ils retentissaient sans cesse dans sa tête: 'David? Voici Evelyne. Ecoute bien. Ne t'inquiète pas de moi. Je n'aurai des problèmes que si tu fais quelque chose d'idiot. Il faut que tu restes là; quelqu'un se mettra en contact avec toi.'

5 A family disagreement (NIEB)   *Time allowed: 30 minutes*

Sur le coup de six heures, comme nous rentrions, un renard traversa rapidement le petit chemin de Saint-Aventurin. Mon père eut à peine le temps d'épauler son fusil et de tirer dans la haie où le renard venait de rentrer.

Nous l'en retirâmes, mort.

– Vous avez de bons yeux, André! s'exclama mon oncle.

Je vous laisse à penser quel fut le succès de notre retour. Mon frère et moi, nous portions le renard attaché par les pattes à une grosse branche, comme les Nègres quand ils ont tué un lion.

L'oncle Michel nous suivait de près, tenant au bout de chaque bras, par les oreilles, les deux plus gros lapins qu'on avait attrapés. Mon père qui fermait la marche sifflait son air favori.

C'est ainsi que nous arrivâmes à la maison. L'enthousiasme tomba tout à fait lorsque nous aperçûmes, à la porte, notre mère qui paraissait plutôt irritée.

– Vous n'avez pas entendu la cloche?

– Quelle cloche? répondit innocemment mon père.

Elle haussa les épaules.

– Il n'y a qu'une cloche dans le pays: la nôtre. Voilà trois fois que je la fais sonner. Le maire de Soledot est venu te voir. Il s'agit de ce poste dont il t'a déjà parlé et qu'il tient beaucoup à t'offrir.

– Mais je n'en veux pas! cria mon père, tu sais bien que je n'en veux pas.

6 (SUJB)   *Time allowed: 1 hour*

Partis de la ville vers neuf heures du matin, les quatre jeunes gens marchaient déjà depuis sept heures, et maintenant ils s'avançaient péniblement le long d'un chemin de campagne poussiéreux et interminable. Ils se dirigeaient vers l'auberge de la jeunesse à Armenton, et comme on était au mois d'août, il faisait un temps chaud et plutôt lourd.

'Il nous reste combien de kilomètres à faire?' s'écria la petite Agnès. Paul, chef du groupe, déplia sa carte. 'Encore dix kilomètres,' répondit-il enfin. 'Impossible,' sanglota Agnès. 'Je suis epuisée, et mes pieds me font mal.' 'Il n'y a pas de raccourci?' demanda Roger. 'Si l'on traversait ces prés, par exemple? Armenton, c'est bien vers l'est, n'est-ce pas?' 'Mais regardez un peu cet écriteau,' fit Paul. Il lut à haute voix l'avertissement: 'Défense d'entrer. Taureau dangereux.'

Ils se reposèrent pendant quelques minutes, et se baignèrent les pieds dans un ruisseau avant de continuer leur chemin. Enfin ils aperçurent devant eux l'ancien moulin, converti en auberge. Ils virent aussi l'avis cloué à la porte: 'Auberge fermée à cause d'incendie.'

Ils s'assirent découragés au bord de la route, et Agnès fondit en larmes. Soudain ils entendirent une voix d'homme. 'Qu'est-ce qu'il y a, les petits?' Ils expliquèrent leur embarras, et le nouveau venu se mit à rire. 'Pas de problème,' dit-il. 'Ma ferme est tout près. Ma femme va vous préparer quelque chose à manger. Nous avons de la place dans la maison pour les jeunes filles. Quant aux garçons, vous pourrez vous installer dans la grange. Un lit de paille vous suffira, n'est-ce pas?'

9 Reading comprehension

Almost all O-level and CSE Examination Boards set some form of reading comprehension to test the candidates' ability to understand written French. The type of test varies according to the requirements of the different Boards. You should check the current syllabus of your particular Examination Board to see which of the following types of test are set by your Board.

Types of O-level reading comprehension test

1 A passage of French (the approximate number of words is normally specified and can vary between 300–600 words).

2 Two or three shorter passages of French (approximately 150 words each in length).

Both these may be tested in the following ways:

(a) Questions in French to be answered in French. This is sometimes called a 'manipulation of the language' test as the candidate usually has to manipulate, i.e. change, the tense or the person of the verb in some way.

(b) Questions in English to be answered in English.

3 Two or three sentences in French, followed by a choice of statements in French. The candidate must choose which statement is most likely to be made in the given situation.

4 Incomplete statements in French. The candidate must insert the most appropriate word, from a list of words given, to complete the statement.

Each candidate must not only check carefully to see which type of reading comprehension test is set by his Examination Board, but also *how long* the test takes. In your exam preparation you must practise answering questions within the time allocated. This is a very useful preparation technique which should give you added confidence in the examination itself.

Types of CSE reading comprehension test

At CSE level a wide variety of tests are set on this section of the paper. Some tests are based on passages of French ranging from 150–350 words. Others are based on single sentences. The tests vary in length from half an hour to an hour. Listed below are the main types of reading comprehension test set at CSE level.

1 A passage of French with questions in French to be answered in French. As at O level, this is sometimes called a 'manipulation of the language' test.

2 A passage of French with questions in English to be answered in English.

3 A passage of French followed by incomplete sentences in English. Multiple-choice answers in English are given and candidates must choose the answer which completes the sentence most satisfactorily.

4 Short pieces of conversation in French. Multiple-choice answers in French are given. The candidate must choose the correct answer to identify the speaker.

5 As 4 above, but the correct answer will identify the place where the conversation has supposedly taken place.

6 One or two sentences in French, with multiple-choice answers given in French. The candidate must decide which remark is most likely to be made in the given situation.

7 A passage of French, followed by incomplete sentences in French. Multiple-choice answers given in French. The candidate must choose the correct word or words to complete the sentences.

How to approach the reading comprehension test

As the title states, these tests are designed to find out if a candidate is able to understand what he/she reads in French. The emphasis is on *reading,* and you should spend time reading and re-reading, where necessary, the passage in front of you before attempting to answer the questions.

Do not attempt to translate the passage into English. This will only waste valuable time. Practise reading passages of French regularly in the weeks before the examination and imagine that you are going to explain to someone who cannot read French what the passage is about.

QUESTIONS IN ENGLISH

1 (Oxford)   *Time allowed: 30 minutes*

Read the following passage carefully and answer the questions set on it. The answers must be entirely in English. No credit will be given for anything written in French.

Hiring a motor-caravan

Après deux heures de voyage, j'étais entré dans un garage pour faire vérifier mon moteur qui ne marchait pas très bien. Cela durait un peu et, pendant que je parlais sans grand espoir avec le mécanicien, ma femme alla traîner devant la boutique d'accessoires automobiles. Elle revint, puis repartit vers une autre vitrine d'où elle m'appela. Elle me montra une sorte de petite camionnette blanche, de marque anglaise, tout à fait confortable avec son grand lit, sa cuisine, et son bloc-toilette, le tout peint en beige et bleu pâle.

   – Regarde! dit-elle. On le loue! Est-ce que c'est très cher?

   – Non. Pas excessif, dis-je en regardant l'écriteau.

   – En plus, cela nous permettrait une rude économie d'hôtels, dit ma femme.

   – C'est vrai, mais il n'y a pas de baignoire.

   – On peut se laver à petits morceaux, soigneusement.

   Le garagiste s'approcha et en parla avec enthousiasme. On pouvait, en moins d'un quart d'heure, donner quelques signatures et partir au volant. Nous étions pressés de conclure. Je présentai mon permis de conduire et ma carte internationale d'assurance, et nous payâmes avec un chèque de voyage. On fit vite le plein d'essence, et on me montra comment faire écouler l'eau sale, et comment me servir de la bouteille de gaz.

   Je confiai ma voiture au garage, après avoir transféré les valises. Ma femme installa nos vêtements et nos affaires de toilette dans les placards. Puis, avant de sortir de cette ville inconnue, nous fîmes dans un supermarché des achats de nourriture et de boissons, et nous nous mîmes en route pour les montagnes.

(a) Why do the author and his wife stop at the garage? (2)
(b) What do the husband and wife do while waiting? (2)
(c) What features of the inside of the caravan do they notice? (3)
(d) What do they think about its cost? (2)
(e) What is its disadvantage? (1)
(f) What formalities are necessary before they can hire it? (3)
(g) What does the garage do to see them on their way? (4)
(h) What do the author and his wife do before they are finally on their way? (3)

Note that the title is given in English. This is there to help you and should not be ignored. Do not worry about individual items of vocabulary which you might not know, but try to grasp the main ideas of the story **before** you look at the questions. Read carefully the instructions given at the beginning of the question. This is especially important when instructions are given about the length of the answer required (whether complete or partial sentences are acceptable). Do not leave gaps or any question unanswered. If you are in doubt about an answer, write down what you think the answer might be. After all, you might be right! A few marks for a partially correct answer are better than no marks for a question unanswered. Always give yourself time to check your work thoroughly.

   Try to keep to the following procedure:

1 Read the passage carefully.

2 Re-read the passage equally carefully.

3 Read through all the questions. This is necessary as you might be inclined to give too much information in one answer, information which is required in a subsequent answer.

4 If the marking scheme is given, as in the above question, check to see if any of the questions has more marks attached to it than the others. If so, you must make sure that you answer that question fully.

5 Answer the questions carefully, checking back to the passage if necessary.

2 (WJEC)
Read carefully the following passage, which is not to be translated, and then answer, in English, the questions which follow. Answers should be selective but should include all the details necessary to make them complete answers to the questions. A complete answer will normally require more than one detail.

A policeman follows a suspect to his hotel
Il était à peu près cinq heures et demie, car les lampes étaient allumées depuis un bon moment, quand l'inspecteur Maloin aperçut l'Anglais qui sortait du bureau de poste. Il pressa le pas afin de le suivre à distance et tous deux marchèrent ainsi le long des vitrines.

   Qu'est-ce que l'homme avait fait depuis le matin? Avait-il dormi? S'était-il promené près du port? C'était improbable, car Maloin y était passé une dizaine de fois et il l'aurait rencontré.

   Il marchait vite. Il faisait froid. Le brouillard régnait toujours et la sirène continuait à gémir au bout de la jetée.

Après le magasin d'antiquités, l'homme tourna à droite et ce fut presque tout. Une rue étroite menait à la digue, à courte distance de l'hôtel de Newhaven. L'hôtel était signalé par deux boules en verre poli qui flottaient dans le brouillard comme des lunes. A gauche, dans le noir absolu, on sentait l'haleine de la mer.

L'Anglais eut-il l'impression qu'on le suivait? Il ne se tourna pas, marcha plus vite, mais c'était peut-être parce qu'il arrivait à destination.

L'hôtel comportait d'abord un large vestibule meublé de chaises, de fauteuils, de porte-manteaux. Au fond, ce vestibule s'élargissait encore, devenait hall, avec un bureau à gauche, un bar américain à droite.

Un homme était assis dans un fauteuil, son chapeau melon sur les genoux, et il était si calme, il regardait devant lui avec tant de patience, qu'il avait l'air d'être installé dans un train. Ce qu'il regardait, c'était le vestibule éclairé au bout duquel la nuit humide se dressait comme un mur. Soudain il vit sortir de l'ombre l'imperméable de l'Anglais. De sa place, la patronne qui terminait une addition ne voyait rien, mais elle reconnaissait toujours les gens au bruit de leurs pas.

– C'est justement M. Brown, dit-elle en souriant.

Alors que M. Brown était à mi-longueur du vestibule, une silhouette apparut sur le trottoir, resta quelques instants et s'en alla. C'était Maloin.

L'Anglais ne savait pas qu'on l'attendait et il regardait à terre en marchant. Quand il leva la tête, il n'était plus qu'à trois pas du fauteuil. Il fit une grimace en voyant le visiteur qui s'était levé et qui dit en anglais, la main tendue:

– Enchanté de vous rencontrer, monsieur Brown.

Il lui serrait la main longuement, vigoureusement, comme s'il ne devait plus la lâcher.

L'hôtelière, aimable, expliqua:

– Votre ami est arrivé que vous veniez à peine de sortir. Par ce brouillard il a préféré attendre que vous chercher en ville.

(a) What was the Englishman doing when Maloin first caught sight of him? How did Maloin react and why?

(b) What did Maloin think the Englishman might have been doing since the morning and why did he reject the second of these ideas?

(c) What objects enabled the outside of the hotel to be recognised and how did they appear that evening?

(d) Describe the interior of the ground floor of the hotel.

(e) Where did the man sitting in the hotel lobby look as if he was? What created this impression?

(f) What was the hotel proprietress doing? Why was it surprising that she recognised the Englishman when he came in and how did she do this?

(g) What happened when the Englishman was half-way across the lobby?

(h) How did the visitor greet the Englishman?

(i) What did the hotel proprietress say to the Englishman about his visitor?

3 (LREB)

Read the following passage carefully, then read the questions. When you have done so, answer the questions in English. The questions follow each other in order through the passage and some call for more than one piece of information. No marks will be given for answers written in French.

A trip to Paris

Un jeudi soir, Paul Lanvin rentra chez lui vers cinq heures. Sa femme, Sophie, qui était dans le salon en train de regarder la télévision, ne l'attendait pas avant six heures et demie.

– Tiens! dit-elle. Pourquoi es-tu rentré de si bonne heure? Tu n'es pas malade?

– Non, répondit-il, mais je dois aller à Paris demain matin; j'ai une réunion à deux heures et je serai libre à six heures du soir. Viens avec moi; nous pourrons rentrer dimanche soir et nous aurons presque deux jours ensemble.

– Oh, oui, dit Sophie en battant des mains. Il fait si beau à Paris au mois de mai et j'ai besoin d'une nouvelle robe d'été.

– Attends, dit Paul. Je vais téléphoner à l'agence de tourisme pour demander s'il y a deux places dans l'avion.

– Ça ira, dit-il après deux minutes, nous prendrons l'avion qui part à onze heures.

Le lendemain matin, pendant que Sophie lavait les tasses et les assiettes, Paul sortait la voiture. Quelques instants plus tard, ils étaient en route pour l'aéroport où ils arrivèrent vers dix heures. Après avoir laissé la voiture dans un parking, ils entrèrent dans la salle d'attente.

– Je voudrais bien une tasse de café, dit Sophie.

– Excellente idée, répondit Paul. Je vais en chercher une. Reste ici avec les bagages.

Il revint avec deux tasses de café et, peu de temps après, on les appela pour prendre place dans l'avion. En quelques minutes ils étaient partis. Paul regarda sa montre.

– Dix heures moins vingt, dit-il. Ah, mais ma montre ne marche pas!

Malheureusement, l'avion entra bientôt dans les nuages et ils ne virent rien par les hublots. Sophie regarda le journal tout en pensant à la robe qu'elle allait acheter à Paris. Paul avait du travail à faire avant sa réunion mais, au bout de vingt minutes, il s'endormit.

Une fois arrivés à Paris, ils déjeunèrent et Paul partit pour sa réunion. Sophie resta à table pour prendre une deuxième tasse de café.

– D'abord, se dit-elle, je vais aller Place de l'Opéra en Métro; je me souviens d'une boutique où je trouverai peut-être une robe.

Elle se dirigeait vers la station de Métro quand elle entendit une voix qui l'appelait – Sophie! Sophie Lanvin! Elle se retourna pour voir une ancienne amie d'enfance. Les deux femmes décidèrent de passer l'après-midi ensemble. Elles allèrent à la boutique où Sophie réussit à trouver une robe et ensuite elles prirent le thé à la terrasse du Café de la Paix.

A six heures et demie Sophie retrouva Paul et ils dinèrent dans un petit restaurant non loin de la tour Eiffel.

– Que faire avant de nous coucher? demanda Paul. Veux-tu aller au théâtre ou au cinéma?

– Non, répondit Sophie. Allons nous promener sur les boulevards.

(a) What was Sophie doing when her husband arrived home?
(b) What did she fear was wrong?
(c) How long was Paul's meeting in Paris likely to last?
(d) What two reasons did Sophie have for welcoming the chance of accompanying Paul?
(e) What did Paul have to do as soon as she agreed to go?
(f) What did Sophie do while Paul got the car out?
(g) What did Paul do when they reached the waiting room?
(h) What did he ask Sophie to do?
(i) How did Sophie pass the time in the plane?
(j) What did Paul do?
(k) Why did Sophie go to the Place de l'Opéra?
(l) What happened to Sophie on her way to the Métro?
(m) How did she spend the afternoon?
(n) Why did Paul and Sophie go in the direction of the Eiffel Tower?
(o) What did they do later in the evening before going to bed?

4 (WJEC)

Read the following passage carefully. Then answer, *in English,* in complete sentences, the questions which follow it.

Je rentrais en chemin de fer après avoir assisté à une conférence dans le nord du pays. Je m'étais installé dans un compartiment de première classe, car la maison de commerce, pour laquelle je travaillais, payait tous les frais de voyage. Quoique fatigué, je décidai de lire quelques documents que j'avais reçus au cours de la dernière séance et dont je devais prendre connaissance avant d'arriver au bureau le lendemain.

– Votre billet, s'il vous plaît, monsieur.

Le contrôleur était devant moi. Je cherchai mon billet, mais ne le trouvai pas à sa place habituelle, c'est-à-dire dans la poche droite de ma veste, ni ailleurs.

Je me levai et continuai à explorer mes poches. Le contrôleur attendait, visiblement impatienté, son appareil de poinçonnage à la main. Je fis un rire forcé.

– J'ai dû le mettre dans un endroit impossible ou bien je l'ai jeté par erreur.

Bien sûr mes voisins s'intéressaient à la scène; quelques-uns se montraient franchement amusés, d'autres avaient l'air même indignés.

– Vous n'avez même pas un billet de seconde classe? demanda le contrôleur d'un ton méprisant.

– Pas question d'un billet de seconde classe, répondis-je, agacé. J'avais un billet de première. Mais je ne peux vous faire attendre davantage; donnez m'en un autre.

Je sortis mon portefeuille, mais celui-là haussa les épaules, fit demi-tour et quitta le compartiment.

A la gare suivante il revint, me fit signe de le suivre et se dirigea vers le bureau du chef de gare.

(a) Where has the writer been?

(b) Why had he chosen a first-class compartment?

(c) What did he decide to do during the journey?

(d) Where did the writer expect to find his ticket?

(e) What did he think he must have done with it?

(f) What was the reaction of the other passengers to this incident?

(g) What suggests that the ticket collector did not believe his story?

(h) Why did the writer offer to buy another ticket?

(i) What was the ticket collector's reaction to this offer?

(j) What happened at the next station?

QUESTIONS IN FRENCH

This type of test is sometimes called 'reading comprehension and manipulation of the French language'. You may be asked to change the tense of the verb in your answer. Always read the instructions carefully before attempting to answer the questions.

1 (AEB)   *Time allowed: 40 minutes for three passages*

Answer the questions following *each* of the passages A, B and C. N.B. The passages must *not* be translated and the past historic tense, e.g. il donna, should *not* be used in your answers.

A. Pierre et Michel étaient deux frères, qui aimaient beaucoup faire le jardinage, et qui habitaient d'ailleurs dans la même rue. Un jour ils se rencontrèrent dans la rue, et se mirent à parler, comme d'habitude, de leur passe-temps préféré.

– Tu cultives des tomates cette année? demanda Michel.

– Oui, mais elles ne réussissent pas très bien, répondit son frère. Je crois que chez moi la terre n'est pas très bonne pour les tomates. Et toi?

– Oui. L'année dernière j'ai eu le même problème que toi, mais cette année j'essaie une nouvelle variété, et ça va très bien.

Pierre demanda à Michel de les lui montrer, disant en même temps qu'elles devaient être plus grosses que les siennes. Les deux frères allèrent donc à la maison de Michel, où Pierre vit de belles tomates rouges aussi grandes que des pommes.

– Mon Dieu! s'exclama-t-il. Elles sont énormes!

(a) Comment Pierre et Michel passaient-ils leur temps libre?

(b) Quelle a été la première indication que Pierre n'était pas content de ses tomates? (Ne donnez pas ses mots exacts.)

(c) Quelle raison Pierre a-t-il donné de son manque de succès? (Ne donnez pas ses mots exacts.)

(d) Qu'est-ce qui indique que Michel n'avait pas eu de succès l'année précédente?

(e) Qu'est-ce que Michel avait fait cette année pour avoir plus de succès?

(f) Quand Michel a dit à Pierre que ses tomates allaient bien, qu'est-ce que Pierre lui a dit? (Donnez ses mots exacts.)

B. Une fois sorti de la station de Métro, Henri alla tout de suite à la maison qui lui avait été indiquée. Il sonna, et aussitôt la porte s'ouvrit; il reconnut l'homme qui lui avait parlé la veille.

– Entrez, dit celui-ci, et faites vite.

Après avoir écouté ce qu'Henri avait à dire, l'homme parla à son tour.

– Allez trouver Gaston, dit-il.

– Où est-il, Gaston?

L'homme soupira comme s'il avait affaire à un imbécile, puis il reprit la parole. Il dit à Henri de prendre l'avenue qu'il verrait en face de lui en sortant, puis de s'arrêter au tabac qu'il trouverait à sa gauche, et de demander au patron de lui dire où il pourrait trouver Gaston.

(g) Qu'est-ce qu'Henri a fait avant d'aller à la maison qui lui avait été indiquée?

(h) Comment l'homme savait-il qu'Henri était à la porte?

(i) Quand l'homme a ouvert la porte, qu'est-ce qu'il a demandé à Henri de faire?

(j) Quelles instructions l'homme a-t-il données à Henri pour l'aider à trouver Gaston? (Donnez ses mots exacts.)

C. La fermière, comme son mari, était vieille et grosse. J'appris très vite la raison de cette grosseur, et je crois que j'aurais grossi moi-même si j'y étais resté plus longtemps, parce que je dois avouer que, comme eux, j'adore la bonne cuisine. J'arrivai chez eux un soir vers sept heures, et la fermière mit tout de suite devant moi un repas énorme. Le lendemain matin je me levai, et, me trouvant sans appétit, je lui dis que je sortais et que je ne rentrerais que le soir. Elle me demanda si je n'aurais pas faim si je sortais sans déjeuner.

– Asseyez-vous, me dit-elle, et je vous préparerai un déjeuner que vous n'oublierez jamais.

C'est avec difficulté que je résistai à cette promesse, mais le repas du deuxième soir fut encore plus grand que celui du premier!

(k) Comment étaient-ils, le fermier et sa femme?

(l) Qu'est-ce que la fermière a fait tout de suite après l'arrivée de l'auteur?

(m) Qu'est-ce qui indique que l'auteur ne passerait pas la journée à la ferme?

(n) Quelle question la fermière a-t-elle posée à l'auteur? (Donnez ses mots exacts.)

(o) Qu'est-ce que la fermière a dit à l'auteur de faire?

(p) Quelle promesse la fermière a-t-elle faite à l'auteur?

Points to remember when answering the above questions

The narrative tense of the above passages is the past historic tense. In the questions, however, the perfect tense is used instead of the past historic tense. You will find that the tense used in the question is almost certainly the tense you will need in the answer.

In reading comprehension questions of this type (questions in French to be answered in French), there is a strong temptation to 'lift' entire sentences from the passage and to copy out these sentences for your answers. This usually proves disastrous. Far too often candidates seize on a word in the passage and then copy out the sentence or sentences in which that word occurs. This is one of the reasons why, in a reading comprehension test with questions in French, you are asked to manipulate the language of the passage by using a different tense.

When preparing to answer this type of question, you should read the passage thoroughly as always, and then concentrate on the structure of the sentences in the passage. Always check that your answer fits the question both logically and grammatically.

When you are asked to give someone's exact words, as in questions **(f)**, **(j)**, and **(n)** above, you should imagine that *you* are speaking those words. Ask yourself first of all which form of address you would use in the given situation – **tu** or **vous**.

In questions **(f)** and **(j)** above, you are telling somebody to do something. Care must be taken therefore to use the correct form of the imperative. (If you are unsure of the imperative, check Grammar Revision section 28.)

Question **(f)** also requires you to know the correct position of the pronouns with the imperative.

Question **(j)** requires you to change not only the verbs but also pronouns (e.g. **vous** arrêter, **vous** dire) and possessive adjective (**votre** gauche).

Question **(n)** requires the **vous** form of address. Care must also be taken to use the correct tense with **si**. (See Grammar Revision section 32 if you are unsure of this.)

2 (NIEC)

Read carefully the following passage which is *not* to be translated. Answer the questions in Sections A and B which follow it.

A young teacher's problems

Deux jours avant le début des vacances de Nöel, Jean Calmet fut convoqué chez le Directeur. M. Grapp était un homme grand, il était chauve et il portait toujours des lunettes noires.

– Je ne vais pas mâcher mes mots, Monsieur Calmet, dit le Directeur d'une voix forte. Vous êtes aimé dans ce lycée, nous apprécions tous votre haute conscience professionnelle. Vos élèves travaillent, vous êtes capable de les enthousiasmer, je sais par de nombreux parents combien vous êtes respecté et admiré. C'est ce qui m'autorise à vous parler aujourd'hui très fermement.

Il fit une pose, sourit de toutes ses dents. Jean Calmet s'apprêta à être dévoré.

– Je n'ai pas voulu vous en parler tout de suite, Monsieur Calmet. Vous deviez vous reprendre et réfléchir. Il s'agit de l'incident du Fanal. Plusieurs amis m'en ont parlé, et des parents m'ont fait part de leur étonnement. J'ajoute que j'ai reçu un coup de téléphone de la police qui voulait savoir s'il était question de drogues. Que s'est-il passé, Monsieur Calmet? Aviez-vous bu? Un moment d'égarement bien compréhensible. Dites-le-moi, Monsieur Calmet. Après tout, je pourrais être votre père. . . .

Jean Calmet fit un affreux effort pour fixer ses lunettes mystérieuses: il ne pouvait parler, sa main mouillée de sueur tremblait sur l'accoudoir du fauteuil.

– J'ai eu un malaise, dit-il enfin. Je ne me suis plus contrôlé, poursuivit Jean d'une voix faible. J'ai dit des choses incohérentes . . . Je ne voyais plus rien. . . .

– L'ennui c'est que vous les avez criées, ces choses, coupa durement le Directeur. Dans votre position, c'est très regrettable. Il y avait plus de trente élèves dans ce café. Vous conviendrez, Monsieur Calmet, que votre attitude a été parfaitement scandaleuse.

Jean l'admit en balbutiant.

– Avez-vous les nerfs malades, Monsieur Calmet? Faudrait-il vous soigner, vous faire traiter quelques semaines en clinique?

Jean sursauta, horrifié.

– Est-ce que vous buvez, Monsieur Calmet? On vous voit souvent à des tables d'élèves, avec des bières. Vous devriez vous marier, Monsieur Calmet, dit le Directeur. Il n'est pas bon que l'homme soit seul. Et vous qui sortez d'une grande famille, vous devez vous trouver d'autant plus solitaire, maintenant. J'ai bien connu votre cher père, vous le savez; voilà un homme qui a vécu pour les siens, et pour ses malades. On en manque, de gens comme lui, aujourd'hui.

Section A

Answer the following questions in *French*. While you may use words and phrases from the passage, you will not gain full marks if you copy unaltered a portion of the passage as your complete answer.

(a) Qu'est-ce que Jean Calmet a dû faire avant les vacances de Noël?
(b) Que pensait-on de M. Calmet au lycée?
(c) Comment le Directeur a-t-il entendu parler de l'incident?
(d) Pourquoi la police s'était-elle intéressée à l'incident?
(e) Comment sait-on que Jean a mis si longtemps à répondre au Directeur?
(f) Qu'est-ce que Jean a dit pour s'excuser?
(g) Pourquoi le Directeur a-t-il trouvé l'attitude de Jean scandaleuse?
(h) Pourquoi Jean a-t-il été horrifié par ce que lui a dit le Directeur?
(i) Quel était le conseil qu'a donné le Directeur?
(j) Quelle était la profession du père de Jean?

Section B

(a) Which of the following words from the passage fits the proverb:
   C'est dans le malheur qu'on reconnaît ses
   A lunettes
   B amis
   C élèves
   D bières

(b) Choose the most appropriate ending, based on your reading of the passage, to the following sentence:
   Le Directeur avait appelé Jean chez lui
   A pour le présenter à ses collègues.
   B pour lui poser des questions.
   C pour lui offrir une bière.
   D parce que c'était le début des vacances.

(c) Choose the most suitable answer to the following question:
   Pourquoi la main de Jean était-elle mouillée de sueur?
   A parce qu'il l'avait posée sur l'accoudoir du fauteuil.
   B parce que le Directeur lui faisait peur.
   C parce qu'il avait bu quelque chose.

(d) Give a word from the text similar in meaning to each of the following:
   A paroles
   B tout à fait
   C fréquemment

(e) Rewrite the following two sentences, giving an alternative for the words underlined:
   A Aviez-vous <u>bu</u>?
   B Il ne pouvait <u>parler</u>.

(f) Explain in French the meaning of the following two words:
A chauve
B café

(g) Change the tense of the following sentences as indicated in the brackets:
A Il s'agit de l'incident du Fanal. (*Imperfect*)
B Jean fit un affreux effort. (*Pluperfect*)
C Voilà un homme qui a vécu pour les siens. (*Present*)

3 (EAEB)　　*Time allowed: 45 minutes*

Read carefully the following passage and answer, in *French,* the questions which follow it. Answer in complete sentences as fully as you can while keeping to the point. The tense and form of your answer should suit those of the questions, and no marks will be gained by simply copying out irrelevant portions of the text.

Aventure en faisant de l'auto-stop (faire de l'auto-stop = *to hitch-hike*)
Jacqueline et moi, nous étions sur la Route Nationale 31 entre Soissons et Reims. Nous avions quitté Soissons, où nous habitons, à huit heures ce matin-là, espérant aller assez vite pour arriver à Metz avant la nuit. Nous faisions de l'auto-stop parce que nous n'avions pas assez d'argent pour voyager par chemin de fer.

'Soixante-deux! soixante-trois!' Je comptais les voitures et les camions qui passaient sans s'arrêter. Nous commencions à en avoir assez.

'Françoise,' m'a dit mon amie, 'si nous nous reposions à l'ombre de cet arbre, là-bas? Ces conducteurs ne sont pas gentils. Ils ne s'arrêtent pas.'

Alors nous nous sommes reposées. Mes pieds commençaient à me faire mal et j'ai enlevé mes chaussures et mes chaussettes, et en prenant une bouteille d'eau, j'en ai versé la moitié sur mes pieds. 'Ça les rafraîchira un peu,' ai-je pensé. 'Doucement avec l'eau,' m'a dit Jacqueline. 'C'est tout ce qu'il y a à boire.'

Vers onze heures nous nous sommes remises en route. Cette fois nous avons eu plus de chance – au moins, c'est ce que nous pensions quand nous avons vu une Peugeot 505 ralentir et s'arrêter tout près de nous. A notre étonnement, deux gendarmes en sont descendus. C'était une voiture de police!

'Nous cherchons deux jeunes filles qui ont disparu,' a expliqué un des gendarmes. 'Ce sont des élèves d'un collège à Soissons, et elles manquent depuis hier matin. Vous ressemblez à la description qu'on nous a donnée.'

Et les deux gendarmes ont commencé à nous interroger. Ils voulaient s'assurer que nous n'étions pas les deux jeunes filles échappées. Enfin, ils nous ont emmenées jusqu'à Reims, où ils nous ont offert une tasse de café à la gendarmerie.

(a) Quelle ville Jacqueline et son amie habitaient-elles? (2)
(b) A quelle heure ont-elles quitté la maison ce matin-là? (2)
(c) Quelle était leur destination? (2)
(d) Pourquoi les deux jeunes filles n'ont-elles pas pris le train pour aller à leur destination? (2)
(e) Pourquoi les deux jeunes filles commençaient-elles à en avoir assez? (3)
(f) Qu'est-ce qu'elles allaient faire à l'ombre d'un arbre? (3)
(g) Pourquoi Françoise a-t-elle versé de l'eau sur ses pieds? (3)
(h) Pourquoi Françoise devait-elle faire attention avec l'eau? (3)
(i) Qui conduisait la Peugeot 505? (2)
(j) Pourquoi est-ce que la police cherchait deux jeunes filles? (2)
(k) Depuis quand les jeunes filles manquaient-elles? (3)
(l) Comment les gendarmes se sont-ils assurés que Jacqueline et Françoise n'étaient pas les jeunes filles échappées? (3)

MULTIPLE-CHOICE QUESTIONS IN FRENCH

This type of test requires the candidate to read carefully not only the passage (or sentence) but also several suggested answers to the given question.

The procedure for this type of question should be as follows:

1 Read and re-read the passage (or sentence) until you understand its meaning.
2 Read the question carefully.
3 Read *all* the suggested answers carefully.

4 Choose your answer carefully. Never choose an answer just because the same word appears in both the passage (or sentence) and one of the suggested answers.

5 Check back to the passage to see that you have understood both the passage and the question.

In multiple-choice questions, some Examination Boards will ask you to write out the correct answer, others will ask you to give the correct letter reference, e.g. C. Do *read the instructions* on the examination paper carefully.

1 (AEB)   *Time allowed: 50 minutes*

In each of the first ten questions, a situation is described. Indicate the response which is most appropriate.

1 Marcel n'est pas du tout sportif, il se passionne plutôt pour les voitures modernes. Il s'intéresse aussi au cinéma et au théâtre. Un jour, son oncle préféré l'invite à assister à un grand match de football avec lui. Comme il est toujours très poli, et surtout comme son oncle vient d'acheter une nouvelle voiture fantastique, il dit:

    A Non merci, je préfère aller au cinéma.

    B Non merci, je ne suis pas du tout sportif.

    C Merci bien, je viendrai avec plaisir.

    D Merci bien, mais je préfère aller au théâtre.

2 Loin de chez eux, la voiture de M. et Mme Pivard s'arrête au milieu d'un carrefour. M. Pivard descend pour voir ce qui ne va pas. Sa femme lui dit:

    A Si seulement j'avais appris à conduire.

    B Tu aurais dû tourner à gauche.

    C Nous avons fait une belle promenade, n'est-ce pas?

    D Tu es sûr qu'il y a de l'essence dans le réservoir?

3 Michèle a rendez-vous avec son amie Estelle devant le cinéma dans la ville où habite celle-ci. Lorsqu'elle arrive à l'arrêt d'autobus, près de chez elle, elle découvre qu'elle a manqué le dernier autobus du soir. Elle rentre vite à la maison, mais ses parents sont déjà sortis en voiture et elle sait que son amie n'a pas le téléphone chez elle. Alors, elle dit à son frère:

    A J'ai manqué l'autobus de huit heures et je ne veux pas attendre le prochain.

    B J'ai manqué l'autobus, je dois vite téléphoner chez Estelle.

    C Sois gentil et emmène-moi en ville sur ta motocyclette!

    D Peut-être que papa m'emmènera en ville dans la voiture.

4 Dans une ville qu'il ne connaît pas, Monsieur Leclerc, accompagné de sa femme et de ses deux enfants, trouve facilement un parking pour la voiture et ils entrent tous dans un restaurant. Monsieur Leclerc dit au maître d'hôtel:

    A Ma femme va nous rejoindre dans quelques minutes.

    B Mes enfants vont venir; ils cherchent à garer la voiture.

    C Je vais me plaindre – c'est une ville où il est impossible de trouver un parking.

    D Quatre couverts, dans un coin tranquille si c'est possible.

5 Ayant entendu sonner le facteur, Monsieur Delépine descend ramasser un assez gros courrier. Il n'y a absolument rien pour lui. Il dit à son fils:

    A Ta sœur sera contente. Il y a huit lettres pour elle.

    B Tu vas mettre à la poste toutes ces lettres.

    C Aujourd'hui le facteur n'a pas sonné assez fort.

    D Je devrai répondre à toutes ces lettres tout de suite.

6 Madame Lefèvre vient de laver une énorme quantité de linge dans sa machine à laver lorsqu'elle découvre que le séchoir électrique est en panne. Dehors il pleut à verse. Alors elle va chez sa voisine et dit:

    A Je n'ai pas lavé beaucoup, ça va sécher devant les radiateurs électriques.

    B Ma machine à laver est en panne, pouvez-vous laver mon linge pour moi?

    C Je vais mettre mon linge dehors; ça va vite sécher au soleil.

    D Est-ce que vous pouvez faire sécher mon linge dans votre séchoir électrique?

7 Etienne a une faim de loup. Il s'empresse de se mettre à table quand sa mère annonce que le repas est prêt; par accident il renverse une tasse vide comme il est en train de saisir un sandwich, et elle tombe par terre. Son père en regarde les morceaux et crie:

    A Mais, Etienne, voyons, tu as renversé le thé!

    B Que tu es maladroit, Etienne!

C Idiot, tu as gâté les sandwichs!

D As-tu tellement soif, Etienne?

8 En descendant d'un autobus qui vient de s'arrêter, un vieux monsieur glisse et tombe par terre. Un passant dit:

A Il faut arrêter l'autobus.

B Il s'est fait mal peut-être.

C Il n'a pas attendu l'arrêt de l'autobus.

D L'autobus allait trop vite.

9 En sortant de la piscine, un jeune homme trouve que son vélo a disparu. Il va au commissariat et raconte l'incident. L'agent lui dit:

A Il faut faire attention quand on monte à vélo.

B Quel est le numéro de votre cabine, monsieur?

C Vous êtes sûr que vous ne l'avez pas laissé ailleurs?

D Est-ce que vous avez appris à nager?

10 Un jeune homme, en vacances en France, tombe de son vélo en ville. Il n'est pas blessé et ses vêtements ne sont pas déchirés, mais son unique veste est mouillée et couverte de boue. Il va donc au pressing et dit:

A Voulez-vous téléphoner à un médecin, s'il vous plaît. Je suis tombé de mon vélo et je suis blessé.

B Je voudrais faire réparer cette veste aussi vite que possible, s'il vous plaît.

C Pouvez-vous me nettoyer cette veste aussi vite que possible, s'il vous plaît.

D Voulez-vous réparer mon vélo, s'il vous plaît?

2 (AEB)

Read the following passage carefully. Ten incomplete statements each followed by four suggested completions are given after the passage. In each case indicate the completion that is best according to the passage. Read the whole passage before attempting the questions.

Décidément elle tournait mal, cette journée. Tout avait commencé avec le temps: trop froid pour sortir sans manteau, surtout parce qu'il risquait de pleuvoir plus tard, mais trop chaud pour mettre un pardessus ou un anorak. Jean-Paul était sorti en pull, mais il était rentré chercher son imperméable et l'avait mis dans sa serviette. C'est à cause de cela qu'il avait manqué l'autobus, son moyen de transport habituel, et qu'il avait décidé de prendre la bicyclette de sa mère, chose qu'il faisait quelquefois lorsqu'il était en retard. Bien sûr, il ne lui avait pas demandé la permission de la prendre, mais sa mère ne s'en servait presque jamais. Sophistiquée, élégante, plus paresseuse qu'athlétique, elle n'était pas du tout le type 'campagnard': elle allait partout dans sa voiture, ou même en taxi, mais jamais à pied!

Alors, le pauvre Jean-Paul, comment aurait-il pu savoir que ce jour-là elle aurait besoin de son vélo? Comment aurait-il pu deviner qu'elle voulait le mettre dans le coffre de sa voiture et qu'elle voulait rentrer à bicyclette après avoir laissé la voiture au garage pour des réparations importantes? Heureusement que sa mère l'avait vu sortir du jardin juste au moment où elle descendait l'escalier, et qu'elle avait eu le temps de l'appeler par la fenêtre de la salle à manger. Autrement, en rentrant de l'école il aurait été grondé par son père, ce qui aurait vraiment été le comble ce jour-là. Il pouvait supporter sans difficulté les mots sarcastiques de sa mère, les paroles cyniques de son professeur et même les remontrances du directeur, mais la colère de son père l'énervait plus que toute autre chose, surtout lorsque rien ne la justifiait.

1 Ce jour-là

A il faisait très froid.

B il faisait assez froid.

C il pleuvait beaucoup.

D il faisait très chaud.

2 Ce matin Jean-Paul portait

A un pullover.

B un imperméable.

C un anorak.

D un pardessus.

3 D'habitude Jean-Paul allait à l'école

A à bicyclette.

B en autobus.

C à pied.

D en taxi.

4 Jean-Paul a pris la bicyclette de sa mère

A parce qu'il risquait de pleuvoir plus tard.

B parce qu'il faisait chaud ce jour-là.

C parce qu'il avait manqué l'autobus.

D parce qu'il aimait se promener à bicyclette.

5 La mère de Jean-Paul se servait de sa bicyclette
A rarement.
B souvent.
C habituellement.
D quelquefois.

6 D'habitude sa mère se promenait
A à pied.
B en taxi.
C à bicyclette.
D en voiture.

7 La mère de Jean-Paul
A aimait se promener à la campagne.
B aimait faire du sport.
C aimait être bien habillée.
D aimait prendre l'autobus.

8 La mère de Jean-Paul avait besoin de sa bicyclette ce jour-là
A parce qu'elle devait la faire réparer au garage.
B parce qu'elle devait laisser sa voiture dans un garage.
C parce qu'elle voulait aller au garage à bicyclette.
D parce qu'elle voulait se promener à la campagne.

9 Quand elle l'a vu sortir, la mère de Jean-Paul était
A dans l'escalier.
B dans le garage.
C dans la salle à manger.
D dans le jardin.

10 Jean-Paul voulait éviter à tout prix
A les remontrances de son professeur.
B la colère de sa mère.
C la colère de son père.
D les remontrances du directeur.

3 (SREB)   *Time allowed: 45 minutes*

Answer all *the questions.*

In every question in this paper four possible answers (A, B, C and D) are given. In each question select the answer you consider to be correct.

Section A
In this section you will read remarks or short conversations. In each case *identify the speaker or speakers.*

Example:
– Voilà madame. Une bouteille de vin rouge, un bon morceau de fromage blanc, et deux tablettes de chocolat.
A Un boulanger
B Un épicier
C Un médecin
D Un garçon de café

Correct answer: B Un épicier

1 – Haut les mains! Ne bougez pas!
A Un criminel à sa victime
B Un professeur à la classe
C Un médecin à un malade
D Un élève à son professeur

2 – Ouvre la bouche et tire la langue.
A Un professeur
B Un dentiste
C Un médecin
D Un boucher

3 – Mais cent vingt à l'heure, ce n'est pas excessif!
– Au contraire, monsieur, vous avez dépassé la limite.
A Un horloger et un client
B Un automobiliste et un gendarme
C Un professeur de mathématiques et un élève
D Un voyageur et un douanier

4 – Non, monsieur, ce n'est pas grave, c'est qu'il n'y a plus d'essence dans le réservoir.
A Un garagiste
B Un pêcheur
C Un médecin
D Un curé

5 – Au mois de mai vous aurez le maximum de confort et vous payerez moins cher.
A Un agent d'assurances
B Un vendeur de voitures
C Un employé d'une agence de voyages
D Un vendeur de meubles

6 – Que faites-vous là?
– Rien. Je regarde.
– Alors, circulez.
A Un guide et un touriste
B Un agent et le spectateur d'un accident
C Un professeur de mathématiques et son élève
D Un marchand de tableaux et son client

7 – Regarde, papa! Le coureur qui porte le maillot jaune est arrivé longtemps après les autres.
– Oui. Peut-être qu'il a crevé en route.
A Deux spectateurs d'une course de chevaux
B Deux coureurs d'une course de vélos
C Deux personnes à la fête du 14 juillet
D Deux spectateurs du Tour de France

8 – Mettez les valises au filet!
– Bien, monsieur.
A Un client et un marchand de poisson
B Un voyageur et un porteur
C Un vendeur et une petite fille
D Un pêcheur et son fils

9 – Pardon, monsieur, est-ce que ce car va au château de Chenonceaux?
   – Non, madame, il vous faut l'arrêt en face.
   A Une cliente et un chauffeur de taxi
   B Une cliente et un garagiste
   C Une dame et un coiffeur
   D Une dame et un passant dans la rue

10 – Tu as de mauvaises notes cette semaine, mon petit.
   A Un professeur de musique à une élève
   B Un épicier à un enfant qui fait des courses pour sa mère
   C Un père à son fils
   D Une femme à son mari

Section B
In this section you will read remarks or short conversations. In each case *identify the place where the remark or remarks are made.*

Example:
– Pardon, monsieur, c'est par là, le bureau de poste?
– Non, mademoiselle, prenez la deuxième rue à gauche et il est en face.
   A En pleine campagne
   B En pleine mer
   C En pleine ville
   D En avion

Correct answer: C En pleine ville

11 – Non, non, Jacques, ne laisse pas entrer le bœuf dans le pré avec les moutons.
   A A la boucherie
   B Au restaurant
   C A la ferme
   D A la cuisine

12 – Jean, va faire la queue à la caisse pendant que je cherche du café.
   A Au supermarché
   B A la gare
   C Au café
   D A la banque

13 – Pour commencer, du saucisson s'il vous plaît.
   – Et après, monsieur?
   – Je prendrai le poisson avec des pommes à l'anglaise.
   A Au restaurant
   B A la rivière
   C A la charcuterie
   D Chez le marchand de poisson

14 – Hé, Philippe, cache les bonbons tout de suite. Monsieur Moreau nous regarde.
   A A la pâtisserie-confiserie
   B En classe
   C A table
   D Dans le parc

15 – Et là, vous voyez, vous avez le choix entre la baignoire et la douche. Et naturellement, il y a le lavabo et le bidet.
   A Au bord de la mer
   B A la piscine
   C Dans une salle de bains
   D Dans une laverie

16 – Vous avez des piles pour mon magnétophone? J'en veux quatre petites comme ça.
   A Chez l'électricien
   B Chez le médecin
   C Au bureau de poste
   D A l'école maternelle

17 – Donnez-moi cinq aubergines, un kilo d'artichauts et une livre de champignons.
   A A l'auberge de jeunesse
   B Chez le marchand de légumes
   C A la librairie
   D Chez le boucher

18 – Il y a un certain Monsieur Lagrange à l'appareil.
   – Dites-lui que je suis sorti; je suis en train de dicter une lettre.
   A A la gare
   B Dans la salle de gymnastique
   C En classe
   D Au bureau

In these final questions in this section you are asked to identify where the following notices are to be found.

19 – Les clients sont priés de ne rien manger dans les chambres.
   A Au restaurant
   B Dans une prison
   C Dans la cuisine
   D A l'hôtel

20 – Pour chasser l'eau, appuyez sur le bouton.
   A Dans un cabinet de toilette
   B Dans un canot
   C Dans les escaliers d'un immeuble
   D Dans une cabine téléphonique

21 – Les clients sont priés de prendre un chariot avant de pénétrer dans le magasin.
   A A la librairie-papeterie
   B Au supermarché
   C Au magasin de sports
   D A l'arène

22 A louer, appartement moderne, quatre pièces, tout confort, chauffage central.
   A Dans un appartement
   B Au théâtre
   C Au Louvre
   D Dans un journal

Section C

In this section you will read remarks or short conversations. In each case *identify what the speakers are doing.*

23 – L'eau de ce robinet n'est pas encore chaude.
   – Utilisez celle qui est dans la casserole et commencez à laver les verres.
   A On fait la lessive.
   B On prépare des boissons.
   C On fait la vaisselle.
   D On prépare un repas.

24 – Par ce vent on ne réussira jamais à la dresser à nous deux.
   – Oui, tu as raison, appelons les voisins pour nous donner un coup de main avec les cordes.
   A On habille le bébé.
   B On fait du camping.
   C On invite des amis à une soirée.
   D On attrape un voleur.

25 – Tu as réglé le réveille-matin? Moi, je vais me brosser les dents et mettre mon pyjama.
   A On va s'habiller.
   B On va se réveiller.
   C On va se coucher.
   D On va se lever.

26 – Maman, qu'est-ce qu'il faut faire maintenant?
   – Voyons, tu ajoutes un peu de sel, tu bats les œufs, et puis tu les verses dans la poêle.
   A On discute un poème.
   B On cherche des poules.
   C On prépare du café.
   D On fait une omelette.

27 – Attache bien la corde au poteau ou le canot va partir tout seul.
   A On sort en bateau.
   B On arrive à la rive.
   C On traverse la Manche.
   D On prépare de la soupe.

28 – On a tout ce qu'il faut?
   – Oui, j'ai les cannes et le filet; toi, tu as la boîte de vers et des sandwichs, n'est-ce pas?
   A On part à la pêche.
   B On prépare un repas.
   C On dîne dans un restaurant.
   D On va à la montagne.

29 – Passe-moi la clef anglaise, s'il te plaît, Jean; je vois pourquoi la roue ne tourne pas.
   A On voyage en Angleterre.
   B On répare un vélo.
   C On entre dans la maison.
   D On examine le plan de la ville.

30 – Encore un coup et ce sera fini; je crois qu'on va bâtir un grand magasin ici.
   A On regarde construire un bâtiment.
   B On prépare un coup d'état.
   C On va se battre.
   D On regarde démolir un bâtiment.

Section D

In this section you will read a series of incomplete sentences. In each case *select the most likely end to the sentence.*

31 Avant de quitter l'école pour la maison . . .
   A j'ai dit au revoir à mes amis.
   B j'ai pris l'autobus.
   C j'ai mis mon uniforme scolaire.
   D j'ai dit au revoir à ma mère.

32 Marie a mis son maillot de bain, puis . . .
   A elle est entrée dans la salle de bains.
   B elle est sortie de la mer.
   C elle s'est couchée sur sa serviette.
   D elle a quitté la piscine.

33 En rentrant à l'hotel le soir, après une journée agréable sur la plage, Monsieur Lebrun . . .
   A a demandé une chambre avec salle de bains.
   B est entré dans le bar prendre une bière.
   C a pris son déjeuner.
   D est allé se coucher après son long voyage.

34 Comme elle voulait écouter le disque avant de l'acheter, Marie . . .
   A a demandé le prix à la vendeuse.
   B a demandé à la vendeuse de le lui passer.
   C a demandé de l'argent à son père.
   D a demandé un tourne-disque comme cadeau de Noël.

35 J'ai mis mon manteau pour aller au travail . . .
   A parce qu'il faisait froid.
   B parce que c'était dimanche.
   C parce qu'il faisait chaud.
   D parce que je prenais l'autobus.

36 Comme elle voulait balayer le plancher dans la cuisine, Mme Legros . . .
   A a mis le balai dans l'armoire.
   B a posé les chaises sur la table.
   C a pris un chiffon.
   D a préparé le déjeuner.

37 En regardant mon emploi du temps pour l'année scolaire, je vois . . .
   A qu'il va faire beau toute l'année.
   B que je vais avoir une nouvelle montre.
   C que je travaillerai dur le dimanche.
   D que j'aurai cinq heures de maths par semaine.

38 Les jeunes Anglais se sont bien amusés à Paris . . .
   A parce qu'il ne faisait que pleuvoir à verse.
   B à participer au Tour de France.
   C quand ils venaient d'arriver en Angleterre.
   D après être arrivés chez leurs correspondants.

Section E
Read the following passage and then complete the statements or answer the questions about it. In each case select the most likely answer.

Robert Lacroix était un jeune parisien de quinze ans et il avait une sœur cadette, Isabelle, qui avait huit ans et demi. Sa grand'mère, qu'il ne voyait pas souvent, habitait sur la Côte d'Azur. Elle avait aussi une maison située dans une forêt en Bretagne où Robert passait chaque année une partie de ses vacances. Il avait également des oncles et des tantes et beaucoup de cousins et de cousines. Quand la famille se réunissait – pour un mariage, par exemple – on était plus de trente personnes! Son oncle favori était l'oncle Jules. Celui-ci avait une voiture de sport et il y a deux ans il a emmené Robert et ses cousins Pierre et Louis faire du camping. Isabelle n'était pas invitée, car elle était trop jeune, mais pour la consoler on lui avait offert un petit lapin très sage qui venait toujours quand on l'appelait. L'oncle Jules espérait les emmener tous camper quand Isabelle serait plus grande.

39 Isabelle était
  A plus âgée que Robert de six ans et demi.
  B plus jeune que Robert de six ans et demi.
  C moins âgée que Robert de huit ans et demi.
  D moins jeune que Robert de huit ans et demi.

40 Robert voyait sa grand'mère
  A très souvent.
  B pendant les vacances.
  C une fois par mois.
  D rarement.

41 Où Robert passait-il une partie de ses vacances?
  A Dans une région où il y avait des bois.
  B Sur la côte d'Azur.
  C Au bord de la mer.
  D En Angleterre.

42 Que savons-nous de la famille de Robert?
  A Il avait autant d'oncles que de tantes.
  B Ils se mariaient souvent.
  C C'était une famille nombreuse.
  D Il avait une trentaine de cousins et de cousines.

43 Combien de personnes sont allés faire du camping?
  A Quatre.
  B Trois.
  C Deux.
  D Cinq.

44 Pourquoi a-t-on acheté un lapin pour Isabelle?
  A Pour son anniversaire.
  B Pour l'emmener à la campagne.
  C Parce qu'elle avait dû rester à la maison.
  D Parce qu'elle était très jeune.

45 Quand Isabelle peut-elle espérer aller faire du camping?
  A L'année prochaine.
  B Tout de suite.
  C Dans quelques années.
  D Jamais.

MULTIPLE-CHOICE QUESTIONS IN ENGLISH

Some Examination Boards test reading comprehension with multiple-choice questions to be answered in English. As with all reading comprehension questions, you must read the passage or sentences very carefully. Never jump to conclusions. Some of the answers may mislead you if you do not read carefully enough. Read *all* the suggested answers before making your choice.

1 (EMREB)   *Time allowed: 45 minutes*

For each question there are four alternative answers, only *one* of which is correct. Read and consider each question carefully, but if you do not know the answer, do not spend too much time on it. If you complete the examination before the time allowed, go back and spend more time on questions about which you are unsure.

Section A

1 Défense de stationner.
This sign means
  A No parking
  B Station security officer
  C No entry to station
  D Supervised parking

2 The notice **Sortie** on a door means
  A Entrance
  B Push
  C Exit
  D Engaged

3 Quand elle a appris la nouvelle, Mme Leduc s'est fâchée.
Mme Leduc
  A was shocked.
  B fainted.
  C became angry.
  D laughed.

4 Le bateau est arrivé en retard à cause du brouillard.
The ship was delayed because of
A the tide.
B a storm.
C fog.
D a breakdown.

5 Les enfants sont admis à tarif réduit.
This tells you that children
A must pay full price for admission.
B are only allowed in with an adult.
C are allowed in at a reduced rate.
D are admitted at certain times only.

6 Il gèle et Marianne va faire une promenade.
Marianne must
A take her umbrella.
B wear her sun glasses.
C put on warm clothes.
D wear light clothes.

7 'Merci', a dit Mme Leroy à la vendeuse, 'mais je cherchais quelque chose de moins cher.'
Mme Leroy was looking for something
A more cheerful looking.
B in a different colour.
C not so expensive.
D more expensive.

8 MM. les campeurs sont priés de jeter leurs ordures dans la poubelle.
This notice on the campsite is asking campers to
A keep order on the campsite.
B place their order as soon as possible.
C put their rubbish in the rubbish bin.
D respect the camp rules.

9 The notice **Sortie de secours** means
A Way out
B No exit
C No entry
D Emergency exit

10 Monsieur Dupont a besoin d'un stylo.
Monsieur Dupont
A has broken his pen.
B needs a pen.
C has lost his pen.
D has bought a pen.

11 A person going into a building marked *P. et T.* could be going to
A buy stamps.
B see a film.
C buy a train ticket.
D take part in some sporting activity.

12 'Je ne sais pas encore ce que je deviendrai, mais j'espère avoir une bonne situation,' a dit Simone.
Simone was talking about
A what she does in her spare time.
B her family circumstances.
C what she will do when she leaves school.
D where she will spend her holidays.

13 Jean-Paul a pris son maillot et une serviette.
Jean-Paul was going to
A get washed.
B have a meal.
C knock in some tent pegs.
D go swimming.

14 Marie n'aime pas la cuisine anglaise.
Marie doesn't like
A her English cousin.
B English cooking.
C her English teacher.
D English kitchens.

15 'Je ne peux pas accepter ce que vous dites, Charles: vous n'avez pas raison,' a dit M. Raymond.
M. Raymond cannot accept what Charles says, because
A Charles is unreasonable.
B there is no reason why he should.
C Charles is wrong.
D Charles is dishonest.

Section B

Read the passage printed below. You should then answer all *ten* questions on this section. You are advised to attempt them in the order in which they appear on the paper.

Madame Duval allait en ville faire ses achats. Elle y allait tous les quinze jours. Le temps était nuageux, avec très peu de vent. Mme Duval prit son parapluie, car elle était sûre qu'il allait pleuvoir plus tard.

Mme Duval avait une voiture, mais elle prenait le car pour aller en ville, parce que le stationnement en ville était très difficile. Elle prenait généralement le car de neuf heures, mais ce jour-là, elle le manqua et elle dut attendre le prochain, une demi-heure plus tard.

Mme Duval avait acheté le journal, mais au lieu de le lire en attendant le car, elle passa le temps à écouter une dame qui attendait avec elle parler de sa famille.

Quand elle descendit du car, Mme Duval alla tout d'abord à la boulangerie acheter deux baguettes. Puis elle alla à l'épicerie, où elle acheta beaucoup de choses. Mademoiselle Latour, l'épicière, connaissait bien Mme Duval. Elle mit les achats dans son filet, et, comme il n'y avait pas d'autres clients dans le magasin, les deux dames bavardèrent un peu.

'Où allez-vous passer les vacances cette année, Madame Duval?' demanda Mlle Latour. 'A la campagne? Ou à la montagne, peut-être?'

'Nous sommes allés à la campagne l'année dernière,' répondit Mme Duval. 'Nous espérons faire un séjour au bord de la mer.'

Mme Duval était sur le point de quitter le magasin. 'Zut! J'allais oublier,' dit-elle. 'Il me faut un kilo de sucre. Il m'en faut pour la visite de ma sœur et de sa famille demain. Ils viennent chez nous tous les samedis.'

16 Mme Duval went to town every
  A fortnight.
  B week.
  C five weeks.
  D few days.

17 The weather when she left the house was
  A very windy.
  B cold.
  C rainy.
  D cloudy.

18 She went to town by bus because
  A she hadn't got a car.
  B parking was difficult in town.
  C her husband had taken the car.
  D she found driving in town difficult.

19 Mme Duval caught the bus at
  A 10 o'clock.
  B 9 o'clock.
  C 10.30
  D 9.30

20 While waiting for the bus, Mme Duval
  A went to buy a newspaper.
  B read the newspaper.
  C listened to a lady talking about her family.
  D talked to a lady about her family.

21 When she arrived in town, Mme Duval went first of all to the
  A grocer's.
  B butcher's.
  C baker's.
  D handbag shop.

22 How many customers, including Mme Duval, were in the grocer's?
  A One.
  B Two.
  C Three.
  D Four.

23 The Duvals were hoping to spend their holidays
  A with Mme Duval's mother.
  B at the seaside.
  C in the mountains.
  D in the countryside.

24 Mme Duval nearly forgot
  A her sister's visit.
  B her bag of groceries.
  C to pay for her purchases.
  D to buy some sugar.

25 On what day of the week did Mme Duval's visit to town take place?
  A Tuesday
  B Thursday
  C Friday
  D Saturday

10 Listening comprehension

Listening comprehension tests are included in almost all O-level and CSE examinations in French. There are, however, differences in the methods of testing. Some Examination Boards ask questions in French to be answered in French. Others ask questions in English to be answered in English. Some Examination Boards ask multiple-choice questions in French and others ask multiple-choice questions in English. Check your examination syllabus to find out which type of listening comprehension test you will have to do.

Some listening comprehension tests will be based on a passage of French read to you. Others are based on short remarks or conversations, which you will hear. The material used in the listening comprehension test will be repeated at least once, sometimes three times, depending on the length of the test. During the first reading, you should try to grasp the main idea of the passage or conversation. Do not worry about individual vocabulary items which might puzzle you at this stage, but concentrate on the main point or ideas.

After the first reading, you will normally be allowed to study the questions. With the exception of multiple-choice questions, where the technique is slightly different, the questions should help you to understand the passage or conversation. The questions will normally be in chronological order when a passage is used for listening comprehension.

The passage or conversation will then be read for the second time and at the end of the second reading you will be allowed to answer the questions. If a passage of French is used, there is sometimes a third reading, during which you should check the answers you have written and listen carefully to find the answers to those questions of which you are not sure. Do not leave any question unanswered. Even if you are not absolutely sure of the answer to a certain question, always write down what you think the answer might be. You might be right after all!

Multiple-choice questions

In this type of listening comprehension test, the answers to the comprehension questions are actually given on your paper. It is up to you to choose the right answers from amongst the other three or four incorrect answers. You must listen just as carefully as for the other types of listening comprehension test, and use your common sense when choosing your answer.

Given below are examples of the various types of listening comprehension test. You must remember, of course, that you would not see the words printed below, only the questions. If possible, ask someone who speaks French to read the passages to you.

QUESTIONS IN ENGLISH

1 (SEB)　　*Time allowed: 30 minutes for the two passages*

Passage A: A handy lamp-post/Un lampadaire utile
– Tu es sûre que tu n'as pas ta clef?

M. Antoine posait cette question à sa femme devant la porte de l'immeuble où ils habitaient. Un taxi venait de les déposer à une heure du matin. Et M. Antoine ne trouvait pas sa clef non plus.

– Il va falloir passer par une fenêtre, a dit M. Antoine finalement.

Seulement les Antoine habitaient au deuxième étage.

– On va sonner, a protesté Madame Antoine. Mais son mari ne l'écoutait pas. Il grimpait déjà un lampadaire qui arrivait au deuxième étage juste sous la fenêtre de leur chambre.

Mais au moment où M. Antoine ouvrait la fenêtre, le lampadaire s'est cassé. Horrifiée, Madame Antoine a vu son mari tomber.

Heureusement pour lui, il y avait un magasin au rez-de-chaussée. Sur le trottoir devant le magasin il y avait des sacs pleins de papiers. M. Antoine est tombé sur les sacs.

A l'hôpital on a trouvé que M. Antoine n'avait rien de cassé. Et on a retrouvé la clef de l'appartement. Elle était dans la poche de son pantalon.

1 Why could the Antoines not get in?
2 What time was it exactly?
3 How did M. Antoine propose to get in?
4 What floor was their flat on?
5 What was Mme Antoine's suggestion?
6 Why was her husband not listening?
7 What use did he make of the lamp-post?
8 (a) What went wrong?
　　(b) What was M. Antoine doing at the time?
9 What saved M. Antoine from serious injury?
10 What discoveries were made in hospital?

Passage B: A hearty eater/Un gros gourmand
Tout le monde connaissait Bouboule; Bouboule était le nouvel apprenti de notre magasin de vêtements. Il travaillait chez nous depuis quelques mois.

A seize ans, ce petit jeune homme était déjà gros. Ce n'était pas étonnant; il mangeait tout le temps. A midi il mangeait deux fois plus que les autres à la cantine. Et après, dans l'arrière-boutique, il mangeait deux bananes ou peut-être un paquet de biscuits.

Mais Bouboule était gentil. Si un collègue n'avait pas eu le temps de prendre son petit déjeuner, Bouboule allait tout de suite lui chercher un sandwich dans ses réserves.

Un jour nous avons beaucoup ri. Un client a surpris Bouboule en train de manger un sandwich sous le comptoir.

– Vite, il me faut une chemise, jeune homme, a dit le client qui était très pressé. Bouboule avait déjà caché son sandwich sous une chemise blanche qui se trouvait sur le comptoir.

– Je prends celle-là, a déclaré le client. Tout confus, Bouboule a enveloppé la chemise blanche. Et le client est parti, tout content, avec sa chemise . . . et le sandwich de Bouboule.

1 (a) Who was Bouboule?
  (b) What kind of shop did he work in?
2 Why was he so fat?
3 What shows that he had a huge appetite
  (a) at mealtimes
  (b) afterwards?
4 How do we know that he was not selfish about his food?
5 What was he doing when taken by surprise one day?
6 What did he do to conceal the evidence?
7 What happened to Bouboule's sandwich?

2 (LREB)   *Time allowed: 30 minutes*

On holiday in Paris

Jean-Pierre et son amie Pauline passaient trois jours à Paris. Ils y étaient arrivés vendredi soir dans la petite voiture de Pauline. Le samedi matin, après avoir pris le petit déjeuner, ils ont décidé de faire une promenade à pied le long de la Seine. Ils ont vu les bateaux qui passaient sur la rivière, et ils ont regardé les livres vendus par les bouquinistes. Enfin, vers midi, ils se sont trouvés devant la cathédrale de Notre-Dame.

– J'ai faim, a dit Pauline. Allons trouver un restaurant, veux-tu? Nous pourrons visiter la cathédrale plus tard.

Ils sont donc entrés dans une rue tranquille où ils ont bientôt trouvé un restaurant. Dans une petite cour se trouvaient quelques tables à l'ombre des arbres. Les deux amis ont lu la carte du jour qui leur paraissait très intéressante. Ils se sont décidés à y entrer. Ils ont mangé un excellent repas bien cuit et bien servi et ils ont bu une demi-bouteille de vin blanc. Enfin le garçon a apporté l'addition. Jean-Pierre l'a regardée mais n'a pas pu trouver le prix du vin.

– Garçon, a-t-il dit, je ne vois pas le vin.

– Ah! C'est vrai, a répondu le garçon. J'ai oublié de le marquer. Je vous en remercie, monsieur.

Après leur déjeuner ils se sont rendus à la cathédrale où il y avait un groupe d'enfants qui parlaient une langue étrangère.

– Ce sont sans doute des élèves anglais, a dit Jean-Pierre. Et regarde, voilà leur professeur.

En sortant, les deux amis ont trouvé devant la cathédrale une petite fille qui pleurait.

– Qu'est-ce qu'il y a? lui a demandé Pauline.

– J'ai perdu mon professeur, a répondu la petite fille.

– Viens avec moi, a dit Pauline. Je crois qu'il est par ici. Tu es anglaise, n'est-ce pas?

Pauline a pris la petite fille par la main et lui a montré le professeur.

1 How long were the two young people staying in Paris?
2 How did they travel to Paris?
3 How did they intend to move around Paris on Saturday morning?
4 Where did they intend to go?
5 What did they find to look at during their morning?
6 What did the girl suggest that they should do later in the afternoon?
7 What appealed to them about the restaurant they found?
8 What are you told about their meal?
9 What was peculiar about the bill?
10 Whom did the two friends see in the Cathedral of Notre-Dame?
11 How did they know that these people were not French?
12 How did Pauline deal with the little girl who was in distress?

QUESTIONS IN FRENCH

The signalman/L'aiguilleur (Oxford)

Rambert partait chaque soir à la même heure, exactement six minutes avant huit heures. Sa maison, avec deux ou trois autres, était bâtie sur la falaise et, en sortant, il voyait à ses pieds la mer, le port et, plus à gauche, la ville de Dieppe. Comme on était en plein hiver, on voyait partout, à cette heure-là, beaucoup de lumières: les rouges et vertes du port, les lumières blanches des quais, enfin toutes les lumières de la ville.

Rambert était parti de mauvaise humeur, mais il n'avait pas oublié de prendre le pain et le beurre et le saucisson que sa femme avait préparés. Puis il a descendu la colline, a tourné à gauche et s'est dirigé vers le pont. A huit heures, il commençait à monter l'échelle de fer conduisant à sa cabine. Il était aiguilleur. Les autres aiguilleurs avaient leur cabine plantée parmi les chemins de fer et les signaux, mais celle de Rambert était en ville, et tout près du port.

Sa gare n'était pas une vraie gare, mais une gare maritime. Les bateaux qui arrivaient d'Angleterre deux fois par jour, à une heure et à minuit, se rangeaient le long du quai. Le train de Paris, quittant la gare ordinaire, à l'autre bout de Dieppe, traversait la ville et s'arrêtait à quelques mètres du navire. Rambert avait trente-deux marches à monter et au sommet de l'échelle il trouvait la cabine vitrée où son assistant mettait déjà son pardessus.

Section A

1 Qu'est-ce que Rambert faisait tous les soirs?
2 Où se trouvait la maison de Rambert?
3 Que voyait-on en sortant de cette maison?
4 Quelles lumières voyait-on?

Section B

5 Qu'est-ce que Rambert a emporté avec lui?
6 Qu'est-ce que Rambert a fait après avoir descendu la colline?
7 Où se trouvait la cabine de Rambert?

Section C

8 Qu'est-ce qui se passait deux fois par jour?
9 Que faisait le train de Paris entre les deux gares?
10 Qu'est-ce qui se passait quand Rambert est entré dans la cabine?

MULTIPLE-CHOICE QUESTIONS IN ENGLISH

(EMREB)   *Time allowed: 45 minutes*

Section A

You will hear 15 short sentences spoken in French. Each sentence will be read to you twice. You will be allowed 20 seconds in which to read each question and decide which of the four answers is correct. Only *one* answer is correct.

Here is an example of a question.
    – Je voudrais une chambre avec deux lits, s'il vous plaît.
The speaker is
    A buying a train ticket.
    B booking a room in a hotel.
    C arranging to have his car repaired.
    D ordering a meal in a restaurant.
The answer to this question is B, booking a room in a hotel.

1 – Un litre de lait et six œufs, s'il vous plaît.
You would most likely hear this in a
A dairy.
B garage.
C baker's.
D sweetshop.

2 M. et Mme Bourdon et leurs quatre enfants habitent au numéro cinq, rue de la Gare.
How many are there in the Bourdon family?
    A 7
    B 4
    C 5
    D 6

3 – Pouvez-vous me dire où se trouve la banque, s'il vous plaît?
The speaker is asking
A when the bank opens.
B if there is a bank.
C who has found the bank.
D the way to the bank.

4 Il fait beaucoup de vent dans le Midi.
This person is talking about
A his work.
B the grape harvest.
C the weather.
D the time.

5 – Dans cet hôtel il n'y a pas de télévision dans les chambres, mais il y a un poste dans le salon.
In this hotel, there is
A television in the bedrooms only.
B television in the lounge only.
C no television at all.
D television in the bedrooms and the lounge.

6 – Qu'est-ce que vous aimez manger, Michel?
Michel is being asked
A what he is going to eat.
B if he has eaten.
C if he would like to eat.
D what he likes to eat.

7 – La carte des vins, s'il vous plaît.
This person is
A buying a postcard.
B asking for the wine list.
C playing cards.
D asking for a map.

8 – Ce café est très fort, a dit Mme Rousseau.
Mme Rousseau finds
A the café is very crowded.
B the coffee very cold.
C the café very expensive.
D the coffee very strong.

9 – Essaie de rester un peu, Marie, a dit Mme Duval.
Mme Duval was trying to get Marie to
A sit down and rest a bit.
B try to stay a short while.
C try to rest a little.
D stay sitting down a while.

10 – Je suis enchanté de faire votre connaissance.
You would say this if you were
A wishing someone a happy birthday.
B apologising to someone.
C arranging to meet someone.
D being introduced to someone.

11 Yvonne est allée faire une promenade au bord de la mer.
Yvonne
A walked along the promenade.
B went for a boat trip.
C went for a walk by the seaside.
D went for a walk with her mother.

12 – Vous devez prendre l'autobus numéro quatre-vingt-quinze, madame.
The lady is being told she must catch bus number
A 85
B 25
C 95
D 75

13 – Mon fils va bientôt avoir cinq ans, a dit Mme Bresson.
Mme Bresson's son is
A only just four.
B five.
C fifteen.
D nearly five.

14 – Nous arriverons vers neuf heures.
The speaker is saying that they will arrive
A about 9 o'clock
B at 9 o'clock.
C before 9 o'clock.
D after 9 o'clock.

15 – Des timbres? Alors, le guichet numéro quatre, madame.
You would most likely hear this in a
A railway station.
B café-tabac.
C post office.
D supermarket.

Section B

A longer passage of French will now be read to you. During the first reading there will be no pauses. You will then have two minutes to study the questions. The passage will then be read again in three parts, with a short pause after each part to allow you twenty seconds to answer each question on that part. A third reading without pauses will then be made, after which you will be allowed two minutes to check your answers.

Mme Prévert: Bonjour, Monsieur Lebel. Comment allez-vous?

M. Lebel: Ça va, merci, Madame Prévert. Et vous?

Mme Prévert: Très bien, merci. Quelle belle journée, n'est-ce pas? Après toute cette pluie hier.

M. Lebel: Oui, mais je crois qu'il va faire froid plus tard.

Mme Prévert: Vous n'êtes pas au travail aujourd'hui, Monsieur Lebel? Vous avez congé peut-être?

M. Lebel: Non, c'est l'heure du déjeuner. Je vais à la pharmacie chercher une ordonnance pour ma femme. Elle est enrhumée.

Mme Prévert: Oh, la pauvre. J'espère que ce n'est pas trop grave?

M. Lebel: Non, heureusement, Dieu merci.

Mme Prévert: Vous êtes prêts à partir en vacances?

M. Lebel: Oui, d'habitude nous faisons du camping, mais cette année nous allons au bord de la mer en Angleterre.

Mme Prévert: Vous êtes déjà allés en Angleterre?

   M. Lebel: Ma femme n'y est jamais allée, mais moi, j'ai passé deux semaines à Londres il y a un an. Londres est très beau, et les gens étaient charmants, mais il y a trop de monde partout. Et vous, Madame Prévert, connaissez-vous l'Angleterre?

Mme Prévert: Nous allons souvent en Angleterre, mon mari et moi. Nous aimons beaucoup les magasins anglais. Nous rapportons toujours beaucoup de choses.

   M. Lebel: Vous n'avez pas eu de problèmes à la douane?

Mme Prévert: Jamais. Les douaniers sont toujours si aimables.

   M. Lebel: Vous comprenez l'anglais, Madame Prévert?

Mme Prévert: Un peu. Pas beaucoup. La première fois que je suis allée en Angleterre j'ai eu peur. J'étais très jeune et je ne parlais pas du tout anglais . . . Eh bien, excusez-moi, Monsieur Lebel. Je dois m'en aller chercher le pain.

   M. Lebel: Au revoir, Madame Prévert.

Part 1

16 At the time of this conversation, it is
  A foggy.
  B raining.
  C fine.
  D cold.

17 M. Lebel is not at work because
  A it is his lunch hour.
  B his wife is ill.
  C he has a holiday.
  D he is going to meet his wife.

Part 2

18 Mme Prévert asks M. Lebel
  A if he has had his holidays.
  B where he has been for his holidays
  C if he is ready for his holidays.
  D if it will soon be time for his holidays.

19 M. Lebel and his wife usually spend their holidays
  A in the countryside.
  B camping.
  C at the seaside.
  D in England.

20 How long was M. Lebel in England?
  A Two weeks
  B Ten weeks
  C One month
  D A year

21 What comment does M. Lebel make about London?
  A It is very big.
  B The policemen were charming.
  C Everyone goes there.
  D It was very crowded.

Part 3

22 When Mme Prévert and her husband go to England, they
  A have lots of things to report.
  B do a lot of sightseeing.
  C take a lot of luggage.
  D bring back lots of things.

23 Mme Prévert says that the Customs officers are always so
  A rude.
  B pleasant.
  C thorough.
  D busy.

24 The first time that Mme Prévert went to England, she
  A was afraid.
  B went with her father.
  C went as an 'au pair' girl.
  D spoke only a little English.

25 When Mme Prévert finishes talking to M. Lebel, she intends going
  A to get some wine.
  B to church.
  C to the breadshop.
  D to someone's house.

MULTIPLE-CHOICE QUESTIONS IN FRENCH

In this type of listening comprehension test you might hear short sentences spoken in French. Sometimes it may be a dialogue. You will then be asked to choose one of the written suggested answers to indicate such things as who the speaker(s) is (are), where the conversation is taking place, or information of a similar nature.

On the next page are examples of the type of test material you might *hear,* and their multiple-choice questions, which you would *see.*

Section A

Where would you most likely hear:

1 – Le service n'est pas compris, Monsieur.
  A Dans une église.
  B Dans un restaurant.
  C Au marché.
  D A la bibliothèque.

2 – Je voudrais deux kilos de pommes de terre, s'il vous plaît.
  A Dans un restaurant
  B Au garage
  C A la gare
  D Au marché

3 – Deux timbres à trois francs, s'il vous plaît.
  A A la station-service
  B Au bureau de poste
  C Chez le coiffeur
  D Au bord de la mer

4 – J'ai oublié ma serviette, mais je vais nager quand même.
  A A la piscine
  B Au bureau
  C Au poste de police
  D A la gare

5 – Bonjour, mademoiselle. Nous venons d'arriver à Chamonix. Pouvez-vous nous indiquer un bon hôtel, s'il vous plaît?
  A Dans un hôtel
  B A la banque
  C Au théâtre
  D Au syndicat d'initiative

Who is the speaker most likely to be?

6 – Je regrette, mais nous n'avons pas de croissants aujourd'hui.
  A Le facteur
  B Le professeur
  C Le curé
  D Le boulanger

7 – Vous devez prendre deux comprimés trois fois par jour.
  A Le médecin
  B Le chef de gare
  C Un bébé
  D Le coiffeur

Who are the speakers most likely to be?

8 – Oui madame, vous désirez?
  – Vingt litres de super, s'il vous plaît.
  A Une élève et son professeur
  B Une dame et son coiffeur
  C Une dame et un employé de gare
  D Une automobiliste et un garagiste

9 – Pour aller à la Tour Eiffel, monsieur?
  – Il faut aller tout droit, monsieur.
  A Un touriste et un passant
  B Un médecin et son client
  C Un élève et son professeur
  D Un garagiste et son mécanicien

10 – Regarde la pendule! Tu es en retard pour le premier cours.
  – Oui monsieur. Je regrette, monsieur, mais je n'ai pas fini mes devoirs non plus.
  A Un employé et son patron
  B Un élève et son professeur
  C Un garçon et son père
  D Un athlète et son entraîneur

Section B

Le voyageur: Excusez-moi, monsieur, mais à quelle heure part le prochain train pour Paris?
L'employé: A onze heures moins le quart, monsieur.
Le voyageur: Et de quel quai, s'il vous plaît?
L'employé: Du quai numéro seize, monsieur.
Le voyageur: Merci, monsieur. Ce train aura un wagon-restaurant?
L'employé: Non, monsieur, mais vous pouvez prendre quelque chose ici dans le Buffet de la gare.
Le voyageur: Et la salle d'attente, s'il vous plaît?
L'employé: La voilà, à gauche, derrière le kiosque à journaux.
Le voyageur: Merci, monsieur.

1 Le voyageur désire savoir . . .
  A à quelle heure le train de Paris est parti.
  B à quelle heure le train de Paris est arrivé.
  C à quelle heure partira le train de Paris.
  D à quelle heure arrivera le train de Paris.

2 L'employé a dit à . . .
  A 10.15   C 10.45
  B 11.45   D 11.15

3 On trouvera le train au quai . . .
  A 6   C 17
  B 16   D 7

4 Le voyageur désire savoir s'il pourra . . .
  A prendre un repas dans le train.
  B fumer dans le train.
  C dormir dans le train.
  D mettre tous ses bagages dans le train.

5 Devant la salle d'attente, on peut . . .
  A téléphoner.
  B acheter des sandwichs.
  C acheter un journal.
  D voir l'indicateur.

Suggested answers to examination practice questions

All the answers in this section, except for answers to multiple-choice questions, are suggestions only. They are designed to give you an idea of how to answer the different types of question, but obviously, particularly in translations, there can be no 'right' answer, and many variations will be acceptable.

ORAL COMPOSITION

Set questions on pictures

1 (p. 92)

(a) Cette scène se passe dans un port.
(b) Il fait beau.
(c) Il est midi dix.
(d) Il vend des bijoux, des ceintures et des sacs à main.
(e) J'en vois quatre.
(f) Il lit un journal.
(g) J'en vois cinq.
(h) Il décharge des bouteilles d'un camion.
(i) L'agence se trouve à côté de la pharmacie.
(j) Ils jouent au football.

2 (p. 93)

(a) La voiture est devant la maison.
(b) Le chat est sur une valise sur la galerie de la voiture.
(c) Il y a un sac et une valise dans le coffre.
(d) Cette scène se passe en été.
(e) Il y a un garage à droite de la maison.
(f) Il y en a deux.
(g) Il tient une canne à pêche à la main droite.
(h) Elle prend une petit valise.
(i) Il est dans la voiture.
(j) La famille va au bord de la mer.

3 (p. 93)

(a) Cette scène se passe à la piscine.
(b) Il fait beau.
(c) Elle est en train de prendre une photo.
(d) Elle se couche au soleil.
(e) Ils jouent avec un ballon.
(f) On nage dans une piscine.
(g) On porte un maillot (caleçon) de bain pour nager.
(h) Elle s'est couchée sur une serviette.
(i) Il va plonger dans l'eau.
(j) Oui, je sais nager./Non, je ne sais pas nager.

4 (p. 94)

(a) Cette scène se passe en hiver.
(b) Il neige./Il fait froid.
(c) Les enfants font un bonhomme de neige.
(d) Ils jettent des boules de neige.
(e) Ils font de la luge.
(f) Elle porte une veste, une jupe, une écharpe, un bonnet et des bottes.
(g) Il est tombé dans l'eau à travers la glace.
(h) La forêt se trouve à gauche au loin.
(i) Il y a le mot 'danger'.
(j) Je jette des boules de neige à mes amis.

FREE COMPOSITION

Picture composition type 2

1 (p. 118)

(a) Cette scène se passe dans un café.
(b) J'en vois quatre.
(c) Elles prennent du café.
(d) Il verse du café.

2 (p. 119)

(a) Il porte un panier.
(b) Les vaches sont dans un champ.
(c) Il fait beau./Le soleil brille.
(d) On va manger des sandwichs, des gâteaux et des pommes.

3 (p. 119)

(a) Il lit un journal.
(b) Il est assis dans un fauteuil.
(c) Ils regardent par la fenêtre.
(d) On est au salon.

4 (p. 120)

(a) Cette scène se passe au bord de la rivière.
(b) Il est en train de pêcher./Il pêche.
(c) Il porte un maillot rayé, un pantalon et un béret.
(d) Le chien est sur un bateau.

5 (p. 120)

(a) Cette scène se passe dans une salle de classe.
(b) J'en vois cinq.
(c) Non, elle est ouverte.
(d) Il écrit sur le tableau noir.

6 (p. 121)

(a) Il arrive à une ferme.
(b) Il est arrivé à vélo.
(c) Il est venu voir son ami.

7 (p. 121)

(a) Il y a quatre personnes.
(b) La famille déjeune.
(c) Les deux enfants rient parce que le petit enfant a jeté sa tasse sur le plancher.

8 (p. 121)

(a) Elles sont dans le salon.
(b) Elle écoute des disques.
(c) Elle lui dira de fermer le tourne-disques.

9 (p. 121)

(a) Cette scène se passe pendant la récréation.

(b) Il va gronder deux élèves méchants.

(c) Ils fumaient.

10 (p. 121)

(a) Il est Anglais.

(b) Il va lui dire, 'Mais vous êtes fou!'

(c) Il y a eu un accident parce que l'Anglais a conduit à gauche au lieu de conduire à droite.

11 (p. 122)

(a) J'en vois trois.

(b) Ils passent leurs vacances à vélo.

(c) Ils poussent leurs vélos parce qu'il y a une grande colline.

(d) Ils ont très chaud.

(e) Ils vont passer la nuit au bord d'une rivière.

(f) Il va préparer un repas.

(g) Il y va chercher du lait.

(h) Il dresse la tente.

(i) Pendant la nuit il commence à pleuvoir à verse. Le fermier arrive avec son chien. Il invite les garçons à venir passer la nuit à la ferme.

(j) Ils ont décidé de passer la nuit dans la grange.

(k) Elle est venue à la grange leur porter quelque chose de chaud à boire.

(l) Il leur dit bonne nuit.

(m) Ils portent des imperméables et des bottes.

Dialogue continuation

4 (p. 123)

(a) (i) Il a six ans.

    (ii) Il est gros et il a les yeux bleus. Il a les cheveux roux.

    (iii) Il porte un short et un pull.

    (iv) Nous étions au premier étage.

    (v) Je l'ai cherché dans tout le magasin.

(b) (i) Je devais prendre le train de six heures.

    (ii) Je suis arrivé trop tard à la gare.

    (iii) J'ai attendu une heure et demie.

    (iv) J'ai lu un livre.

    (v) Je n'avais pas de monnaie.

TRANSLATION: ENGLISH TO FRENCH

1 (p. 126)

Pierre était en colère. En été il aimait aller voir ses cousins qui habitaient à la campagne. Là, lui et sa sœur pouvaient faire beaucoup de bruit, jouer au bord du lac et se promener aux bois. Ils y allaient généralement au mois d'août pendant leurs vacances, et ils s'amusaient bien. Un autre oncle venait de téléphoner de Paris. Pierre ne le connaissait pas très bien. Cet oncle l'invitait à passer un mois entier en France pour apprendre à parler français comme un Français. Pierre ne voulait pas accepter cette invitation. Il croyait que ce serait difficile et qu'il ne comprendrait pas ce que disaient les gens. Peut-être qu'il n'aimerait pas les repas. Toute la famille en a parlé longtemps. Enfin, son père a dit qu'il pourrait y aller en avion. 'D'accord,' a dit Pierre, 'achète-moi un billet, s'il te plaît.'

2 (p. 127)

Je m'appelle Philippe. L'été dernier, ma mère et moi avons passé quelques semaines en Écosse avec quelques amis qui avaient loué une maison au bord de la mer. Nous avons fait le voyage par le train.

    Un soir, je me promenais seul quand j'ai remarqué deux garçons qui jouaient sur des rochers. Tout à coup, l'un d'eux a glissé et est tombé dans la mer.

    D'abord j'ai cru qu'il allait se noyer, car il ne savait pas nager. Puis, heureusement, un touriste, qui pêchait tout près, a réussi à le sauver avec sa ligne.

    L'homme était trempé, mais au lieu de se fâcher, il s'est tourné vers le garçon et lui a dit gentiment: 'Si tu es sage, tu apprendras à nager aussi vite que possible.'

3 (p. 128)

C'était la première fois que Robert avait quitté ses hôtes depuis son arrivée en France la semaine dernière. Monsieur Deschamps avait des devoirs à faire en ville, et le correspondant de Robert, Pierre, voulait aller à la bibliothèque. Robert les a donc accompagnés, et puis il est allé à la foire au jardin public, où ses amis le rejoindraient plus tard. Il a erré parmi les foules et a essayé même quelques-unes des attractions. Tout à coup il a éprouvé un choc et a failli tomber par terre. Il s'est retourné et a vu un jeune homme barbu, qui a murmuré: 'Pardon, mon petit,' et s'est sauvé. C'était seulement plus tard qu'il a découvert que son portefeuille n'était plus dans sa poche.

    Quand les Deschamps sont arrivés, il leur a raconté ce qui s'était passé. 'Y avait-il beaucoup d'argent dans le portefeuille?' a demandé M. Deschamps. 'Environ dix francs seulement,' a-t-il répondu. 'Tout de même, nous devons aller voir mon vieil ami le commissaire de police.'

    Le commissaire a écouté d'un air sérieux leur histoire et la description que Robert a donnée du jeune homme. 'Je crois que ce doit être Robert Aramis,' a-t-il dit. 'C'est un criminel bien connu. Mes hommes l'interrogeront. Votre argent ne vous sera probablement pas rendu, mais nous verrons.'

4 (p. 128)

Il y a quelques jours je venais de finir le petit déjeuner quand on a frappé à la porte. 'C'est le facteur. Va voir ce qu'il nous a apporté, Robert,' a crié maman, qui était dans la cuisine.

Quand j'ai ouvert la porte, le facteur, que je connaissais bien, m'a donné un paquet. 'Comment va ton père aujourd'hui?' a-t-il demandé, car il savait que papa était malade depuis plusieurs semaines.

'Il va beaucoup mieux, merci. Il espère se lever bientôt,' ai-je répondu. En entrant dans la cuisine, j'ai remarqué qu'il était presque huit heures et demie. 'Dépêche-toi,' a dit ma mère. 'Tu ne seras pas à l'école avant neuf heures.'

J'habite à trois kilomètres environ de l'école et il n'y a pas de car. J'ai pris mes livres, j'ai dit au revoir et je me suis mis en route tout de suite.

5 (p. 128)

Mon oncle, qui habite à la campagne, vient nous rendre visite à Londres une fois par an. Ma sœur et moi lui demandons toujours de nous emmener au théâtre. Il aime le faire parce qu'il ne voit jamais de pièce de théâtre dans son petit village. Tout le monde est donc content et sa visite est un grand succès.

Cette année il est arrivé la veille de mon anniversaire. 'Alors,' a-t-il dit, 'Tu auras seize ans demain. Je crois que nous devrions entendre un opéra au lieu de voir une pièce. Aimerais-tu cela?' J'ai répondu que cela me plairait beaucoup, et ma sœur, qui joue du violon, était ravie.

'Ne faites pas trop d'attention à l'histoire. Elle vous paraîtra probablement un peu stupide, mais l'art et la vie sont deux choses différentes. Écoutez la musique.' C'était une soirée intéressante. Nous avons pris un repas magnifique après, pendant lequel mon oncle a expliqué tout ce que nous n'avions pas compris.

6 (p. 128)

L'année dernière, après avoir passé deux semaines à Paris, Jean a décidé de prendre le train de midi à la Gare du Nord. Il faisait beau temps et le soleil brillait ce jour-là. Pendant son séjour à Paris, Jean s'était bien amusé et il était triste de quitter une si belle ville.

A onze heures et demie il a quitté l'hôtel à pied, car il n'avait pas beaucoup de bagages et il aimait toujours se promener. Arrivé à la gare, il a acheté un journal et un magazine. Après les avoir achetés, il s'est rendu compte qu'il ne lui restait que cinq francs, mais il avait toujours de l'argent anglais qu'il pourrait dépenser sur le ferry. Il espérait que la traversée serait calme et qu'il n'aurait pas le mal de mer. L'année prochaine il espérait retourner en France, mais cette fois en avion.

7 (p. 128)

Un matin d'hiver, Pierre et sa mère, qui habitaient un petit appartement près du centre de la ville, sont sortis faire des commissions. Pierre n'avait que trois ans et n'allait pas encore à l'école. Louise, sa sœur ainée qui avait treize ans, était élève au Collège d'Enseignement Secondaire. Elle aimait beaucoup son école mais elle avait toujours beaucoup de devoirs à faire.

Pierre aimait faire des commissions avec sa mère parce qu'elle lui achèterait une tablette de chocolat s'il était sage. Sa mère s'inquiétait parce que le temps faisait si froid et Pierre était souvent malade en hiver.

'Mets tes gants et ton écharpe, Pierre,' a-t-elle dit avant de sortir. 'Tu ne dois pas t'enrhumer.'

8 (p. 129)

'Lève-toi tout de suite!' a dit papa à Annette. 'Ta mère est dans la cuisine et le petit déjeuner est prêt.'

'J'ai mal à la tête et je ne veux pas me lever,' a répondu Annette.

'Qu'est-ce qu'il y a?' a crié maman de la cuisine.

'Annette dit qu'elle a mal à la tête et qu'elle ne veut pas se lever,' a dit papa.

Mme Leclerc savait que sa fille était très paresseuse et qu'elle faisait semblant d'être malade. Aujourd'hui Annette devait aider sa mère à faire le ménage et Annette était toujours malade quand il y avait du travail à faire.

'Si elle a mal à la tête, elle ne prendra pas le petit déjeuner,' a répondu maman.

Annette, qui avait toujours faim, ne voulait pas manquer son petit déjeuner. Elle a donc décidé de se lever tout de suite et de descendre à la cuisine.

TRANSLATION: FRENCH TO ENGLISH

1 Mother-in-law problems (p. 131)

My mother-in-law, who came to see us whenever she was bored, arrived while I was giving a private lesson to a third-year[1] pupil. When I went into the sitting-room, after seeing the child to the door, she was still there.

We exchanged a few words about the coming holidays and the continuing heatwave. By the way she was examining me, I suspected that she had been talking about me again, about what I hadn't done and what I ought to have done.

So I escaped as quickly as I could into the room which I used as an office. I could hear mother and daughter carrying on their conversation. The succession of questions and answers made me think that there was a plot, but I did my best not to look up.

When my wife Danièle came to tell me that her mother was staying for dinner, I shrugged my shoulders indifferently, which perhaps wasn't very nice, for she sighed and whispered to me:

'You could at least come and keep us company. . . .'

When the meal was over I got up from the table on the pretext that I had some marking to finish. They were not taken in by this. However, I leant out of the window and smoked several cigarettes without thinking of anything in particular.

Outside their front doors, people were sitting on chairs, enjoying the fresh air. Danièle, however, was doing the washing-up and a little of her bad mood must have got into her movements, for the plates were knocking against each other with more noise than usual.

My mother-in-law finally went away. From the hall she shouted, at the top of her voice:

'Don't disturb Andrew, since he's working. . . .'

Danièle came and joined me immediately. She said reproachfully:

'You'll always be the same . . . She is my mother. . . .'

Then:

'I'm going to bed. Today's exhausted me. . . .'

2 Incident at the Arc de Triomphe (p. 132)

A group of workmen in blue overalls were making their way towards the Arc de Triomphe. The white-haired man was following a few steps behind them.

'There he is!' shouted Kader, pointing a finger. 'Behind those men!' The two children rushed off. They easily avoided the vehicles, but not the policeman who was waiting for them.

They wasted a few minutes arguing. Kader didn't say anything, trying to be diplomatic, but Gilles spoiled everything by declaring that the policeman was blind. Fortunately for them, a tourist in German dress intervened and asked for permission to take a photo of the group busy arguing. While the policeman was dealing with him, the two friends made haste to dodge round the monument and put some thousands of tons of stones between themselves and the Law.

'It's annoying!' Gilles complained, tapping himself hard on the forehead. 'The white-haired man must have gone up!'

'He wasn't carrying anything,' said Kader. 'He'll come down again for lunch. No doubt someone will be able to tell us what time the workmen stop work.'

They found an excessively talkative man to give them the information. They had to listen to the whole history of the monument before getting the answer they had come in search of: midday.

3 A missing boy (p. 132)

It was four o'clock in the morning. Marcel had not come home and hadn't sent any message. So at exactly four o'clock Germaine decided to make another phone-call.

'Hello? Is that you, Yvette? Were you asleep? Don't get annoyed . . . Germaine here . . . Would you do me a big favour? Get dressed quickly, any old how. To save time, I'm going to phone for a taxi for you. See you soon . . .'

A quarter of an hour later Yvette climbed the stairs. Germaine opened the door for her.

'You must have been surprised,' she said. 'Marcel hasn't come back. I'll explain it all to you later.'

'Where must I look for Marcel?' asked Yvette.

'You're going to stay here. I'm the one who must go out. If anyone calls, write down the messages carefully. If it's Marcel, tell him who you are. He knows you. Say that I've gone out

[1] N.B. In France classes are numbered in inverse order, so English Form I = la sixième.

but that I'll be back soon. And if he comes back, tell him the same thing, tell him I was worried and went out to look for him.'

'Half past four,' observed Yvette. 'It's hardly worth my getting undressed again.'

4 A worried man (p. 132)

David looked at his watch again: ten past six. He had obviously fallen asleep in the armchair; and he must have slept deeply, for rays of sunlight were already entering the room, in spite of the fact that he had not yet drawn the curtains. He got up, and went into the kitchen. The events of the previous day had not yet begun to preoccupy him, and, mechanically, he boiled some water to make some coffee. After all, that was what he usually did – but of course, normally he was not dressed at that time. He was even about to pour a cup for Evelyne, when he suddenly remembered that she wasn't there. He went up to the bedroom to make sure that she had not returned whilst he was sleeping. But as he was coming back down the stairs he began to think about everything that had happened, and about what he could do. It was indeed a complicated situation, if not to say worrying, and he must not act without having thought for a long time about what he should do.

After having a shower he looked for some paper and sat down at the table. He began by writing the words that Evelyne had used on the phone. He had no difficulty in remembering them – they were ringing incessantly in his head: 'David? This is Evelyne. Listen carefully. Don't worry about me. I won't have any problems unless you do something stupid. You must stay there; someone will contact you.'

5 A family disagreement (p. 133)

On the stroke of six, as we were going home, a fox rushed across the little path leading to Saint-Aventurin. My father scarcely had time to aim his gun and fire into the hedge into which the fox had just gone. We pulled him out, dead.

'You have good eyes, Andrew!' exclaimed my uncle.

I leave you to imagine the success of our return. My brother and I carried the fox tied by its paws to a large branch, like Negroes when they have killed a lion.

Uncle Michael followed close behind us, holding in each hand, by their ears, the two biggest rabbits that we had caught. My father, who brought up the rear, was whistling his favourite tune.

Thus it was that we arrived at the house. Our enthusiasm vanished completely when we saw, at the door, our mother who seemed rather annoyed.

'Didn't you hear the bell?'

'What bell?' our father answered innocently.

She shrugged her shoulders.

'There is only one bell around here; ours. I've rung it three times. The mayor of Soledot has come to see you. It's about the job which he has already spoken to you about and which he very much wants to offer you.'

'But I don't want it!' shouted my father. 'You know very well that I don't want it.'

6 (p. 133)

Having left the town at about nine o'clock in the morning, the four young people had already been walking for seven hours, and now they were moving painfully along a dusty, endless country road. They were making their way towards the Youth Hostel at Armenton, and as it was August the weather was warm and rather heavy.

'How much further is it?' cried little Agnes. Paul, the leader of the group, unfolded his map. 'Another ten kilometres,' he answered at last. 'Is there no short cut?' asked Roger. 'What if we cut across these fields, for example? Armenton is over to the east, isn't it?' 'But take a look at this notice,' said Paul. He read aloud the warning: 'No entry. Dangerous bull.'

They rested for a few minutes, and bathed their feet in a stream before going on their way. Finally they saw in front of them the old mill, converted into a hostel. They also saw the notice nailed to the door: 'Hostel closed because of fire.'

They sat down despondently at the side of the road, and Agnes burst into tears. Suddenly they heard a man's voice. 'What is the matter, little ones?' They explained their difficulty and the newcomer began to laugh. 'No problem,' he said. 'My farm is close by. My wife will make you something to eat. We have room in the house for the girls. As for you boys, you can make yourselves at home in the barn. A straw bed will be all right for you, won't it?'

READING COMPREHENSION

Questions in English

1 (p. 134)

(a) The author and his wife stop at the garage to have the engine of their car checked as there is something wrong with it.

(b) While waiting, the husband chats to the mechanic and his wife goes to look in the window of the car-accessory shop.

(c) They notice that inside the motor-caravan there is a large bed, a kitchen and a toilet compartment.

(d) They think that it is not too expensive, and would save on hotel bills.

(e) Its disadvantage is that it does not have a bath.

(f) Before they can hire it, they have to sign some papers and the author has to show his driving-licence and his international insurance certificate.

(g) To see them on their way, the garage fills up the motor-caravan with petrol, and shows them how to get rid of the waste water and how to use the bottled gas. The garage will also keep their car for them while they are away.

(h) Before they are finally under way, the author and his wife put their belongings in the cupboards in the motor-caravan, go shopping in a supermarket to buy food and drink to take with them, and leave their car at the garage.

2 (p. 135)

(a) The Englishman was coming out of the post office when Maloin first caught sight of him. Maloin began to hurry so that he could follow him.

(b) Maloin thought that the Englishman might have been sleeping, or walking near the port. He rejected the second of these ideas because he had already been to the port several times and he would have seen the Englishman if he had been there.

(c) The outside of the hotel could be recognised by two round, glass lamps which looked like moons that particular evening.

(d) On the ground floor of the hotel there was an entrance hall, a larger inner hall, an office and an American bar.

(e) The man sitting in the lobby looked as if he was in a train. The fact that he had his bowler hat on his knees and was looking patiently straight ahead created this impression.

(f) The hotel proprietress was adding up a bill. It was surprising that she recognised the Englishman because she did not look up. She recognised him by the sound of his footsteps.

(g) When the Englishman was half-way across the lobby, a shadow appeared on the pavement outside, and remained there for a moment before disappearing.

(h) The visitor said that he was delighted to meet Mr Brown.[1]

(i) The hotel proprietress said that the visitor had arrived just after Mr Brown had gone out and that he had decided to wait for his return instead of going to look for him, as it was so foggy.[1]

3 (p. 136)

(a) Sophie was watching television.

(b) She thought that her husband might be ill.

(c) His meeting was likely to last for four hours.

(d) She said that Paris was beautiful in May and that she needed a new summer dress.

(e) Paul had to telephone the travel agency to see if there were two plane tickets available.

(f) She washed the dishes.

(g) He went to get some coffee.

(h) He asked Sophie to stay with the luggage.

(i) She looked at the newspaper and thought about the dress she would buy.

(j) He had some work to do but he soon fell asleep.

(k) She went to the Place de l'Opéra because she remembered there was a shop there where she might find a dress.

(l) On her way to the Métro station she met a childhood friend.

---

[1] In a reading comprehension test, when you are asked what someone said, use indirect speech for your answer; i.e. 'He said that . . .' or 'She said that . . .'. Remember that this is *not* a translation test.

(m) She spent the afternoon with this friend. They went to the shop where Sophie found a dress and then they had a cup of tea together at the Café de la Paix.

(n) They went in the direction of the Eiffel tower to have dinner in a small restaurant.

(o) They went for a walk along the boulevards.

4 (p. 137)

(a) The writer had been to a conference in the north of the country.

(b) He had chosen a first-class compartment because the firm for which he worked was paying his expenses.

(c) He decided to read some documents which had been given to him at the conference.

(d) He expected to find his ticket in the right-hand pocket of his jacket.

(e) He thought that he must have put it in an impossible place or that he had thrown it away by mistake.

(f) Some of them found it amusing, but others found it annoying.

(g) He asked scornfully if the passenger hadn't even a second-class ticket.

(h) He offered to buy another ticket because he didn't want to keep the ticket-collector waiting.

(i) He shrugged his shoulders and left the compartment.

(j) The ticket-collector came back and asked the man to follow him to the station-master's office.

Questions in French

1 (p. 138)

A.

(a) Ils passaient leur temps libre à faire le jardinage.

(b) Il a dit que ses tomates ne réussissaient pas très bien cette année.

(c) Il a dit que la terre chez lui n'était pas très bonne pour les tomates.

(d) Il a dit que l'année précédente il avait eu le même problème que Pierre.

(e) Il avait essayé une nouvelle variété.

(f) Pierre lui a dit: 'Montre-les-moi! Elles doivent être plus grosses que les miennes.'

B.

(g) Il a pris le Métro.

(h) Henri a sonné à la porte.

(i) Il a demandé à Henri d'entrer et de faire vite.

(j) Il a dit: 'Prenez l'avenue que vous verrez en face de vous en sortant, puis arrêtez-vous au tabac que vous trouverez à votre gauche et demandez au patron de vous dire où vous pourrez trouver Gaston.'

C.

(k) Ils étaient vieux et gros.

(l) Elle a mis tout de suite devant lui un repas énorme.

(m) Le matin, quand il sortait, il a dit qu'il ne rentrerait que le soir.

(n) Elle lui a demandé: 'Tu n'auras pas faim si tu sors sans déjeuner?'

(o) Elle lui a dit de s'asseoir.

(p) Elle a promis de lui préparer un déjeuner qu'il n'oublierait jamais.

2 (p. 139)

Section A

(a) Il a dû aller voir le Directeur.

(b) On l'aimait au lycée.

(c) Des amis et des parents d'élèves lui en ont parlé.

(d) La police voulait savoir s'il était question de drogues.

(e) Parce que l'auteur dit que d'abord Jean ne pouvait pas parler, puis il a parlé, 'enfin'.

(f) Il a dit qu'il avait eu un malaise, et qu'il ne s'était plus contrôlé.

(g) Parce que Jean avait crié les choses devant plus de trente élèves dans un café.

(h) Parce que le Directeur a demandé s'il faudrait le faire traiter en clinique pour les nerfs malades.

(i) Le Directeur lui a conseillé de se marier.

(j) Le père de Jean était médecin.

Section B

(a) B amis.

(b) B pour lui poser des questions.

(c) B parce que le Directeur lui faisait peur.

(d) A mots

B parfaitement

C souvent

(e) A Aviez-vous pris quelque chose à boire?

B Il ne pouvait rien dire.

(f) A Sans cheveux.

B Un endroit où on peut acheter à manger et à boire.

(g) A Il s'agissait de l'incident du Fanal.

B Jean avait fait un affreux effort.

C Voilà un homme qui vit pour les siens.

3 (p. 141)

(a) Elles habitaient Soissons.

(b) Elles ont quitté la maison à huit heures ce matin-là.

(c) Leur destination était Metz.

(d) Elles n'avaient pas assez d'argent pour voyager par chemin de fer.

(e) Elles commençaient à en avoir assez parce que les voitures et les camions passaient sans s'arrêter.

(f) Elles allaient se reposer.

(g) Elle a versé de l'eau sur ses pieds parce que ses pieds commençaient à lui faire mal.[1]

(h) Elle devait faire attention avec l'eau parce que c'était tout ce qu'il y avait à boire.

(i) Un gendarme conduisait la Peugeot 505.

(j) La police cherchait deux jeunes filles parce que deux jeunes filles avaient disparu.

(k) Elles manquaient depuis hier matin.

(l) Ils les ont interrogées.[2]

Multiple-choice questions in French

1 (p. 142)

1 C Merci bien. Je viendrai avec plaisir.

2 D Tu es sûr qu'il y a de l'essence dans le réservoir?

3 C Sois gentil et emmène-moi en ville sur ta motocyclette!

4 D Quatre couverts, dans un coin tranquille si c'est possible.

5 A Ta sœur sera contente. Il y a huit lettres pour elle.

6 D Est-ce que vous pouvez faire sécher mon linge dans votre séchoir électrique?

7 B Que tu es maladroit, Etienne!

8 B Il s'est fait mal, peut-être.

9 C Vous êtes sûr que vous ne l'avez pas laissé ailleurs?

10 C Pouvez-vous me nettoyer cette veste, aussi vite que possible, s'il vous plaît?

2 (p. 143)

1 B il faisait assez froid.

2 A un pullover.

3 B en autobus.

4 C parce qu'il avait manqué l'autobus.

5 A rarement.

6 D en voiture.

7 C aimait être bien habillée.

8 B parce qu'elle devait laisser sa voiture dans un garage.

9 A dans l'escalier.

10 C la colère de son père.

[1] Care must be taken here to use the correct pronoun, **'lui'**, and not the pronoun **'me'** which is used in the passage. Always keep to the structure used in the question when answering.

[2] A preceding direct object agreement is used here. Check Grammar Revision section 23 if you are still not sure about this rule.

3 (p. 144)

Section A

1 A Un criminel à sa victime
2 C Un médecin
3 B Un automobiliste et un gendarme
4 A Un garagiste
5 C Un employé d'une agence de voyages
6 B Un agent et le spectateur d'un accident
7 D Deux spectateurs du Tour de France
8 B Un voyageur et un porteur
9 D Une dame et un passant dans la rue
10 C Un père à son fils

Section B

11 C A la ferme
12 A Au supermarché
13 A Au restaurant
14 B En classe
15 C Dans une salle de bains
16 A Chez l'électricien
17 B Chez le marchand de légumes
18 D Au bureau
19 D A l'hôtel
20 A Dans un cabinet de toilette
21 B Au supermarché
22 D Dans un journal

Section C

23 C On fait la vaisselle.
24 B On fait du camping.
25 C On va se coucher.
26 D On fait une omelette.
27 B On arrive à la rive.
28 A On part à la pêche.
29 B On répare un vélo.
30 D On regarde démolir un bâtiment.

Section D

31 A j'ai dit au revoir à mes amis.
32 C elle s'est couchée sur sa serviette.
33 B est entré dans le bar prendre une bière.
34 A parce qu'il faisait froid.
35 B a demandé à la vendeuse de le lui passer.
36 B a posé les chaises sur la table.
37 D j'aurai cinq heures de maths par semaine.
38 D après être arrivés chez leurs correspondants.

Section E

39 B plus jeune que Robert de six ans et demi.
40 D rarement.
41 A dans une région où il y avait des bois.
42 C C'était une famille nombreuse.
43 A Quatre.
44 C Parce qu'elle a dû rester à la maison.
45 C Dans quelques années.

Multiple-choice questions in English

Section A (p. 147)

1 A No parking.
2 C became angry.
3 C Exit.
4 C fog.
5 C are allowed in at a reduced rate.
6 C put on warm clothes.
7 C not so expensive.
8 C put their rubbish in the rubbish bin.
9 D Emergency exit.
10 B needs a pen.
11 A buy stamps.
12 C what she will do when she leaves school.
13 D go swimming.
14 B English cooking.
15 C Charles is wrong.

Section B (p. 148)

16 A fortnight.
17 D cloudy.
18 B parking was difficult in town.
19 D 9.30.
20 C listened to a lady talking about her family.
21 C baker's.
22 A One.
23 B at the seaside.
24 D to buy some sugar.
25 C Friday.

LISTENING COMPREHENSION

Questions in English

1 (p. 150)
Passage A

1 They could not find their keys.
2 It was just after one o'clock in the morning.
3 He proposed to get in through a window.
4 Their flat was on the second floor.
5 She suggested that they ring the bell.
6 He was climbing up a lamp-post.
7 He was using it to reach the window.
8 (a) The lamp-post broke.
   (b) He was opening the window.
9 He fell on some sacks full of paper.
10 He had nothing broken and they found the key in the pocket of his trousers.

Passage B

1 (a) He was the new apprentice.
   (b) He worked in a clothes shop.
2 He was always eating.
3 (a) He ate twice as much as the others.
   (b) He ate two bananas or a packet of biscuits.

4 If a colleague had not had time for breakfast, he would give him one of his sandwiches.

5 He was eating a sandwich under the counter.

6 He hid it under a white shirt on the counter.

7 The customer took it away with the shirt.

2 (p. 151)

1 They were staying in Paris for three days.

2 They travelled to Paris in Pauline's car.

3 They intended to move about Paris on foot on Saturday morning.

4 They intended to walk along the Seine.

5 They saw boats on the river and books being sold by the secondhand booksellers on the banks of the river.

6 She suggested that they should visit the Cathedral of Notre Dame later in the afternoon.

7 It was in a quiet street with a small, shady courtyard.

8 It was well-cooked and well-served.

9 The waiter had forgotten to charge for the wine.

10 They saw a group of children with their teacher.

11 They were speaking a foreign language.

12 She found her teacher for her.

Questions in French

The Signalman (L'Aiguilleur) (p. 151)
Section A

1 Il partait toujours à la même heure, six minutes avant huit heures.

2 Elle se trouvait sur la falaise près de Dieppe.

3 On voyait la mer, le port et la ville de Dieppe.

4 On voyait les lumières rouges et vertes du port, les lumières blanches des quais, et puis les lumières de la ville.

Section B

5 Il a emporté le pain, le beurre et le saucisson préparés par sa femme.

6 Il a tourné à gauche et s'est dirigé vers le pont.

7 Sa cabine se trouvait en ville, tout près du port.

Section C

8 Les bateaux arrivaient d'Angleterre.

9 Il traversait la ville de Dieppe.

10 Son assistant était en train de mettre son pardessus.

Multiple-choice questions in English

Section A (p. 152)

1 A dairy.

2 D 6.

3 D the way to the bank.

4 C the weather.

5 B television in the lounge only.

6 D what he likes to eat.

7 B asking for the wine list.

8 D the coffee very strong.

9 B try to stay a short while.

10 D being introduced to someone.

11 C went for a walk by the seaside.

12 C 95.

13 D nearly five.

14 A about 9 o'clock.

15 C post office.

Section B (p. 153)

16 C fine.

17 A it is his lunch hour.

18 C if he is ready for his holidays.

19 B camping.

20 A two weeks.

21 D It was very crowded.

22 D bring back a lot of things.

23 B pleasant.

24 A was afraid.

25 C to the breadshop.

Multiple-choice questions in French

Section A (p. 155)

1 B Dans un restaurant

2 D Au marché

3 B Au bureau de poste

4 A A la piscine

5 D Au syndicat d'initiative

6 D Le boulanger

7 A Le médecin

8 D Une automobiliste et un garagiste

9 A Un touriste et un passant

10 B Un élève et son professeur

Section B (p. 155)

1 C à quelle heure partira le train de Paris.

2 C 10.45

3 B 16

4 A prendre un repas dans le train.

5 C acheter un journal.

Faux amis

Check the following words carefully. They resemble English words but in fact have different meanings.

Note the following in reverse:

assister à	to be present at	to assist	aider
les cabinets	lavatories	cabinets (*furniture*)	les meubles (mpl) à tiroir
le car	coach	car	l'auto (f), la voiture
causer	to chat	to cause (to be done)	faire (faire)
la cave	cellar	cave	la caverne
la crêpe	pancake	crape	le crêpe
le délit	crime, offence	delight	les délices (fpl), le plaisir
se dresser	to rise up	to dress	s'habiller
la figure	face	figure	la taille (*body*), le chiffre (*number*)
la journée	day	journey	le voyage
la lecture	reading	lecture	une conférence
la librairie	bookshop	library	la bibliothèque
la location	hiring, renting	location	l'emplacement (m), la situation
le médecin	doctor	medicine	le médicament
la ménagère	housewife	manager	le directeur, le gérant
le Métro	underground railway (*not* a car)	Metro car	*la* Metro (N.B. all cars are feminine)
la monnaie	(loose) change	money	l'argent (m)
passer	to spend (*time*)	to pass	réussir à (*succeed*), croiser (*e.g. person in the street*)
le pensionnaire	boarder	pensioner	le (la) retraité(e)
le pétrole	crude oil	petrol	l'essence (f)
le photographe	photographer	photograph	la photographie
la place	square	place	l'endroit (m)
le plat	dish	plate	l'assiette (f)
le record	record (e.g. sports, *not* music)	record (*musical*)	le disque
rester	to stay	to rest	se reposer
le robinet	tap	robin	le rouge-gorge
sensible	sensitive	sensible	raisonnable, sensé
travailler	to work	to travel	voyager
la veste	jacket	vest	le maillot
le water(-closet)	W.C., toilet	water	l'eau (f)

Useful idioms

aussitôt dit, aussitôt fait	no sooner said than done
casser la croûte	to have a snack
C'est du gâteau.	It's a piece of cake.
courir à toutes jambes	to run quickly (*person*)
courir à plat ventre	to run quickly (*animal*)
crier à tue-tête	to shout at the top of one's voice
donner un coup de main	to give a helping hand
dormir comme une souche	to sleep like a log
l'avoir échappé belle	to have a lucky escape
faire l'école buissonnière	to play truant
faire la grasse matinée	to sleep late
Au feu!	Fire!
mouillé jusqu'aux os	soaked to the skin
sain et sauf	safe and sound
Au secours!	Help!
un temps de chien	foul weather
tourner le bouton	to switch on
Tout est bien qui finit bien.	All's well that ends well.
travailler d'arrache-pied	to work very hard

COMMON PITFALLS

Listed below are some of the words most frequently misspelt or misunderstood by O-level and CSE candidates.

agent	policeman	habiter	to live in
argent	money	s'habiller	to get dressed
le bois	wood	monter	to go up
la boisson	drink	montrer	to show
chevaux	horses	payer	to pay *for*
cheveux	hair	plusieurs	several
combien **de** or **d'**	how much, how many	raconter	to tell (*a story*)
		rencontrer	to meet

Combien **de** pommes veux-tu?
How many apples do you want?

la veille	the day before/eve
la vieille	the old woman

but Combien **des** pommes sont rouges?
How many of the apples are red?

French–English vocabulary

A

une **abeille,** bee
abîmer, to spoil
aboyer, to bark
abriter, to shelter
accabler, to overwhelm
d' **accord,** agreed, all right
s' **accoutumer à,** to get used to
acheter, to buy
achats: faire des achats, to go shopping
achever, to finish
d' **acier,** steel
les **actualités** (fpl), news (*e.g. T.V.*); current affairs
actuellement, now, at this present time
l' **addition** (f), bill
les **affaires** (fpl), business
une **affiche,** notice, poster
affreux, awful
agacer, to annoy
s' **agenouiller,** to kneel
agir, to act
s' **agir,** to be a question of; **il s'agit de,** it is a question of
aider, to help
aigre, bitter
une **aiguille,** needle
l' **ail** (m), garlic
une **aile,** wing
ailleurs, elsewhere
aimer mieux, to prefer
aîné, elder
ainsi, so, thus
air: avoir l'air, to look like, to have the appearance of
ajouter, to add
l' **alimentation (générale),** food shop
une **allée,** path, drive
l' **Allemagne** (f), Germany
aller chercher, to fetch
allumer, to light

les **allumettes** (fpl), matches
alors, then, well
l' **alpinisme** (m), mountaineering
amarrer, to moor
l' **Ambassade** (f), Embassy
améliorer, to improve
une **âme,** soul
amer, bitter
l' **amertume** (f), bitterness
l' **amitié** (f), friendship
une **ampoule,** light-bulb; blister (*on foot*)
s' **amuser,** to enjoy oneself
un **âne,** donkey
un **ange,** angel
anglais, English
l' **Angleterre** (f), England
l' **angoisse** (f), anguish
animé, busy (*e.g. street*)
un **anneau,** ring
un **anniversaire,** birthday, anniversary
apercevoir, to notice
apparaître, to appear
un **appareil,** camera
un **appartement,** a flat
appartenir à, to belong to
apporter, to bring
s' **apprêter,** to get ready
appuyer, to lean
l' **araignée** (f), spider
l' **arc-en-ciel** (m), rainbow
l' **argent** (m), money
l' **armoire** (f), cupboard
arracher, to tear (away, out)
l' **arrêt** (m) **(d'autobus),** bus stop
s' **arrêter,** to stop
l' **arrivée** (f), arrival
un **arrondissement,** district (of Paris)
un **ascenseur,** a lift
l' **aspirateur** (m), vacuum-cleaner
un **assassinat,** murder
s' **asseoir,** to sit down
l' **assiette** (f), plate

assister, to help
assister à, to be present at
un **atelier,** workshop
un **âtre,** fireside, hearth
atteindre, to reach
attendre, to wait for
s' **attendre à,** to expect
atterrir, to land
attirer, to attract
attraper, to catch
l' **aube** (f), dawn
une **auberge,** inn
l' **auberge de jeunesse,** Youth Hostel
aucun(e), any
ne... **aucun(e),** none
au-dessous de, below
au-dessus de, above, over
augmenter, to increase
aujourd'hui, today
auparavant, before, previously
aussitôt, immediately
autant, as much
l' **automobiliste** (m & f), motorist
l' **autoroute** (f), motorway
l' **auto-stop** (m), hitch-hiking
autour de, around
autrefois, formerly
autrement, otherwise
avaler, to swallow
s' **avancer,** to advance
avare, miserly
avis: changer d'avis, to change one's mind
l' **avenir** (m), the future
une **averse,** a shower
avertir, to warn
l' **avertissement** (m), warning
aveugle, blind
l' **avis** (m), notice; opinion
l' **avocat** (m), barrister
avouer, to admit, confess
ayant, having

B

le **baccalauréat,** French school-leaving certificate
les **bagages** (mpl), luggage
la **bague,** ring
la **baguette,** long French loaf
se **baigner,** to bathe
baîller, to yawn
se **baisser,** to bend down
balayer, to sweep
balbutier, to stammer
la **banlieue,** suburbs
la **banquette,** bench, seat
la **baraque,** hut
la **barbe,** beard
la **barque,** (small) boat
bas(se), low
la **basse-cour,** farm-yard
le **bassin,** pond
le **bâtiment,** building
bavarder, to chat, gossip
le **beau-père,** father-in-law
bêcher, to dig
la **belle-mère,** mother-in-law
le **berceau,** cradle
la **berge,** (steep) bank (*of a river*)
le **berger,** shepherd
la **besogne,** job, task, work
besoin: avoir besoin de, to need
bêtises: faire des bêtises, to act the fool
le **béton,** concrete
le **beuglement,** bellowing
la **bibliothèque,** library
bientôt, soon
la **bienvenue,** welcome
le(s) **bijou(x),** jewel(s)
le **billet,** note, ticket
le **bistrot,** pub
bizarre, strange
le **blé,** corn
les **blés,** cornfields
(se) **blesser,** to injure
la **blessure,** wound
boire, to drink
la **boisson,** drink
boiter, to limp
le **bol,** bowl
bon marché, cheap(ly)
bond: faire un bond, to leap
bondir, to leap
le **bonheur,** happiness
le **bonhomme,** chap, fellow
la **bonne,** maid (servant)
la **bonté,** kindness
le **bord,** edge
bouche bée, open-mouthed
le **bouchon,** cork
la **boue,** mud
bouger, to move
la **bougie,** candle
bouillir, to boil
bouleverser, to overthrow, upset
bousculer, to jostle
la **boum,** party
le **bout,** end
la **bouteille,** bottle
la **boutique,** shop
le **brancard,** stretcher
le **bras,** arm
brasse: nager à la brasse, to swim breast-stroke
brave, good, honest
bricoler, to do odd jobs
briller, to shine
le **briquet,** (cigarette) lighter
briser, to break
brosser, to brush
la **brouette,** wheelbarrow
le **brouillard,** fog
bronzé, sunburnt, tanned

le **bruit,** noise
brûler, to burn
la **brume,** mist
brusquement, quickly
bruyamment, noisily
le **buisson,** bush
le **bureau,** desk, office
le **but,** aim, goal

C

(se) **cacher,** to hide
le **cachet,** tablet
le **cadavre,** corpse
le **cadeau,** present
cadet(te), younger
le **caillou,** pebble
la **caisse,** cash-desk
le **caleçon de bain,** swimming-trunks
le **camarade,** friend
le **cambrioleur,** burglar
le **camion,** lorry
la **canne,** walking-stick
la **canne à pêche,** fishing-rod
le **carnet,** notebook
le **carrefour,** crossroads
la **carte,** map
le **carton,** cardboard
la **casserole,** saucepan
le **cauchemar,** nightmare
causer, to chat
la **ceinture,** belt
célèbre, famous
le **célibataire,** bachelor
cesser, to stop
chacun(e), each
chahuter, to make a row; to play up in class
la **chaleur,** heat
la **chance,** luck; **avoir de la chance,** to be lucky
le **chandail,** sweater
la **chanson,** song
chaque, each
charger, to load
le **chariot,** trolley
le **chauffage,** heating
chauffer, to warm
les **chaussures** (fpl), shoes
chauve, bald
chavirer, to capsize
le **chevet,** bedside table
le **chiffre,** figure (*number*)
le **choix,** choice
un **chômeur,** unemployed person
chuchoter, to whisper
le **ciel,** sky
le **cierge,** candle
la **circulation,** traffic
clair, bright, clear, light
la **clarté,** brightness
la **clé (clef),** key
le **client,** customer
le **clochard,** tramp
la **cloche,** bell
le **clou,** nail
le **cœur,** heart
le **coin,** corner
la **colère,** anger; **être en colère,** to be angry
le **colis,** parcel
le **collège,** secondary school
le **collier,** necklace
la **colline,** hill
les **comestibles** (mpl), food
commander, to order
commissions: faire des commissions, to do the shopping
complet, full (up)
le **complet,** suit
le **complot,** plot

composer un numéro, to dial a number
comprendre, to understand
compter, to count
le **comptoir,** counter
le **concierge,** caretaker
conduire, to drive
la **confiture,** jam
confus, embarrassed
le **congé,** holiday, leave
la **connaissance,** acquaintance
connaître, to know
conseiller, to advise
construire, to build, construct
contre, against
le **copain,** chum, pal
la **copine,** chum, pal
la **corbeille,** basket
le **corps,** body
la **côte,** coast
le **côté,** side
le **coteau,** hillside
le **couchant,** setting sun
coudre, to sew
couler, to flow
un **coup d'œil,** glance
couper, to cut
couramment, fluently
le **courrier,** post, mail
la **course,** race
courses: faire des courses, to go shopping
court, short
le **couvercle,** lid
craindre, to fear
le **crépuscule,** twilight
creuser, to dig, hollow out
la **crevaison,** puncture
crever, to burst
croire, to think, believe
croiser, to cross, pass someone (e.g. in a street)
cueillir, to gather, pick
le **cuir,** leather
cuire: (faire) cuire, to cook
le **curé,** priest

D

le (la) **dactylo,** typist
d'abord, at first
d'ailleurs, moreover
davantage, more, more so
débarrasser (la table), to clear (the table)
se **débarrasser de,** to get rid of
se **débattre,** to struggle
debout, standing
se **débrouiller,** to manage
le **début,** beginning
décharger, to unload
déchirer, to tear
la **découverte,** discovery
découvrir, to uncover, disclose
décrocher, to lift (*telephone receiver*)
déçu, disappointed
dedans, inside
défendre, to forbid
le(s) **dégât(s),** damage
dégeler, to thaw
dehors, outside
déjà, already
le **délit,** crime, offence
demain, tomorrow
démarrer, to set off (*e.g. car*)
déménager, to move house
demeurer, to live, remain
démodé, out of date
la **denrée,** commodity
se **dépêcher,** to hurry
dépenser, to spend

déplier, to unfold
déposer, to put down
depuis, since
déranger, to disturb
dériver, to drift
à la dérobée, stealthily
désolé, sorry
dès que, as soon as
dessiner, to draw
les dessins animés, cartoon films
se détendre, to relax
détruire, to destroy
devenir, to become
deviner, to guess
devoir, to owe, to have to
les devoirs (mpl), homework
Dieu, God
digne, worthy
se diriger vers, to make towards
discuter, to discuss
disparaître, to disappear
disponible, available
se disputer, to quarrel
le disque, record
distinguer, to distinguish, to make out
se distraire, to amuse oneself
distrait, absent-minded
le doigt, finger
le (la) domestique, servant
dommage: c'est dommage! it's a pity!
  quel dommage! what a pity!
donc, so, therefore
donner sur, to overlook
le dos, back
la Douane, Customs
doubler, to overtake
doucement, gently
la douche, shower
la douleur, pain, sorrow
se douter de, to suspect
le drap, sheet
le drapeau, flag
se dresser, to rise up
la drogue, drug(s)
le droit, law, right
à droite, on the right
droit: tout droit, straight on
drôle, funny
durer, to last

E

écarter, to separate, open (*curtains*)
échanger, to exchange
s' échapper, to escape
une échelle, ladder
éclairer, to light
éclater de rire, to burst out laughing
les économies (fpl), savings
écosser, to shell (*peas*)
s' écouler, to go by (*time*)
écouter, to listen to
s' écrier, to exclaim
l' écriteau (m), signpost, board
effrayer, to frighten
effroyable, frightful
égal, equal
s' égarer, to lose one's way, to wander
s' élancer, to dash, rush (forward)
l' électrophone (m), record-player
s' éloigner, to move away
embêter, to annoy
l' embouteillage (m), traffic jam
embrasser, to kiss
une émission, broadcast
emmener, to take (*a person*)
emplettes: faire des emplettes, to go
  shopping
s' emparer de, to get hold of, to take
  possession of
empêcher, to prevent

emporter, to carry, take, away
s' emporter, to lose one's temper
s' empresser de, to hasten to
emprunter, to borrow
ému, thrilled
enchanté, delighted
encombré, crowded, packed
s' endormir, to go to sleep
un endroit, place, spot
énerver, to get on someone's nerves
s' enfuir, to flee
enlever, to take off, away
ennuyer, to annoy, to bore
s' ennuyer, to be bored
enregistrer, to record (*on tape*)
s' enrhumer, to catch a cold
l' enseignement (m), teaching
ensemble, together
ensuite, afterwards, then
entendre, to hear
entendu: bien entendu, of course
entourer, to surround
entre, between
entreprendre, to undertake
entr'ouvert, half-open
envie: avoir envie de, to feel inclined to
environ, about
les environs (mpl), surrounding area
s' envoler, to take off (*plane*)
envoyer, to send
épatant, amazing, splendid
l' épaule (f), shoulder
une époque, period, time
épouser, to marry
épouvantable, dreadful
les époux (mpl), married couple
éprouver, to experience, feel
épuiser, to exhaust
l' équipe (f), team
errer, to wander
un escalier, stairs
espérer, to hope
l' espoir (m), hope
essayer, to try
l' essence (f), petrol
essoufflé, out of breath
essuyer, to wipe
l' est (m), east
un étage, floor, storey
éteindre, to put out
s' étendre, to lie, stretch
une étoile, star
s' étonner, to be astonished
étouffer, to stifle, suffocate
un étranger, foreigner, stranger
étroit, narrow
s' évanouir, to faint
s' éveiller, to wake up
un événement, event
éviter, to avoid
expliquer, to explain
l' exposition (f), exhibition
exprès, on purpose

F

en face (de), opposite
se fâcher, to get angry
faible, weak
faillir (faire) quelque chose, to nearly
  miss (doing something)
faim: avoir faim, to be hungry
la falaise, cliff
fatiguer, to tire
féliciter, to congratulate
fêter, to celebrate
la feuille, leaf
les feux (mpl), traffic lights
la fiche, form, piece of paper
fier, fière, proud
la figure, face

se figurer, to imagine
la fin, end
flâner, to idle, loiter
le fleuve, large river
les flots (mpl), waves
la fois, occasion, time
le fond, bottom, end (*e.g. of corridor*)
fondre en larmes, to burst into tears
formidable, terrific
fort, strong
fou, folle, mad
fouiller, to search
la foule, crowd
le fracas, din
frais, fraîche, fresh
franchir, to cross
freiner, to brake
frissonner, to shudder
les frites (fpl), chips
froncer les sourcils, to frown
frotter, to rub
fumer, to smoke
le fusil, gun

G

gâcher, to spoil, waste
gagner, to win
la gaieté, cheerfulness
le gamin, urchin
garder, to keep
la gare, (railway) station
gaspiller, to waste
gâter, to spoil, damage
le gazon, lawn, turf
geler, to freeze
gémir, to groan, moan
gêner, to annoy, hinder
le(s) genou(x), knee(s)
la gentillesse, kindness
le gérant, manager
le geste, gesture, movement
le gîte, lodging, resting-place
glisser, to slip, slide
le gosse, kid
le goût, taste
goûter, to taste, to have tea
le goûter, tea (*meal*)
la grange, barn
gratuit, free
grave, serious
le grenier, loft
la grève, strike
grimper, to climb
la grippe, 'flu
gronder, to scold
la guêpe, wasp
ne... guère, scarcely
guérir, to cure
se guérir, to get better
la guerre, war
le guichet, booking-office

H

s' habiller, to get dressed
les habits (mpl), clothes
d' habitude, usually
une habitude, habit
la haie, hedge
par hasard, by chance
hausser les épaules, to shrug one's
  shoulders
heureusement, fortunately
(se) heurter, to bump (into), knock
hocher la tête, to shake one's head
honte: avoir honte de, to be ashamed of
l' horaire (m), time-table
l' humeur: (la bonne, mauvaise) humeur,
  (good, bad) temper
hurler, to yell

I

ignorer, to be unaware of
l' île (f), island
un immeuble, block of flats
un imperméable, raincoat
imprévu, unexpected
à l' improviste, unexpectedly
inattendu, unexpected
un incendie, fire
un inconnu, stranger
incroyable, unbelievable
une inondation, flood
s' inquiéter, to be anxious
insolite, unusual
s' installer, to settle down (into)
à l' insu de, unknown to
inutile, useless
un invité, a guest
ivre, drunk

J

jadis, formerly
jeter, to throw
le jeu, game
la jeunesse, youth
joindre, to join
jouer, to play
jouir de, to enjoy
la journée, day
le jumeau, la jumelle, twin
la jupe, skirt
jurer, to swear
jusqu'à, as far as, until

K

le képi, peaked cap
klaxonner, to sound the horn

L

lâcher, to let go
laid, ugly
la laine, wool
laisser, to leave
lancer, to throw
la langue étrangère, foreign language
le lapin, rabbit
la larme, tear
las(se), tired
léger, light
le légume, vegetable
le lendemain, the next day
lent, slow
lentement, slowly
la lessive, washing
la lèvre, lip
libre, free
lier, to tie, bind
le lieu, place, spot
lire, to read
le lit, bed
le (la) locataire, tenant
loin, far
le loisir, leisure
longer, to go along (the side of)
lorsque, when
louer, to hire
lourd, heavy
la lueur, light, glow
la lutte, struggle

M

machinalement, mechanically
le magnétophone, tape-recorder
maigre, thin
le maillot, vest, tee-shirt
le maillot de bain, swimming-costume
maint(es), many
la mairie, town-hall
la maison de commerce, business firm

mal, badly
malade, ill
maladroit, clumsy
malgré, in spite of
le malheur, misfortune
malheureux, unhappy
la Manche, English Channel
la manière, manner, way
manquer, to fail, lack
le manteau, coat
maussade, sullen, sulky
mauvais, bad
le médicament, medicine
se méfier de, to mistrust
meilleur, better (*adjective*)
même, same, even
menacer, to threaten
ménage: faire le ménage, to do the
    housework
mener, to lead
le mensonge, lie
mentir, to tell lies
mériter, to deserve
le métier, profession, trade
le Métro, the Underground (railway)
se mettre à, to begin
se mettre en route, to set off
les meubles (mpl), furniture
mieux, better (*adverb*)
mince, thin
moindre, smallest, slightest
moins, less; au moins, at least
la moitié, half
se moquer de, to make fun of
mordre, to bite
morne, gloomy
la mort, death
le mot, word
mouillé, damp, wet
le moulin, mill
mugir, to bellow
le musée, museum

N

nager, to swim
la naissance, birth
la nappe, table-cloth
le naufrage, shipwreck
le navire, ship
la neige, snow
nettoyer, to clean
le neveu, nephew
le nez, nose
nier, to deny
la noce, wedding (party)
Noël, Christmas
la noisette, hazel-nut
la noix, nut, walnut
nouer, to tie
nourrir, to feed
la nourriture, food
nouveau, nouvelle, new
à nouveau, again
les nouvelles, news
se noyer, to drown
le nuage, cloud
nullement, not at all

O

obéir, to obey
l' occasion (f), opportunity
occupé, busy
une œuvre, work
l' ombre (f), shadow
l' or (m), gold
l' orage (m), storm
ordinaire, ordinary, usual
ordonner, to order
l' oreille (f), ear
orgueilleux, proud

l' os (m), bone
oser, to dare
ôter, to take off
oublier, to forget
un ouvrier, workman
ouvrir, to open

P

la paille, straw
paisible, peaceful
le palier, landing
la panne, breakdown
le panneau, board, sign
le paquebot, passenger ship
Pâques, Easter
paraître, to appear
le parapluie, umbrella
le pardessus, overcoat
pareil, like, similar
paresseux, lazy
parfois, sometimes
parmi, among
la parole, word
partager, to share
particulier, private, personal, special
partout, everywhere
parvenir, to manage, succeed
le pas, step
le passage clouté, pedestrian crossing
le patron, boss, proprietor
la patte, paw
la paupière, eyelid
pauvre, poor
le pays, district, country
le paysage, landscape, scenery
la peau, skin
pêcher, to fish
peigner, to comb
peindre, to paint
à peine, scarcely
la peine, difficulty
la peinture, painting
la pelle, shovel, spade
la pelouse, lawn
se pencher, to lean
pendant, during, for
pendant que, while
la pendule, clock
pénétrer dans, to go into
pénible, painful
la pensée, thought
penser, to think
la pente, slope
la Pentecôte, Whitsuntide
perdre, to lose
permettre, to allow
le permis de conduire, driving licence
peser, to weigh
la peur, fear
peut-être, perhaps
le phare, headlamp, lighthouse
le pharmacien, chemist
la pièce, coin, room, play (*theatre*)
le pied, foot
la pierre, stone
le piéton, pedestrian
piquer, to sting
pire, worse
pis: tant pis! too bad!
la piscine, swimming-pool
la piste, track, runway
le placard, cupboard
la place, square
le plafond, ceiling
la plage, beach
plaindre, to pity
plaire, to please
la plaisanterie, joke
le plancher, floor
plat, flat

le **plat,** dish
le **plateau,** tray
plein, full; **faire le plein d'essence,** to fill up with petrol
pleurer, to weep
pleuvoir, to rain
plier, to fold, bend
plonger, to dive
la **pluie,** rain
la **plupart,** most
de **plus en plus,** more and more
plusieurs, several
plutôt, rather
le **pneu,** tyre
le **poids,** weight
le **poignet,** wrist
le **poing,** fist
la **pointure,** size (*of shoe*)
la **poitrine,** chest
la **pompe à incendie,** fire-engine
le **pompier,** fireman
le **portefeuille,** wallet
le **porte-monnaie,** purse
la **portière,** door (*e.g. car, train*)
poser, to put
le **poste (de T.S.F.),** radio
le **poste (d'essence),** petrol-pump
le **poste de police,** police-station
la **Poste,** postal service
le **poteau,** pole, post
le **pourboire,** tip
pourquoi, why
poursuivre, to pursue; **poursuivre son chemin,** to go on one's way
pourtant, however, yet
pousser, to push
la **poussière,** dust
pouvoir, to be able
le **pré,** field, meadow
se **précipiter,** to dash, rush
préféré(e), favourite
prendre, to take
presque, almost
se **presser,** to hurry
prêt, ready
prêter, to lend
le **prêtre,** priest
la **preuve,** proof
prévenir, to warn
prévoir, to anticipate, to foresee
prier, to ask, pray
le **printemps,** spring
la **prise (de courant),** (electric) plug, point
le **prix,** price
prochain, next
proche, near
produire, to produce
profiter de, to take advantage of
profond, deep
le **projet,** plan, project
promettre, to promise
à **propos,** by the way
propre, own; clean
le **proviseur,** headmaster (*secondary school*)
puis, then, next
puisque, since
le **puits,** well

Q

le **quai,** platform; embankment; quay
quand, when
quant à, as for
le **quartier,** district
quelque chose, something
quelquefois, sometimes
quelque part, somewhere
la **queue,** tail, queue

le **quincaillier,** ironmonger
la **quinzaine,** fortnight
quitter, to leave
quoi, what
quoique, although
quotidien, daily

R

raconter, to tell, relate
le **raccourci,** short cut
la **raie,** stripe
raison: avoir raison, to be right
ralentir, to slow down
ramasser, to pick up
ramener, to bring back
se **rappeler,** to remember
se **raser,** to shave
ravi, delighted
rayé, striped
le **rayon,** shelf; ray
le **récepteur,** receiver (*telephone*)
le **receveur,** (bus) conductor
recevoir, to receive
la **réclame,** advertisement (*sign*)
la **réclamation,** complaint
la **récompense,** reward
reconnaissant, grateful
reculer, to move backwards
réfléchir, to think
la **reine,** queen
remarquer, to notice
remercier, to thank
remplir, to fill
remuer, to move, stir
le **renard,** fox
rencontrer, to meet
rendre, to give back
se **rendre compte,** to realise
le **renseignement,** (piece of) information
renverser, to knock over
renvoyer, to dismiss
répondre, to answer, reply
se **reposer,** to rest
la **représentation,** performance (*play*)
respirer, to breathe
rester, to stay
en **retard,** late
retenir, to hold back, to book (*a ticket*)
retentir, to resound, ring
retirer, to pull, draw out
la **retraite,** retirement
la **réunion,** meeting
réussir, to succeed
rêver, to dream
le **réveille-matin,** alarm-clock
se **réveiller,** to wake up
revenir, to come back
le **réverbère,** street-lamp
le **rez-de-chaussée,** ground floor
le **rhume,** cold (*medical*)
le **rideau,** curtain
rire, to laugh
les **rires (mpl),** laughter
le **rivage,** shore
la **rive,** bank, shore (*of river*)
le **robinet,** tap
la **roche,** rock
le **rocher,** rock
le **roi,** king
le **roman,** novel
rompre, to break
ronfler, to snore
la **roue,** wheel
rougir, to blush, redden
rouler, to drive, travel, roll
roux, rousse, auburn, red
la **rue,** street
le **ruisseau,** stream
la **ruse,** trick

S

le **sable,** sand
le **sac de couchage,** sleeping-bag
sage, well-behaved, wise
saisir, to seize
sale, dirty
salut! hello!
le **sang,** blood
le **sanglot,** sob
sans, without
la **santé,** health
sauf, except
sauter, to jump
sauvage, wild
se **sauver,** to run away
savoir, to know
le **savon,** soap
le **seau,** bucket
sec, sèche, dry
secouer, to shake
au **secours!** help!
le **séjour,** stay
selon, according to
la **semaine,** week
semblable, similar
sembler, to seem
le **sens,** direction
le **sentier,** path
le **sentiment,** feeling
sentir, to feel
serrer, to squeeze; **serrer la main à,** to shake hands with
la **serrure,** lock
la **serviette,** briefcase; napkin; towel
seulement, only
le **siècle,** century
le **siège,** seat
siffler, to whistle
signe: faire signe à, to signal, wave (to)
singulier, curious, strange
la **situation,** job, post, situation
soif: avoir soif, to be thirsty
soigner, to look after
sinon, otherwise, except
le **sol,** ground
les **soldes (mpl),** sale(s)
le **soleil,** sun
sombre, dark, gloomy
sommeil: avoir sommeil, to be sleepy
songer, to dream, think
sonner, to ring
le **sort,** destiny, fate
la **sortie,** exit
sortir, to go out
le **sou,** penny
le **souci,** care, worry
soudain, sudden(ly)
souffler, to blow
souhaiter, to wish
le **soulagement,** relief
le **soulier,** shoe
souligner, to underline
soupçonner, to suspect
soupirer, to sigh
le **sourcil,** eyebrow
sourd, deaf
sourire, to smile
la **souris,** mouse
le **sous-sol,** basement
se **souvenir de,** to remember
souvent, often
le **sparadrap,** sticking-plaster
le **stationnement,** parking
le **stylo à bille,** ball-point pen, biro
subir, to undergo
subit, sudden
le **sud,** south
suivre, to follow
sur-le-champ, at once
le **surlendemain,** the day after tomorrow

sursauter, to jump, start up
surtout, especially
le **Syndicat d'Initiative,** Tourist Information Office

T

le **tableau,** picture
le **tablier,** apron
la **tâche,** job, task
tâcher, to try
la **taille,** figure, size, waist
se **taire,** to be quiet
le **talon,** heel
tandis que, whilst
tant, so much
tant pis! too bad!
taper, to tap
taquiner, to tease
la **tasse,** cup
le **taureau,** bull
tellement, so
la **tempête,** storm
le **temps,** time, weather
tendre, to hold out
terminer, to end
le **terrain,** ground
tiède, luke-warm
le **timbre,** stamp
tirer, to pull, shoot
le **tiroir,** drawer
la **toile,** canvas, cloth, linen
le **toit,** roof
le **tonnerre,** thunder
tort: avoir tort, to be wrong
tôt, early
toujours, always, still
se **tourmenter,** to worry
tout à coup, suddenly
tout de suite, at once
tout le monde, everybody

toutefois, however, yet
traduire, to translate
en **train de,** in the process of
le **trait,** feature, trace; **d'un trait,** at one go
le **trajet,** journey
travailler, to work
à **travers,** across
traverser, to cross
la **traversée,** crossing (*voyage*)
trempé, soaked
le **trésor,** treasure
tricher, to cheat
tricoter, to knit
le **trimestre,** term (*school*)
triste, sad
se **tromper,** to make a mistake
trop, too much
le **trottoir,** pavement
le **trou,** hole
trouver, to find
tuer, to kill
à **tue-tête,** at the top of one's voice

U

unique, one and only
l' **usine** (f), factory
utile, useful

V

les **vacances** (fpl), holidays
vaisselle: faire la vaisselle, to do the washing-up
la **valise,** suitcase
valoir, to be worth
la **veille,** eve, day before
le **vélo,** bicycle
vendre, to sell
le **vent,** wind

le **ventre,** stomach
le **verger,** orchard
vérifier, to check
la **vérité,** truth
le **verre,** glass
le **verrou,** bolt
vers, towards
verse: pleuvoir à verse, to pour with rain
verser, to pour (out)
vert, green
le **vestibule,** hall
les **vêtements** (mpl), clothes
le **veuf,** widower
la **veuve,** widow
la **viande,** meat
vide, empty
la **vie,** life
le **vieillard,** old man
vieux, vieille, old
vilain, bad, nasty
le **visage,** face
vite, quickly
la **vitesse,** speed
la **vitre,** window-pane
la **vitrine,** shop-window
vivre, to live
voir, to see
le **voisin,** neighbour
la **voix,** voice
le **vol,** flight; theft
le **volant,** steering-wheel
voler, to fly; to steal
le **voleur,** thief
vouloir, to want, wish
le **voyou,** hooligan
vraiment, really, truly

Y

les **yeux** (mpl), eyes

English–French vocabulary

A

able: to be able, pouvoir
about (= *approximately*), à peu près, environ, vers; (= *concerning*), à propos de, au sujet de; **to be about to,** être sur le point de
above, en haut, au-dessus (de)
abroad, à l'étranger
to **accept,** accepter
across, à travers
to **add,** ajouter
afraid: to be afraid, avoir peur
after, après
again, de nouveau, encore une fois
against, contre
ago, il y a
alarm-clock, le réveil, le réveille-matin
all, tout; **all the same,** tout de même
to **allow,** permettre
almost, presque

alone, seul
along, le long de
aloud, à haute voix
already, déjà
also, aussi
although, bien que, quoique
always, toujours
among, parmi
angry: to be angry, être en colère; **to get angry,** se fâcher
to **annoy,** agacer, ennuyer
another, un(e) autre
to **answer,** répondre
anxious: to be anxious, s'inquiéter
to **appear,** apparaître
to **approach,** s'approcher (de)
area, la région
to **argue,** disputer
armchair, le fauteuil
around, autour de

arrival, l'arrivée (f)
as, comme; **as far as,** jusqu'à; **as much as,** autant; **as soon as,** aussitôt que
ashamed: to be ashamed of, avoir honte de
to **ask,** demander
asleep, endormi; **to fall asleep,** s'endormir
astonished: to be astonished, s'étonner
attraction, l'attraction (f)
aunt, la tante
to **avoid,** éviter
away: to go away, s'en aller, partir
awful, affreux

B

baby, le bébé
back, le dos
back: to come back, revenir; **to give back,** rendre; **to go back,** retourner, rentrer

bad, mauvais; **too bad!** tant pis!
badly, mal
bag, le sac
bank, la banque
bank (*of river*), le bord, la rive
bar (*e.g. chocolate*), la tablette
to **bark,** aboyer
barn, la grange
basket, le panier
bath: to have a bath, to bathe, se baigner
bathroom, la salle de bain(s)
beach, la plage
beard: with a beard, barbu
to **beat,** battre
because, parce que
because of, à cause de
to **become,** devenir
bed, le lit; **to go to bed,** se coucher
bedroom, la chambre (à coucher)
before, (*place*) devant; (*time*) avant
beggar, le mendiant
to **begin,** commencer (à), se mettre à
behind, derrière
to **believe,** croire
bell: to ring the bell, sonner
to **belong,** appartenir
below, en bas
beside, à côté de
besides, d'ailleurs
best, (*adj.*) le meilleur; (*adv.*) le mieux
better, (*adj.*) meilleur; (*adv.*) mieux; **it is better (to)** . . ., il vaut mieux . . .
between, entre
birthday, l'anniversaire (m)
to **bite,** mordre
blanket, la couverture
to **book** (*e.g. room, tickets*), retenir
to **bore,** ennuyer; **to be bored,** s'ennuyer
born, né; **to be born,** naître
to **borrow,** emprunter
boss, le patron
both, tous les deux
to **bother,** déranger
bottle, la bouteille
bottom: at the bottom of, au fond de
box, la boîte
to **break,** briser, (se) casser
breakfast, le petit déjeuner
breath: out of breath, essoufflé
to **bring,** (*person*) amener; (*object*) apporter
to **brush,** (se) brosser
building, le bâtiment
bull, le taureau
burglar, le cambrioleur
to **burn,** brûler
to **burst out laughing,** éclater de rire
business, les affaires (fpl), les devoirs (mpl)
bus stop, l'arrêt (m) d'autobus
busy, (*e.g. town*) animé; (*e.g. person*) occupé
but, mais
to **buy,** acheter
by, (*near*) près de; (*on the edge of*) au bord de

C

to **call,** appeler; **to be called,** s'appeler
camping: to go camping, faire du camping
can (*to be able*), pouvoir
card, la carte
careful: to be careful, faire attention
carefully, avec soin
caretaker, le (la) concierge
carpet, le tapis
cart, la charrette
case, (*briefcase*) la serviette; (*suitcase*) la valise

to **catch,** attraper, prendre
century, le siècle
Channel: the (English) Channel, la Manche
to **chat,** bavarder, causer
cheap, bon marché
chemist, le pharmacien
chimney, la cheminée
to **choose,** choisir
Christmas, Noël
Christmas Eve, la veille de Noël
church, l'église (f)
cinema, le cinéma
city, la ville
clean, propre
to **clean,** nettoyer
clever, habile, intelligent
cliff, la falaise
to **climb,** grimper
clock, (*in a house*) la pendule; (*on a public building*) l'horloge (f)
close (by), tout près
to **close,** fermer
clothes, les vêtements (mpl)
cloud, le nuage
coach, le car
coast, la côte
coat, le manteau
coin, la pièce
cold: to be cold, avoir froid; **it is cold,** il fait froid; **to catch cold,** s'enrhumer; **to have a cold,** être enrhumé
to **collect,** collectionner
to **collide with,** entrer en collision avec
colour, la couleur
to **come,** venir
to **come back,** revenir
to **come down,** descendre
to **come in,** entrer
to **come out,** sortir
to **come up,** monter
comfortable, confortable
compartment, le compartiment
to **complain,** se plaindre
complete, complet, entier
comprehensive school, le Collège d'Enseignement Secondaire
to **continue,** continuer
to **cook,** (faire) cuire
cool, frais, fraîche
corner, le coin
corridor, le couloir
cost, le prix
to **cough,** tousser
to **count,** compter
country, le pays
countryside, la campagne
of **course,** bien entendu, évidemment, naturellement
to **cover,** couvrir
covered with, couvert de
criminal, le criminel
to **cross,** traverser
crossing, (*by boat*) la traversée; (*pedestrian*) le passage clouté
crossroads, le carrefour
crowd, la foule
to **cry,** crier; (*tears*) pleurer
cupboard, l'armoire (f), le placard
to **cure,** guérir
curtain, le rideau
customer, le (la) client(e)
Customs, la Douane
customs officer, le douanier

D

to **dance,** danser
dangerous, dangereux
to **dare,** oser
dark, noir, obscur, sombre

dawn, l'aube (f)
day, le jour, la journée; **the day after,** le lendemain; **the day before,** la veille
dead, mort
dear, cher, chère
death, la mort
to **decide,** décider
to **declare,** déclarer
deep, profond
delighted, enchanté, ravi
to **depart,** partir
to **describe,** décrire
to **deserve,** mériter
diary, le journal, l'agenda (m)
to **die,** mourir
difficult, difficile
dirty, sale
to **disappear,** disparaître
disappointed, déçu
disco(theque), la discothèque, le dancing
to **discover,** découvrir
to **discuss,** discuter
dishes: to wash the dishes, faire la vaisselle
distance: in the distance, au loin
district, (*country*) la région; (*town*) le quartier
to **disturb,** déranger
to **dive,** plonger
doubtless, sans doute
downstairs, en bas
drawer, le tiroir
dreadful, affreux
to **dream,** rêver
dress, la robe; **to get dressed,** s'habiller
to **drink,** boire
to **drive,** conduire
driving-licence, le permis de conduire
to **drop,** laisser tomber
to **drown,** se noyer
dry, sec, sèche
during, pendant
dust, la poussière

E

each, chaque
each one, chacun(e)
ear, l'oreille (f)
early, de bonne heure
to **earn (one's living),** gagner (sa vie)
easily, facilement
Easter, Pâques
easy, facile
to **eat,** manger
edge: at the edge of, au bord de
empty, vide
end, la fin; **at the end of,** au bout de
to **end,** finir, terminer
to **enjoy oneself,** s'amuser
enough, assez
to **escape,** s'échapper
especially, surtout
even, même
every, chaque
everybody, tout le monde
everyone, tout le monde
everywhere, partout
examination, un examen
except, sauf
to **exclaim,** s'écrier, s'exclamer
exit, la sortie
to **expect,** attendre
expensive, cher, chère; coûteux, coûteuse
to **explain,** expliquer
extremely, extrêmement
eye, un œil (pl. les yeux)

F

face, la figure, le visage
factory, l'usine (f)
to fall, tomber
false, faux, fausse
famous, célèbre
far, loin; as far as, jusqu'à
fast, (*adj.*) rapide; (*adv.*) vite
to fear, avoir peur (de), craindre
to feel, sentir
ferry, le ferry
to fetch, aller chercher
few, peu (de)
a few, quelques
field, le champ, la prairie, le pré
to fill, remplir
to fight, se battre
finally, enfin
to find, trouver
fine: it is fine, il fait beau
finger, le doigt
to finish, finir, terminer
fire, le feu; l'incendie (m)
fireman, le pompier
fireworks, les feux (mpl) d'artifice
first, premier, première
at first, d'abord
to fish, pêcher
flat, un appartement
to flow, couler
flower, la fleur
floor, le plancher
floor (= *storey*), l'étage (m)
fluently, couramment
to fly, voler
foggy: it's foggy, il fait du brouillard
to fold, plier
to follow, suivre
following day, le lendemain
food, la nourriture
on foot, à pied
for, (*conj.*) car; (*prep.*) pour;
     (= *during*) pendant; (= *since*) depuis
to forbid, défendre
foreigner, l'étranger (m)
to forget, oublier
to forgive, pardonner
formerly, autrefois
fortnight, une quinzaine, quinze jours
fortunately, heureusement
free, libre
to freeze, geler
to frighten, effrayer
in front of, devant
fun: to make fun of, se moquer de
funny, drôle
furniture, les meubles (mpl)

G

game, le jeu, la partie, le match
gate, la barrière (*farm*); la grille (*iron*);
     la porte (*garden*)
generally, généralement
gently, doucement
to get, (= *look for*) chercher; (= *find*)
     trouver; (= *obtain*) obtenir
to get up, se lever
gift, le cadeau
to give, donner
glad, content, heureux
to glance, jeter un coup d'œil
glass, le verre
glasses (*spectacles*), les lunettes (fpl)
gloomy, sombre
glove, le gant
to go, aller
to go away, s'en aller
to go down, descendre
to go for a walk, se promener
to go home, rentrer

to go in, entrer
to go on, continuer
to go out, sortir
to go to sleep, s'endormir
to go up, monter
Good evening! Bonsoir!
Good morning! Bonjour!
Good night! Bonne nuit!
good: to have a good time, s'amuser
to gossip, bavarder
grass, l'herbe (f)
great! formidable! sensationnel!
ground, la terre, le terrain
ground floor, le rez-de-chaussée
to grow, cultiver (*plants*); grandir (*person*)
to grumble, grogner
to grumble at, gronder
to guess, deviner
guest, l'invité(e)
gun, le fusil

H

hair, les cheveux (mpl)
hairdresser, le coiffeur, la coiffeuse
half, demi
half of, la moitié de
half an hour, une demi-heure
hand, la main
handkerchief, le mouchoir
handsome, beau
to happen, arriver, se passer
happiness, le bonheur
happy, heureux
harbour, le port
hard, dur
hardly, à peine, ne . . . guère
hat, le chapeau
to hate, détester
to have to, devoir
headache, un mal de tête; to have a
     headache, avoir mal à la tête
headlamp, le phare
headmaster, le directeur, le proviseur
     (*secondary school*)
health, la santé
to hear, entendre; to hear about, entendre
     parler de
heart, le cœur
heat, la chaleur
heavy, lourd
hedge, la haie
Hello! Bonjour! Salut!
to help, aider
here, ici; here is, voici
to hesitate, hésiter
to hide, (se) cacher
high, haut
hill, la colline
to hit, frapper
to hold, tenir
hole, le trou
holidays, les vacances (fpl)
homework, les devoirs (mpl)
to hope, espérer
host, l'hôte (m)
hot, chaud
housework: to do the housework, faire le
     ménage
how, comment, comme, que
how long? combien de temps?
how much? combien?
however, cependant
huge, énorme
hundred, cent
hungry: to be hungry, avoir faim
to hurry, se dépêcher
to hurt, (se) blesser, (se) faire mal à
husband, le mari
hut, le cabanon, la cabane, la hutte

I

ice cream, la glace
idea, l'idée (f)
if, si
ill, malade
illness, la maladie
to imagine, (s') imaginer
immediately, immédiatement
to inform, avertir, prévenir
information, les renseignements (mpl)
inhabitant, un habitant
to injure, (se) blesser
inn, l'auberge (f)
inside, dedans, à l'intérieur
instead of, au lieu de
to intend to, avoir l'intention de
interesting, intéressant
to interrupt, interrompre
to introduce (*person*), présenter
to invite, inviter
island, une île

J

jacket, le veston, la veste
jewel, le bijou (pl. bijoux)
job, l'emploi (m), le métier
to joke, plaisanter
journey, le voyage
to jump, sauter
just: to have just, venir de . . .
just now, tout à l'heure

K

to keep, garder
key, la clef (clé)
to kill, tuer
kind, (*adj.*) aimable; (*noun*) l'espèce (f),
     le genre, la sorte
king, le roi
to kiss, embrasser
kitchen, la cuisine
knee, le genou (pl. genoux)
to kneel, s'agenouiller
knife, le couteau
to knock, frapper; to knock down,
     renverser
to know, (*person*) connaître; (*fact*) savoir

L

ladder, l'échelle (f)
land, la terre
language, la langue
large, grand
last, dernier; at last, enfin
to last, durer
late, tard, en retard
later, plus tard
latter, celui-ci, celle-ci
to laugh, rire
to laugh at, se moquer de
lawn, la pelouse
lazy, paresseux
to learn, apprendre
at least, (*minimum*) au moins; (*at all events*)
     du moins
to leave, (*behind*) laisser; (+ *object*)
     quitter; (= *depart*) partir
left, gauche (*as opposed to right*)
leg, la jambe
to lend, prêter
less, moins
to let (= *allow*), laisser, permettre
library, la bibliothèque
to lie, mentir
to lie down, se coucher
life, la vie
lift, l'ascenseur (m)
to lift, lever, soulever
light (*adj.*), (*weight*) léger; (*colour*) clair

light (*noun*), la lumière
to light, allumer
lighthouse, le phare
to like, aimer
like, comme
line, la ligne
to listen to, écouter
little, petit
to live, demeurer, vivre; **to live in**, habiter
living: **to earn one's living**, gagner sa vie
lock, la serrure
to lock, fermer à clef
to look (*appear*), avoir l'air, paraître
to look after, garder, soigner
to look at, regarder
to look for, chercher
to look like, ressembler à
to look up, lever la tête
lorry, le camion
to lose, perdre; **to lose one's temper**, se mettre en colère
a lot of, beaucoup
loud, fort
low, bas(se)
lucky: **to be lucky**, avoir de la chance
luggage, les bagages (mpl)
lunch: **to have lunch**, déjeuner

M

mad, fou, folle
magazine, le magazine, la revue
main road, la grande route
majority, la plupart
to make, faire
to make for, se diriger vers
to manage (to do), réussir à
manager, le directeur, le gérant
many, beaucoup; **so many**, tant; **as many**, autant
map, la carte
mark, la note
market, le marché
to marry, épouser, se marier avec
marvellous, merveilleux
matter: **what's the matter?** qu'y a-t-il?; **what's the matter with you?** qu'as-tu? qu'avez-vous?
may I? puis-je?
meal, le repas
to meet, rencontrer
midday, (le) midi
middle: **in the middle of**, au milieu de
midnight, (le) minuit
to miss, manquer
mistaken: **to be mistaken**, se tromper
money, l'argent (m)
month, le mois
mood: **in a good (bad) mood**, de bonne (mauvaise) humeur
moon, la lune
moped, le vélomoteur
more, plus
morning, le matin, la matinée; **the next morning**, le lendemain matin
most, la plupart
motorway, l'autoroute (f)
to murmur, murmurer
museum, le musée
music, la musique
must, devoir

N

name, le nom; **what is your name?** comment t'appelles-tu? comment vous appelez-vous?
naturally, naturellement
naughty, méchant
near, près de
nearby, tout près
nearly, presque

to need, avoir besoin de
neighbour, le (la) voisin(e)
neither . . . nor, ni . . . ni . . . (ne)
never, (ne) . . . jamais
new, nouveau, nouvelle; neuf, neuve
newspaper, le journal
next, (*adj.*) prochain; (*adv.*) ensuite, puis
next day, le lendemain
next to, à côté de
nice, aimable
night, la nuit
nightfall, la tombée de la nuit, la nuit tombante
nobody, (ne) . . . personne
noise, le bruit
no longer, ne . . . plus
no more, ne . . . plus
nothing, (ne) . . . rien
not yet, pas encore
note, le billet
notebook, le carnet
to notice, remarquer
now, maintenant; **just now**, tout à l'heure
nurse, un infirmier, une infirmière

O

to obtain, obtenir
obviously, évidemment
to offer, offrir
office, le bureau
often, souvent
old, vieux, vieille
older, aîné
once, une fois
at once, immédiatement, tout de suite
only, ne . . . que, seulement
to open, ouvrir
opposite, en face (de)
orchard, le verger
to order, commander
other, autre
ought, (*conditional tense of*) devoir
out: **to go out**, sortir
outside, dehors, à l'extérieur
over there, là-bas
overcoat, le pardessus
to overtake (*e.g. car*), doubler
to owe, devoir
own, propre; **on one's own**, seul(e)
owner, le (la) propriétaire

P

pain, la douleur
parcel, le colis, le paquet
to park, stationner
particular: **(on) that particular day**, ce jour-là
party, la boum (*young people's*); la soirée
passenger, le passager, le voyageur
passer-by, le passant
path, le sentier, l'allée (f)
patient, le client, le (la) malade
patiently, patiemment
pavement, le trottoir
to pay for, payer
peace, la paix
pebble, le caillou (pl. cailloux)
pen, le stylo
pencil, le crayon
people, les gens (mpl); **a lot of people**, beaucoup de monde
perhaps, peut-être
to permit, permettre
petrol, l'essence (f)
to phone, téléphoner
to pick up, ramasser
picture, le tableau

piece, le morceau
pity: **what a pity!** quel dommage! **it's a pity!** c'est dommage!
to pity, plaindre
place, l'endroit (m)
plan, le projet, le plan
plane, l'avion (m)
plate, l'assiette (f)
platform, le quai
play, une pièce (de théâtre)
to play, jouer
pleasant, agréable
to please, plaire à
please, s'il te (vous) plaît
pleasure, le plaisir
plenty (of), beaucoup (de)
pocket, la poche
point: **to be on the point of**, être sur le point de; **to point out**, indiquer
policeman, l'agent, le policier
police station, le poste de police
police superintendent, le commissaire de police
polite, poli
poor, pauvre
to post, mettre à la poste
postcard, la carte postale
postman, le facteur
post office, le bureau de poste
pound (*money and weight*), la livre
to prefer, préférer, aimer mieux
to prepare, préparer
present, un cadeau
presently, tout à l'heure
to pretend, faire semblant de
pretty, joli
to prevent, empêcher
price, le prix
probably, probablement
programme, le programme, l'émission (f)
to promise, promettre
proprietor, le (la) propriétaire
proud, fier, fière
provided that, pourvu que
to pull, tirer
to punish, punir
pupil, un(e) élève
purse, le porte-monnaie
to pursue, poursuivre
to push, pousser
to put (on), mettre
to put down, poser

Q

to quarrel, se disputer
quay, le quai
queen, la reine
to question, interroger
quick, rapide
quickly, vite
quiet, tranquille; **to be quiet**, se taire
quietly, doucement, silencieusement
quite, assez; (= *completely*) tout à fait

R

racquet, la raquette
railway, le chemin de fer
railway-station, la gare
rain, la pluie
to rain, pleuvoir; **it is raining**, il pleut; **it was raining**, il pleuvait; **it rained**, il a plu
rarely, rarement
rather, assez, plutôt
to reach, arriver à, gagner
to read, lire
ready, prêt; **to get ready**, s'apprêter, se préparer

to **realise,** comprendre, se rendre compte
really, vraiment
to **receive,** recevoir
to **recognise,** reconnaître
to **reflect,** réfléchir
relative, un parent
to **rely on,** compter sur
to **remain,** rester
to **remember,** se rappeler, se souvenir de
to **rent,** louer
to **repair,** réparer
to **repeat,** répéter
to **reply,** répondre
to **resemble,** ressembler à
the **rest** (*others*), les autres
to **rest,** se reposer
to **return,** retourner, revenir; (= *give back*) rendre
to **ride** (*horse, bicycle*), se promener (à cheval, à vélo)
right, droit(e); **on the right,** à droite; **to be right,** avoir raison
to **ring,** sonner
to **rise** (*e.g. smoke*), monter
road, (*in country*) la route; (*in town*) la rue
rock, le rocher
rod (*fishing*), la canne (à pêche)
roof, le toit
room, la pièce, la salle; la chambre (*bedroom*); la place (*space*)
round: to go round, faire le tour de
to **rush (forward),** s'élancer, se précipiter
to **rush** (= *hurry*), se dépêcher

S

sad, triste
same, même; **all the same,** tout de même
sand, le sable
to **save,** sauver; (*money*) faire des économies
scarcely, à peine, ne . . . guère
scarf, (*long*) l'écharpe; (*silk*) le foulard
school, l'école (f)
to **scold,** gronder
to **scratch,** gratter
sea, la mer
sea-sick: to be sea-sick, avoir le mal de mer
to **search (for),** chercher
to **see,** voir
to **seem,** sembler, paraître, avoir l'air
to **seize,** saisir
to **sell,** vendre
to **send,** envoyer
serious, grave, sérieux
to **set off,** se mettre en route
to **set out,** partir
several, plusieurs
shade, l'ombre (f)
to **shake,** secouer; **to shake hands,** serrer la main (à); **to shake one's head,** hocher la tête
to **shave,** se raser
sheet, le drap
shelf, le rayon
to **shine,** briller
ship, le navire, le paquebot
shock, le choc
to **shoot,** tirer
shop, la boutique, le magasin
shopping: to do some shopping, faire des achats (emplettes, courses, commissions)
short, court
to **shout,** crier
to **show,** montrer
shower, (*bathroom*) la douche; (*rain*) une averse

to **shut,** fermer
to **shut up,** se taire
sick, malade, souffrant
side, le côté; **at/by the side of,** à côté de, au bord de; **on the other side,** de l'autre côté
silly, stupide
silver, l'argent (m)
since, (*reason*) puisque; (*time*) depuis
to **sing,** chanter
to **sit down,** s'asseoir
sitting, assis
sky, le ciel
to **sleep,** dormir; **to go to sleep,** s'endormir
to **slip,** glisser
to **slow down,** ralentir
slowly, lentement
small, petit
to **smile,** sourire
smoke, la fumée
to **smoke,** fumer
to **snatch,** arracher
snow, la neige
to **snow,** neiger
so, (= *therefore*) donc; (*extent*) si, tellement
soaked, trempé
somebody, quelqu'un
something, quelque chose
sometimes, quelquefois
somewhere, quelque part
soon, bientôt
sorry! pardon! **to be sorry,** être désolé
sound, le bruit, le son
the **South (of France),** le Midi
to **speak,** parler
spectacles, les lunettes (fpl)
speed, la vitesse
to **spend,** (*money*) dépenser; (*time*) passer
in **spite of,** malgré
to **spoil,** gâter
in **spring,** au printemps
stairs, l'escalier (m)
stamp (*postage*), le timbre (-poste)
to **stand,** se tenir (debout)
to **stand up,** se lever
to **start,** commencer, se mettre à
to **stay,** rester, demeurer
to **steal,** voler
stick, le bâton; **(walking-) stick,** la canne
still, encore, toujours
stone, la pierre
to **stop,** (s')arrêter
storey, l'étage (m)
storm, l'orage (m)
story, l'histoire (f)
straight on, tout droit
strange, étrange
stranger, un étranger, une étrangère; un inconnu, une inconnue
stream, le ruisseau
street, la rue
to **strike** (*hit*), frapper
strike: to go on strike, se mettre en grève, faire (la) grève
strict, sévère
strong, fort
to **study,** étudier
suburbs, la banlieue
to **succeed,** réussir à
success, le succès
such, tel(le)
sudden, soudain
suddenly, tout à coup
suitcase, la valise
in **summer,** en été
sun, le soleil
supermarket, le supermarché
surprised: to be surprised, s'étonner

to **surround,** entourer
sweet-shop, la confiserie
to **swim,** nager

T

to **take,** (= *pick up*) prendre; (*person*) emmener
to **take away,** emporter
to **take off,** enlever, ôter; décoller (*plane*)
to **talk,** parler
tall, grand
tape-recorder, le magnétophone
tea, (*drink*) le thé; (*meal*) le goûter
to **teach,** enseigner
teacher, le professeur; l'instituteur (*junior school*)
team, l'équipe (f)
to **tear,** déchirer
to **telephone,** téléphoner (à)
television, la télévision
television set, le téléviseur
to **tell,** dire, raconter (*relate*)
temper: in a temper, en colère
to **thank,** remercier
then, alors, donc, ensuite, puis
there, (*pronoun*) y; (*adverb*) là
there is (are), il y a
therefore, donc, ainsi
thief, le voleur
thin, maigre
to **think,** croire, penser
thing, la chose
thirsty: to be thirsty, avoir soif
as **though,** comme si
to **threaten,** menacer
through, par, à travers
to **throw,** jeter
ticket, le billet
ticket-office, le guichet
till (= *until*), jusqu'à
time, (*by the clock*) le temps, l'heure; (= *occasion*) la fois; **a long time,** longtemps
time-table, (*school*) un emploi de temps; (*train*) l'horaire (m), l'indicateur (m)
tip, le pourboire
tired, fatigué
today, aujourd'hui
together, ensemble
tomorrow, demain
too, trop (*much*); aussi (*also*)
top, le haut, le sommet
tourist, le (la) touriste
towards, vers
traffic, la circulation
to **travel,** voyager
tree, l'arbre (m)
trip, une excursion
to **trouble,** déranger
true, vrai
truth, la vérité
to **try,** essayer
to **turn off (out),** éteindre
to **turn round,** se retourner
to **turn towards,** se tourner vers
twice, deux fois
twin, le jumeau, la jumelle

U

ugly, laid
umbrella, le parapluie
unbearable, insupportable
under, sous
to **understand,** comprendre
to **undress,** se déshabiller
unfortunately, malheureusement
unhappy, malheureux
unknown, inconnu
unwell, souffrant, malade

until, jusqu'à (ce que)
up: to come up, monter; **to get up,** se lever
upstairs, en haut
to **use,** employer, se servir de, utiliser
useful, utile
useless, inutile
as **usual,** comme d'habitude
usually, généralement, d'habitude
to **utter a cry,** pousser un cri

V

in **vain,** en vain
vegetable, le légume
very, bien, fort, très
very much, beaucoup
to **visit,** (*person*) faire (rendre) visite; (*country, town etc.*) visiter
visitor, le visiteur
voice, la voix

W

to **wait,** attendre
waiter, le garçon
waitress, la serveuse
to **wake up,** se réveiller
to **walk,** marcher, se promener
wall, le mur
wallet, le portefeuille
to **wander,** errer
to **want,** désirer, vouloir
war, la guerre
warm: to be warm, (*person*) avoir chaud; (*weather*) faire chaud
to **warm oneself,** se réchauffer

to **wash,** (se) laver
washing: to do the washing (*clothes*), faire la lessive; **to do the washing-up,** faire (laver) la vaisselle
wasp, la guêpe
to **waste (time),** perdre (son temps)
watch, la montre
to **watch,** regarder
water, l'eau (f)
wave (*sea*), la vague
to **wave,** (*an object*) agiter; (*to someone*) faire signe à
way, la façon, la manière
way (= *path*), le chemin
weak, faible
wealthy, riche
to **wear,** porter
weary, las(se)
weather, le temps
week, la semaine
to **weep,** pleurer
well, bien; **to be well,** aller bien
well-known, célèbre, bien connu
wet, humide, mouillé
what, (*adj.*) quel; **what!** comment!
when, lorsque, quand
where, où
whether, si
while, pendant que
whilst (*contrast*), tandis que
to **whisper,** chuchoter, murmurer
to **whistle,** siffler
whole, entier, tout
why, pourquoi
wide, large
widow, la veuve

widower, le veuf
wife, la femme
wild, sauvage
to **win,** gagner
windy: to be windy, faire du vent
wine, le vin
in **winter,** en hiver
to **wipe,** essuyer
wise, prudent, sage
to **wish,** désirer, vouloir
with, avec
without, sans
to **wonder,** se demander
wonderful, merveilleux
wood, le bois
word, le mot, la parole (*spoken*)
work, le travail
to **work,** travailler
workman, -woman, un ouvrier; une ouvrière
world, le monde
worried, inquiet, inquiète
to **worry,** s'inquiéter
worse, pire (*adj.*); pis (*adv.*)
worth: to be worth, valoir
to **wound,** blesser
to **write,** écrire
wrong: to be wrong, avoir tort, se tromper

Y

year, l'an (m), l'année (f)
yesterday, hier
yet (*still*), encore, déjà; (*however*) cependant
young, jeune

Index